IMPROVING POLICY ANALYSIS

SAGE FOCUS EDITIONS

IMPROVING POLICY ANALYSIS

Edited by
STUART S. NAGEL

SAGE PUBLICATIONS   Beverly Hills   London

For information address:

SAGE PUBLICATIONS,INC.
275 South Beverly Drive
Beverly Hills, California 90212

SAGE PUBLICATIONS LTD.
28 Banner Street
London ECIY 8QE England

Printed in the United States of America

Library of Congress Cataloging in Publication Data

Main entry under title:
Improving policy analysis.
   (Sage focus editions ; 16)
    Bibliography: p.
    1. Policy sciences—Addresses, essays, lectures.
I. Nagel, Stuart S., 1934-   II. Series.
H61.I52   309.1   79-23019
ISBN 0-8039-1390-7
ISBN 0-8039-1391-5 pbk.

FIRST PRINTING

CONTENTS

PART III. POLICY ANALYSIS FROM AN EVALUATION
RESEARCH PERSPECTIVE

PART IV. IMPLEMENTING POLICY ANALYSIS RESEARCH

INTRODUCTION: POLICY ANALYSIS RESEARCH, WHAT IT IS AND WHERE IT IS GOING

Stuart S. Nagel

I. WHAT IS POLICY ANALYSIS RESEARCH?

The purpose of this book is to describe the new developments in the increasingly important field of policy analysis research. By *policy analysis research,* we mean the how-to-do-it methods associated with determining the nature, causes, and effects of governmental decisions or policies designed to cope with specific social problems. In that sense, the research methods could focus on (1) taking policies as givens and attempting to determine what causes them, (2) taking social forces as givens and attempting to determine what policies they are responsible for, (3) taking policies as givens and attempting to determine what effects they have, or (4) taking effects or goals as givens and attempting to determine what policies will achieve or maximize those goals. One new development in policy analysis research is an increasing concern with the fourth type of analysis. That kind of optimizing perspective is emphasized in this book, although we are also concerned with recent developments in the third type of analysis, which is generally associated with evaluation research, and also in the first two types of analysis, which are especially associated with a political science or political perspective. This book is also concerned with new institutions for implementing these relatively recent developments in policy analysis.

The increased concern for evaluating alternative public policies has manifested itself in new articles, books, journals, book series, conference papers, organizations, courses, curricula, grants, job openings, legislative provisions, evaluative agencies, and other indicators of activity. The increased concern began especially in the late 1960s as part of the general public's concern for civil rights, the war on poverty, peace, women's liberation, environmental protection, and other social problems. The implementation of that concern was facilitated by the development and spread of computer software, statistical and mathematical methods, and interdisciplinary relations. The relative attractiveness of the government as an employer and sponsor also increased, as the role of universities in employment and research funding decreased. A more recent stimulant has been the concern for obtaining more government output from reduced tax dollars.

Policy analysts are involved mainly in determining the effects of alternative public policies in working for government agencies, non-university research centers, university research centers, teaching units, or interest groups. The work is generally not full-time policy analysis work, but rather policy analysis tends to be part of a full-time position in public administration, research, or teaching. The government agencies are executive agencies like HEW and HUD, legislative agencies like the Congressional Reference Service and the General Accounting Office, or judicial agencies like the Federal Judicial Center and the National Center for State Courts. The government agencies could also be at the federal, state, or local level.

In order to acquire the training needed for policy analysis work, one normally must acquire a graduate degree in one of the social sciences, preferably economics, political science, social psychology, planning, or one of the newer interdisciplinary policy studies programs. Some of the leading interdisciplinary programs include those at the Harvard Kennedy School, Princeton Woodrow Wilson School, University of Michigan Institute of Public Policy Studies, Berkeley Graduate School of Public Policy, Duke Institute of Policy Sciences and Public Affairs, and the Minnesota Hubert Humphrey Institute of Public Affairs. The methodological training of policy analysts includes courses in social science research methods, especially methods that relate to questionnaires, interviewing, sampling, goal measurement, prediction, causal analysis, data processing, systematic observation, and report writing. The methodological training also includes courses in optimum decision making, such as those offered in business administration, industrial engineering, and economics under titles like operations research or management science. The substantive training of policy analysts generally includes courses that deal with how and why alternative policies get adopted and implemented, and also courses that cover the basic issues and references in various specific policy fields. Most policy analysts combine such general training with expertise concerning at least a few specific policy problems.

The study of governmental policy problems is clearly an interdisciplinary activity, at least in the sense that many disciplines have something to contribute to the study. For any social scientist or practitioner, it would be too much to acquire an expertise in all the relevant perspectives. Indeed, it is too much to become an expert in all the subfields within one's own discipline. Nevertheless, there probably is a consensus that if one is interested in developing competence in policy studies work, he or she should be familiar in a general way with the potential contributions and drawbacks of the various social sciences. Such familiarity will at least enable one to know when to call upon a social scientist or a social science treatise, the way a lay person has a general idea of the meaning of what is said by a doctor or a lawyer.

One particularly interesting set of issues worth raising when discussing public policy analysis is the role of values in policy analysis. Policy analysts cannot be totally value-free since they are seeking to achieve or maximize given values, but they can take extra precautions to keep social or personal values from interfering with their statements of fact. These precautions can include drawing upon multiple sources and individuals for cross-checking information, making available raw data sets for secondary analysis, and making assumptions more explicit. Policy analysts can also attempt to justify the values they are seeking to achieve by showing how they relate to higher, widely-accepted values. They can especially vary the normative and factual inputs into their models to see how that variation or sensitivity analysis affects the policy recommendations. They can also be especially sensitive to democratic political constraints and constitutional legal constraints.

How can one define good policy analysis, or good analysis of the effects of alternative public policies? For one thing, it is empirically valid in the sense of conforming to reality. It is useful to policymakers or policy appliers by providing new insights that are clearly communicated. It is useful to society in aiding in the production of desired social consequences. It is also done with a minimum of time and expense.

What institutional structures in terms of government agencies, policy research centers, and academic units are needed to facilitate good policy analysis? The most appropriate government agencies are those that recognize the value of using social science in program evaluation, that have staff people with program evaluation skills, and that know how and are willing to arrange for outside evaluations which exceed the in-house skills. The most appropriate research centers are those that combine the creativity of academia with the conscientious concern of nonuniversity centers for meeting time and specification deadlines. The most appropriate academic units are probably the interdisciplinary policy studies programs and the disciplinary programs which encourage students to develop a specialty along policy studies lines.

Why should one want to develop skills for evaluating alternative public policies? For researchers in academia, government, or research institutes, doing so may provide opportunities for such things as jobs, grants, articles, books, promotions, conferences, and teaching. Policymakers and other consumers of policy research can take more informed positions on controversial issues if they have an understanding of policy analysis methods. Policy analysis can also be intellectually challenging, and it can produce feelings of social usefulness. In addition to being practical, it is also relevant to developing theories or generalizations concerning the causes and effects of public policies, which is an important part of social science. It is hoped that this book will help to stimulate those benefits which policy analysis can potentially provide.

II. WHAT NEW DEVELOPMENTS DOES
THIS BOOK COVER?

The first section of the book brings out the relevance of deductive modeling and optimizing to policy analysis research. *Deductive modeling* in this context means drawing conclusions concerning the effects of alternative public policies from premises that have been empirically validated or intuitively accepted. *Optimizing* in this context means deducing a conclusion about what policy will maximize benefits minus costs, taking into consideration that policies often have diminishing and uncertain returns and must be analyzed in light of economic, legal, and political constraints. The Nagel-Neef chapter illustrates deductive modeling with various examples, including determining the impact of jury size on the probability of conviction, and it illustrates optimizing with examples like determining an optimum percentage of defendants to hold in jail prior to trial. John Brandl suggests, in his chapter, that decision rules in government often are so complex that they make it unclear, even to their designers, whether they accomplish what is intended. He develops a method for embodying the intentions of the designers in complex decision rules. His chapter also emphasizes the importance of satisfying constraints, obtaining feedback from policy people, and using decision rules in government, especially to make decisions allocating scarce resources. The chapter by Werner Hirsch uses medical malpractice litigation and tenants rights legislation to illustrate the value of the related methodology of economics. In the last chapter in this section, Jack Byrd, from his insider's awareness as an operations researcher, calls for more creativity, understanding of the subject matter, and hard work in developing and using policy models.

The second section of the book deals with a political science or political perspective on policy analysis. Such a perspective emphasizes the role of interest groups, governmental personnel, and governmental procedures in determining policy formation and impact. Economists who advocate a pollution tax to protect the environment often fail to consider the great difficulties involved in passing such legislation over the opposition of affected business groups. Likewise, the economists conducting the negative income tax experiments (which emphasized the relation between dollars granted and ambition to work) might have benefited from political science input, which could have caused the experiments to include an analysis of the ambition effects of alternative delivery systems like a check-in-the-mail versus the compulsory caseworker. The Bardes-Dubnick chapter brings out the differences and similarities across types of policy analysts depending mainly on whether they have a scientific, professional, political, administrative, or personal orientation. The Duncan MacRae chapter puts policy analysis methods into a broad political framework, emphasizing the concept of political feasibility and governmental functions of taxing-spending, public goods, service delivery, regulation, enforcement, socialization, and making policies about policymaking.

The third part of the book deals with evaluation research. Such research has sometimes been distinguished from policy analysis by the fact that evaluation research traditionally requires policies to be adopted before they can be evaluated, and concentrates on the effects of the policies rather than on finding policies that will maximize given goals. The chapter by Cook, Johnson, and Wagner emphasizes that both evaluation research and policy analysis tend to be inadequately integrated into ongoing program administration. They suggest ways of combining administration and experimentation to the possible benefit of both. The paper by Frank Scioli emphasizes problems involved in policy evaluation, such as collecting the data, measuring the key variables, finding adequate research funds, dealing with adminstrators who want to see their programs favorably evaluated, and obtaining balance between a theoretical and an applied orientation. He also deals with various matters that affect the future of policy evaluation, such as performance consciousness in government, university programs, publishing outlets, federal agency activities, and the National Conference of State Legislatures.

The last section of the book discusses how to implement more effectively the work of policy analysis researchers. Peter House and Joseph Coleman provide a perspective of governmental insiders on the realities of day-to-day policy analysis work. Edward Lehman talks about the roles of policy research centers including for-profit, not-for-profit, and academic centers. Karin Knorr is concerned with increasing the utilization of social science results, especially from a cross-national perspective. The final chapter, by Arnold Meltsner, discusses the need for creating a policy analysis profession through the establishment of new organizations, training programs, journals, and other relevant institutions.

Some of these chapters began as part of the interdisciplinary panel on "Methodology Problems in Policy Analysis" at the 1978 American Political Science Association meeting. The chapters by Nagel-Neef, Hirsch, Bardes-Dubnick, Lehman, and Meltsner appeared as the September 1979 issue of *Transaction/Society* under the theme "The Policy Analysis Explosion." We are quite appreciative of being allowed by Irving Horowitz and Scott Bramson of *Transaction/Society* to use those articles in this book.

From this set of chapters, one can conclude there is a great deal of ferment in policy analysis research. It manifests itself in (1) new methods of deductive and optimizing analysis, (2) interdisciplinary integration across political science and the other social sciences, (3) new concerns for more effective data gathering associated with evaluation research, and (4) increased implementation and utilization of policy analysis by way of policy research centers and other indicators of policy analysis professionalism. Given the current ferment, it is anticipated that over the next few years there will be more new developments that will result in even more and better applications of social science to important policy problems.

SUGGESTED READINGS

Dror, Yehezkel. *Design for Policy Sciences*. New York: Elsevier, 1971.

Horowitz, Irving and James Katz. *Social Science and Public Policy in the United States*. New York: Praeger, 1975.

Lasswell, Harold. *A Pre-View of Policy Sciences*. New York: Elsevier, 1971.

MacRae, Duncan, Jr., and James Wilde. *Policy Analysis for Public Decisions*. North Scituate, Mass.: Duxbury, 1979.

Nagel, Stuart and Marian Neef. *Policy Analysis: In Social Science Research*. Beverly Hills: Sage, 1979.

Stokey, Elizabeth and Richard Zeckhauser. *A Primer for Policy Analysis*. New York: Norton, 1978.

PART I. POLICY ANALYSIS FROM A DEDUCTIVE MODELING OR OPTIMIZING PERSPECTIVE

1

WHAT'S NEW ABOUT POLICY ANALYSIS RESEARCH?

Stuart S. Nagel
Marian Neef

All fields of scientific knowledge, but especially the social sciences, are now undergoing an increased concern for being relevant to important governmental policy problems. That increased concern has manifested itself in new articles, books, journals, book series, convention papers, organizations, courses, curricula, grants, job openings, and other indicators of academic activity.

The increased concern began in the late 1960s as part of the general public's concern for civil rights, the war on poverty, peace, women's liberation, environmental protection, and other social problems. The implementation of that concern was facilitated by the development and spread of computer software, statistical and mathematical methods, and interdisciplinary relations. The relative attractiveness of the government as an employer and sponsor also increased, as the role of universities in employment and research funding decreased.

Policy analysis or policy studies can be broadly defined as the study of the nature, causes, and effects, of alternative public policies. Sometimes, policy analysis is more specifically defined to refer to the methods used in analyzing public policies. The main methods, however, are no different from those associated with social science and the scientific method in general, except that they are applied to variables and subject matters involving relations among policies, policy causes, and policy effects. In that sense, policy analysis is not something new methodologically. There are, however, at least two relatively new exciting developments that are becoming increasingly associated with policy analysis.

One new development involves a concern for deducing the effects of alternative public policies before the policies are adopted, as contrasted to the more usual approach of quantitatively or nonquantitatively evaluating policies before and after they have been adopted. Deductive modeling involves drawing conclusions about the effects of policies from empirically tested premises, although the conclusions have not necessarily been empirically tested. A second new development involves a concern for determining an optimum policy or combination of policies for achieving a given goal or set of goals. This evaluative approach can be contrasted with the more common situation where policies are taken as givens and the researcher attempts to determine the extent to which they are achieving their desired effects.

The purpose of this chapter is to present a few general principles concerning these new developments of deducing policy effects and of optimizing policy alternatives, and especially to present some illustrative examples. The examples are taken mainly from the criminal justice field, but one can see by analogy how the basic methods are applicable to a great variety of public policies.

DEDUCING THE EFFECTS OF POLICY CHANGES

GENERAL MATTERS

The main scientific alternative to deducing the effects of alternative public policies involves comparing people or places who have not experienced a certain policy with people or places who have experienced the policy. That approach has a number of methodological and normative defects. On a methodological level, there may be no places or not enough places which have adopted the policy. For example, a leading criminal justice controversy at the present time relates to whether flat sentencing should be adopted whereby legislatures specify the sentences to be administered to defendants convicted of certain crimes and judges have no substantial discretion to deviate from those flat or fixed sentences. We cannot, however, use a purely empirical or observational approach to evaluate that policy proposal since almost none of the states has yet adopted it.

Comparing places which have and have not adopted a policy may also be impossibe for the opposite reason, namely, that no places exist that do not have the policy or that all the relevant places adopted the policy simultaneously. For example, in the controversial Miranda decision, the Supreme Court required all states simultaneously to exclude the results of police interrogations where indigent defendants were not provided with requested counsel. No state had previously adopted that rule; and after the rule was adopted, there was no control group for comparison purposes.

Along related lines, there are policies that have been adopted by some states or places and not others, but the adoption has involved nonrandom self-selection, which tends to make comparisons meaningless. For example, it may not be meaningful to compare murder rates in states that have capital punishment with those that lack capital punishment since there are so many other social characteristics that relate to murder rates besides capital punishment which may also relate to why some states have adopted capital punishment and others have not.

Another defect in the purely empirical approach is that the policy may have been adopted too recently for long-term evaluation. For example, the New Deal rural development program of the 1930s involved the government purchasing bankrupt plantations and large farms for redistributing parcels to small farmers under long-term, low-interest mortgages. The program was judged a failure because so many of the small farmers were unable to keep up the payments and lost their land. However, thirty years later, in the 1960s, it was observed that the leaders of the voting rights movement in the Mississippi Delta were often older black farmers who had been among the recipients of the New Deal land redistribution, rather than young black militants. The older land-owning farmers fought for voting rights because they had more at stake in government programs and because they had less to fear with regard to losing their jobs. It took over thirty years though to observe that effect, and most academics are unwilling to wait that long to publish the results of a before-and-after evaluation.

Another methodological defect often present in making comparisons across places or over time is that sufficient data may not be available for the before period rather than the after period except in persons' memories, which may not be reliable. For example, in a study of the effects of the Supreme Court's 1961 decision requiring the exclusion from state criminal courtrooms of illegally seized evidence, questionnaires were sent to police chiefs, prosecutors, judges, defense attorneys, and officials of the American Civil Liberties Union asking before-and-after questions. One interesting finding was that police chiefs in states that had previously adopted the exclusionary rule often erred in thinking their states never had the rule and that it was imposed upon them by the Supreme Court. On the other hand, the ACLU officials in states that had not previously adopted the exclusionary rule often erred in thinking their states had always had the rule because they could not imagine that their states could be so insensitive to fair procedure as to allow illegally obtained evidence to be admissible in court.

Making comparisons across places or over time has not only methodological defects but also important normative or socially harmful defects even if the methodology were capable of accurately determining the effects of alternative public policies. One undesirable aspect of social experiments as a means of determining the effects of alternative policies is that once the policy is adopted it is quite difficult to withdraw even if accurate evaluation shows that the policy is ineffective or is producing undesirable consequences. This may possibly be the case with some aspects of the Law Enforcement Assistance Administration, which has repeatedly been evaluated as being a relative waste of money in terms of crime reduction or other social indicators. Yet it continues to operate with little change in its methods, mainly because of the vested interests that have now been established on the part of federal, state, and local bureaucrats and grant recipients. The same may be true of farm programs that subsidize types of farming that other governmental evaluators have found to be socially undesirable, such as tobacco farming or farming that is dependent on alien and cheap migrant labor.

Even if a governmental policy that is found to be harmful after adopted is consequently terminated, considerable damage may have been done while the policy was in existence. For example, changing from a twelve-person jury to a six-person jury may substantially increase the conviction rate before the increase is discovered if we have to adopt the six-person jury in order to determine its effects. That increased conviction rate may mean the conviction of a number of innocent people who would otherwise not have been convicted. The damage done by those wrongful convictions cannot be set right by merely terminating the six-person jury policy.

To avoid these methodological and normative defects of the traditional cross-sectional or time series analysis of policies or treatments, one can attempt to deduce the effects of policies from empirically tested premises. That kind of deductive modeling generally takes one of three forms. It can be based on models dealing with group decision making, models of bilateral decision making, or models of individual decision making. A simple illustration can be given of each kind of deductive modeling applied to policy analysis research.

DEDUCTIONS BASED ON A GROUP DECISION-MAKING MODEL

A good illustration of deductive modeling based on a group decision-making model involves attempting to determine the effects on conviction rates of changing from twelve-person juries to six-person juries. At first glance, one might think an appropriate way to determine that relation would be simply to compare the conviction rates in a state that uses twelve-person juries with those of a state that uses six-person juries. That approach is likely to be meaningless, however, because any differences we find in the conviction rates may be determined by other differences, such as the characteristics of the law, the people, or the cases in the two states or two sets of states, rather than by differences in their jury sizes.

As an alternative, one might suggest making before-and-after comparisons in a single state or set of states in order to control for the kinds of characteristics which do not generally change so much over short periods of time. If the conviction rate before was 64 percent with twelve-person juries, the conviction rate afterwards with six-person juries might be substantially lower rather than higher, although most criminal attorneys would predict a higher conviction rate with six-person juries. The conviction rate might, however, fall by virtue of the fact that if defense attorneys predict that six-person juries are more likely to convict, then they will be more likely to plea bargain their clients and to bring only their especially prodefendant cases before the six-person juries. Thus, the nature of the new cases, not the change in jury size, would cause at least a temporary drop in the conviction rate, and there would be no way to hold constant the type of cases heard by the new six-person juries.

As another alternative, one might suggest working with experimental juries, all of whom would hear exactly the same case. Half the juries would be six-person juries, and half would be twelve-person juries. This experimental analysis, however, has the big defect that it involves a sample of only one case, no matter how many juries are used. Whatever differences or nondifferences are found may be peculiar to that one case, such as being proprosecution, prodefense, highly divisive, or simply unrealistic, and the results may thus not be generalizable. What is needed is about one hundred different trial cases on audio or video tape selected in such a way that 64 percent of them have resulted in unanimous convictions before twelve-person juries and 36 percent in acquittals or hung juries as tends to occur in real jury trials. It would, however, be too expensive a research design to obtain and play so many trials before both a large set of twelve-person juries and a large set of six-person juries, especially if the experiment lacks representative realism.

As an alternative to the cross-sectional, the before-and-after, and the simulation approaches, we could try a deductive approach to determine the impact of jury size on the probability of conviction. Figure 1.1 shows in a kind of syllogistic form how such a deduction might be made. The basic premise is the fact that twelve-person juries tend to convict 64 percent of the time and individual jurors on twelve-person juries tend to vote to convict 67.7 percent of the time. If jury decision making involved an independent probability model like coin-flipping, then individual jurors would vote to convict 96.4 percent of the time in order for twelve-person juries to convict 64 percent of the time. If, on the other hand, jury decision-making involved an averaging model analogous to bowling, where the 10 pins tend to stand or fall depending on what happens to the average pin, then individual voters would vote to convict 64.0 percent of the time in order for twelve-person juries to convict 64 percent of the time. Since individual jurors actually vote to convict 67.7 percent of the time, that means jury decision making is much more like the bowling model than the coin-flipping model, or to be more exact, it is about 1.00 to .13, or 8 to 1, more like the bowling model. That information and some simple calculations analogous to calculating a weighted average between the two models enable us to deduce (as Figure 1.1 shows) that if we switch from a twelve-person jury to a six-person jury and everything else remains constant, the conviction rate should rise from 64 percent to 66 percent.

I. Basic Symbols

PAC = probability of an average defendant before an average *jury* being convicted (empirically equals .64 for a 12-person jury shown to two decimal places).

pac = probability of an average defendant receiving from an average *juror* a vote for conviction (empirically equals .677 for a juror shown to three decimal places).

II. Implications of the Coin-Flipping Analogy (Independent Probability Model)

$PAC = (pac)^{NJ}$.

.64 = $(pac)^{12}$, which deductively means the coin-flipping pac is .964.

III. Implications of the Bowling Analogy (Averaging Model)

PAC = pac.

.64 = pac, which deductively means the bowling pac is .640.

IV. Weighting and Combining the Two Analogies

Actual pac = [weight (coin-flipping pac) + (bowling pac)] / (weight + 1)

.677 = [weight (.964) + (.640)] / (weight + 1), which deductively means that the relative weight of the coin-flipping analogy to the bowling analogy is .13.

V. Applying the Above to a Six-Person Jury

PAC = [weight (coin-flipping PAC) + (bowling PAC)] / (weight + 1)

PAC = [.13 $(.964)^{6}$ + (.64)] / 1.13, which deductively means PAC with a 6-person jury is .66.

VI. Applying the Above to a Decision Rule Allowing Two of Twelve Dissenters for a Conviction

PAC = [weight (coin-flipping PAC) + (bowling PAC)] / (weight + 1)

PAC = [.13 (.99) + (.64)] / 1.13, which deductively means that PAC with a 10/12 rule is .68.

Figure 1.1 The Impact of Jury Size on the Probability of Conviction

The reason the conviction rate goes up so little when jury size is reduced from twelve to six is that jury decision making is more like the bowling or averaging model than it is like the independent probability or coin-flipping model. The reason the conviction rate goes up at all is probably that nonconvicting hung juries decrease with a six-person jury since holdouts are less likely to be reinforced by other holdouts than with a twelve-person jury and the number of reinforcing supporters is more important in maintaining a holdout than the number of opponents within the six to twelve range. Knowing the relation between jury size and conviction rates can in turn be relevant information as input into the empirical premises of an optimizing model designed to arrive at an optimum jury size that minimizes the weighted sum of type 1 errors (convicting the innocent) plus type 2 errors (not convicting the guilty). That, however, is a separate optimizing problem rather than a problem of deducing the effects of alternative policies.

DEDUCTIONS BASED ON
A BILATERAL DECISION-MAKING MODEL

A good illustration of deductive modeling based on a two-sided, decision-making model involves attempting to determine the effect of increasing the pretrial release rate on the pretrial jail population. At first glance, one might logically jump to the conclusion that if pretrial release rates are increased, then of course the pretrial jail population will be decreased. That, however, is not necessarily so, as is shown in Figure 1.2. That figure shows an increase in pretrial release has the effect of decreasing guilty pleas by lowering a key cost that defendants otherwise often have to pay when they refuse to plead guilty, namely, the cost of sitting in jail awaiting a trial. If more defendants are released prior to trial, they are less vulnerable to a prosecutor's promise in return for a plea of guilty to recommend a sentence equal to the time already served waiting in jail or to recommend probation, which will also mean the defendant can immediately get out of jail. Thus, a plea bargain is less likely to be struck, since the probability of arriving at a bargain is at least partly a function of the costs to the litigants of not reaching an agreement, or, in this context, of forcing a trial.

If there is a decrease in guilty pleas, there is likely to be an increase in trials, since a defendant pleading not guilty is in effect asking for a trial. If there is an increase in trials, there is likely to be increased delay in the system, since queueing models and common sense indicate that more trials mean more delay for those awaiting trial, in jail or out. If those awaiting trial in jail now have to wait longer, then the

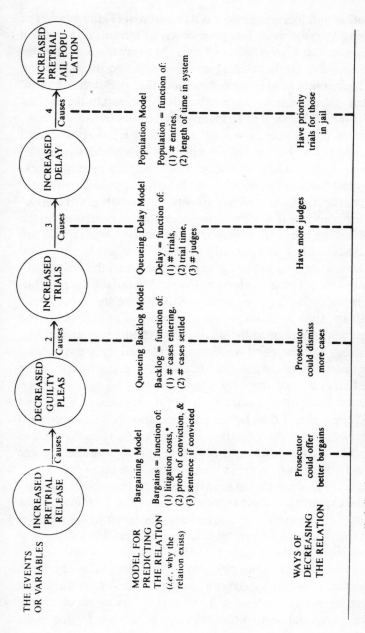

THE EVENTS OR VARIABLES

INCREASED PRETRIAL RELEASE → 1 Causes → DECREASED GUILTY PLEAS → 2 Causes → INCREASED TRIALS → 3 Causes → INCREASED DELAY → 4 Causes → INCREASED PRETRIAL JAIL POPULATION

MODEL FOR PREDICTING THE RELATION (i.e., why the relation exists)

Bargaining Model

Bargains = function of:
(1) litigation costs,*
(2) prob. of conviction, &
(3) sentence if convicted

Queueing Backlog Model

Backlog = function of:
(1) # cases entering,
(2) # cases settled

Queueing Delay Model

Delay = function of:
(1) # trials,
(2) trial time,
(3) # judges

Population Model

Population = function of:
(1) # entries,
(2) length of time in system

WAYS OF DECREASING THE RELATION

Prosecutor could offer better bargains

Prosecutor could dismiss more cases

Have more judges

Have priority trials for those in jail

*including the cost of sitting in jail awaiting trial

Figure 1.2   The Impact of Pretrial Release on the Pretrial Jail Population

23

jail population will increase since it is a function of (1) the number of people going to jail, which has gone down as a result of increased pretrial release, and (2) the length of time they stay there, which has gone up because of the increased pretrial release and its intervening effects. The increase in jail length may more than offset the decrease in jail entries, thereby increasing rather than decreasing the pretrial jail population, all because of an increase in pretrial release.

It is interesting to note how each of the four relations of causal arrows at the top of Figure 1.2 is explained by a deductive model summarized in the middle of Figure 1.2. The first relation is explained by the bargaining model, which says that plea bargains arrived at are a function of the litigation costs, the probability of conviction, and the sentence if a conviction occurs, all as perceived by the defendant and the prosecutor. One of the defendant's most important litigation costs is the cost of possibly having to sit in jail awaiting trial if he demands a trial. By lowering that litigation cost, the defendant's upper limit to his offers is likely to be lowered, reducing the possibility that the defendant's upper limit will be above the prosecutor's lower limit and thereby reducing the possibility of a settlement. The second relation is explained by the queueing model for determining backlog sizes, and the third relation is explained by the queueing model for determining the amount of delay or time consumption per case. The fourth relation involves a population model like that which says the world's population is a function of the number of births and how long people live. Likewise the jail population is a function of (1) the number of people entering the jail by not being released prior to trial, which has gone down, and (2) the length of time the average detained defendant lives in the jail, which has gone up.

It is especially interesting to note that each of the models not only predicts and explains the chain of relations from pretrial release to the size of the jail population but also suggests meaningful ways of lessening the extent to which those undesired relations occur, as is indicated at the bottom of Figure 1.2. The bargaining model suggests that the prosecutor could hold constant the percentage of guilty pleas, even in the face of an increased pretrial release rate, by making better offers to those who are released. The better offers might consist of shorter sentences and more probation than the expected value of the sentence if convicted, discounted by the probability of being convicted. Even if the guilty plea rate goes down, the prosecutor can still hold constant the number of trials by dismissing more cases, since he is under no obligation to prosecute just because the defendant pleads not guilty. Even if the number of cases increases, the amount of delay can be held constant by providing for more judges and other court personnel. If delay does increase, there need not be an increase in the length of time spent in jail awaiting trial if the prosecutor provides for priority trials to those who are in jail whereby their cases are tried ahead of those of defendants who are out of jail).

DEDUCTIONS BASED ON
AN INDIVIDUAL DECISION-MAKING MODEL

A good illustration of deductive modeling based on an individual decision-making model involves attempting to determine the effect that publicizing judicial propensities has on judicial behavior. More specifically, the law provides that when in doubt, a judge should release rather than hold a defendant in jail prior to trial. In reality, however, a judge stands to lose more by making the mistake of releasing a defendant who fails to appear for the court date or who commits a crime while released than by making the mistake of holding a defendant who would appear without committing a crime while released. The reason is that one can tell in an individual case that a held defendant would have appeared without committing a crime since the held defendant is not given an opportunity to do so. Thus, the rational judge when in doubt may tend to hold rather than to release, because his expected cost of holding is less than his expected cost of releasing. The deductive modeling problem involves determining the effect on judicial behavior of publicizing the holding rates of judges in light of this decision-making model.

If the holding rates of the judges serving in a given area are publicized, that is unlikely to bring those holding rates down. In other words, publicizing that the trial court judges in a given city hold 60 percent of all defendants in jail pending trial will not cause any individual judge to decrease his holding, because publicizing that information does not increase his expected costs of holding. Likewise, publicizing the holding rates for each individual judge on the court is not likely to lower the holding rates of the high holders, because they can justify at least to themselves that their high holding is needed in order to decrease nonappearances and the committing of crimes by defendants released prior to trial. If, however, the holding rates of individual judges are publicized along with the appearance rates and non-crime-committing rates they achieve among the defendants they release, then the high holders might come down.

This might be so because empirical studies show that holding rates do vary greatly across judges, but appearance and non-crime-committing rates tend to be almost uniformly high among both high-holding and low-holding judges. Thus, Judge Jones, who holds 80 percent of all defendants, may look bad in comparison with his fellow judges like Judge Smith, who holds only 30 percent of all defendants. But each is likely to have about a 90 to 95 percent appearance rate and non-crime-committing rate for those defendants they release. In other words, it looks as if Judge Jones is holding 50 percent more defendants than he needs to hold in order to have a 90 to 95 percent appearance and non-crime-committing rate, even though we cannot tell in which cases Judge Jones has made a holding error. That kind of publicizing thereby increases the expected cost of holding to Judge Jones, and is likely to cause him to decrease his holding if everything else remains constant. That effect can be further accentuated by also publicizing the undesirable effects and high social costs incurred by holding defendants in jail, such as jail maintenance, lost gross national product, increased number of families on welfare, jail congestion, and the frequency of held defendants being found not guilty or only guilty of crimes involving sentences shorter than the jail time already served awaiting trial.

The same individual decision-making model can be used to deduce the effects of other changes on decreasing the decision to hold. The expected cost of holding relative to releasing is likely to go down if one decreases the costs of releasing by such means as making rearrests more easy through pretrial supervision or decreasing the time from arrest to trial, thereby lessening the time to disappear or commit crimes. The expected cost of releasing also goes down if the probability of appearance and non-crime-committing can be increased through such means as better screening and notification and more vigorous prosecution of those who fail to appear.

OPTIMIZING ALTERNATIVE PUBLIC POLICIES

GENERAL MATTERS

The main scientific alternative to optimizing alternative public policies is the perspective that takes policies as givens and attempts to determine their effects. This is often referred to as impact analysis or evaluation research. An optimizing perspective, on the other hand, takes goals as givens and attempts to determine what policies will maximize those goals.

On a highly general level, the best or optimum policy or set of policies is the one that maximizes benefits minus costs, subject to economic, legal, political, or other constraints. Models for optimizing alternative public policies can be classified in terms of whether they involve finding (1) an optimum policy level where doing too much or too little may be undesirable, (2) an optimum policy mix where scarce resources need to be allocated, or (3) an optimum policy choice among discrete alternatives, especially under conditions of uncertainty.

In optimum-level problems, one needs to relate adoption costs and nonadoption costs to various policy levels. The optimum policy level is then the level or degree of adoption that minimizes the sum of the adoption costs plus the nonadoption costs. In optimum mix problems, one needs to determine the relative slopes or marginal rates of return of each of the places or activities under consideration. If linear relations are present, the optimum mix is then the mix or allocation that gives all of the budget to the most productive places or activities subject to the constraints. If diminishing returns are assumed, the optimum mix is the one that allocates the budget in such a way that the marginal rates of return are equalized across the places or activities so that nothing can be gained by redistributing the budget. In optimum choice problems, one needs to determine the benefits and costs from each choice. The optimum choice is then the one that has the highest benefits minus costs with the benefits and costs being discounted by the probability of their being received.

These general concepts and principles can be greatly clarified by providing a concrete illustration for each of the three major types of optimizing models with regard to determining an optimum level, mix, or choice.

DETERMINING AN OPTIMUM POLICY LEVEL

A good illustration of finding an optimum policy level is the problem of what is the optimum size for juries. That problem is one being faced by many states which have lowered or contemplated lowering jury sizes from twelve to six or even five in order to save the time and money which twelve-person juries supposedly incur. The United States Supreme Court has heard a number of cases in which defendants have questioned the constitutionality of juries smaller than twelve persons. In the 1978 case of Ballew v. Georgia, the Supreme Court favorably referred to some of the policy analysis literature which has attempted to analyze not only the effects on conviction rates of changing jury sizes but also what an optimum jury size might be.

Knowing the relation between jury size and conviction rates can be used as input into the empirical premises of an optimizing model designed to arrive at an optimum jury size that minimizes the weighted sum of type 1 errors of convicting the innocent plus type 2 errors of not convicting the guilty. Figure 1.3 summarizes what is involved in that kind of analysis. The curve of "weighted errors of innocent convicted" was arrived at by using the analysis of Figure 1.1, but operating on the tentative assumption that a twelve-person jury would be likely to convict an innocent person only about 40 percent of the time rather than 64 percent and that about five out of one hundred defendants tried by juries may be actually innocent. The curve of "errors of guilty not convicted" was arrived at with the tentative assumption that a twelve-person jury would be likely to convict a guilty person about 70 percent of the time rather than 64 percent and that about ninety-five out of one hundred defendants tried by juries are probably actually guilty.

The "weighted sum of errors" curve was calculated by simply summing the other two curves after multiplying the points on the first curve by ten to indicate that convicting the innocent is traditionally considered ten times as bad as not convicting the guilty. With those tentative assumptions and that analysis, the weighted sum of errors bottoms out at jury sizes between six and eight. Justice Blackmun in announcing the Court's decision referred favorably to that analysis in deciding that it was meaningful to allow juries to be smaller than twelve but no smaller than six.

In his opinion in the Ballew case, Justice Blackmun indicated agreement with the analysis in Figure 1 and the 10-to-1 trade-off weight. The model, however, is not particularly sensitive to that trade-off weight in the sense that the weight can be reasonably varied and the weighted errors curve will still bottom out at about 7. The

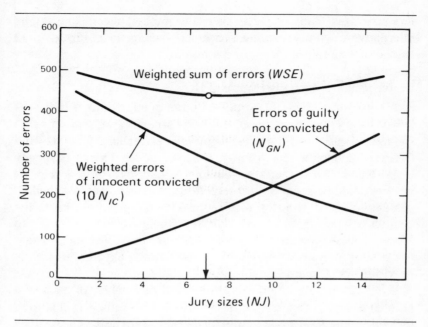

Figure 1.3 Graphing the Number of Errors for Various Jury Sizes

model, however, is particularly sensitive to the assumption that prosecutors operate at a .95 level of confidence in deciding whether a defendant is guilty such that he or she can be brought to trial. If prosecutors are operating substantially below a .95 level, then one would need larger juries to protect those additional innocent defendants from being convicted. If prosecutors are operating substantially above a .95 level, then one could have smaller juries to increase the probability of convicting those additional guilty defendants.

Thus, the optimum jury size mainly depends on what assumption one is willing to make regarding how many jury-tried defendants out of one hundred are truly guilty. People who favor twelve-person juries probably perceive the number of innocent jury-tried defendants as being greater than the number perceived by people who favor six-person juries. Thus, the optimum jury size ultimately depends on normative values rather than on observed relations or relations deduced from empirical premises. Nevertheless, the combination of the predictive model of Figure 1 and the optimizing model of Figure 2 enables us to see better what is involved in choosing among alternative jury sizes. The same analysis can be applied to choosing among alternative fractions required to convict, such as unanimity, a 10/12 rule, or a 9/12 rule.

DETERMINING AN OPTIMUM POLICY MIX

A good illustration of finding an optimum policy mix is the problem of what is the optimum allocation between law reform activities and routine case handling in the legal services agencies funded by the Office of Economic Opportunity. The average legal services agency in 1971 had $67 to spend per client. Of that $67, not less than 10 percent could be spent on law reform activities and not less than 80 percent could be spent on routine case handling, according to the general policies of the national office. The question thus is how to allocate the $67 per client in such a way as to maximize the satisfaction of the program evaluators or how to minimize expenditures while providing a minimum level of satisfaction.

To obtain the optimum mix, one could determine for each of a number of legal services agencies (1) the overall satisfaction score it received in the 1971 evaluations, (2) the number of dollars it spent per client on law reform activities, and (3) the number of dollars it spent per client on case handling activities. One could then fit an equation to that data through the use of linear regression analysis. That equation tells us the relation between satisfaction on the one hand and law reform and case handling on the other, especially if we statistically hold constant other variables that might influence satisfaction. Such an equation indicates that law reform has a higher slope or rate of return than case handling. With that finding, one can say the optimum mix for *maximizing satisfaction* is to give the minimum constraint to case handling and the rest of the budget per client to law reform. One can also say the optimum mix for *minimizing expenditures* is to give the minimum constraint to case handling and the rest of the budget per client to law reform, but just up to the point where a satisfaction score of seven is obtained since that score was considered to represent a minimum satisfaction level.

The actual average allocation was substantially less efficient than either of the above optimums, because many conservative legal services agencies felt such an emphasis on law reform would get them into trouble with the national office as of 1971, and many liberal legal services agencies that were dominated by a client orientation felt law reform was not what the individual clients wanted. The evaluators, on the other hand, tended to be prominent lawyers who had a high regard for the technical competence needed to do law reform work, like appellate case argument, and not such a high regard for the relative lack of competence needed to do much routine case handling, like default divorce cases, regardless of whether the lawyers had conservative or liberal backgrounds. If the evaluators had included more low-income clients rather than lawyers, the slope of law reform may have become lower than the slope of case handling in the regression equation that was developed from the agency-by-agency data. The optimum mix, however, would still be the same if the law reform slope were decreased but still higher than the case handling slope, given the linear nature of the data for the somewhat narrow range of discretionary allocation.

DETERMINING AN OPTIMUM POLICY CHOICE

A good illustration of finding an optimum policy choice is the problem of how a juror should vote with regard to convicting or acquitting a given defendant, and how jurors should be instructed in order to maximize objectivity across jurors and conformity with the principle that convictions should only occur if the defendant is guilty beyond a reasonable doubt.

A rational juror should vote to convict or acquit depending on which choice will give him or her the highest expected value, although expected value calculations are done implicitly rather than explicitly. The expected value of each choice equals the perceived benefits minus costs, discounted by the probability of their being received. The probability in this context is the probability of the defendant actually being guilty. To obtain the highest expected value, a juror should vote to acquit if the perceived probability of guilt is below a threshold probability and vote to convict if the perceived probability of guilt is above a threshold probability. The threshold probability can be determined by knowing the relative value a juror places on avoiding the conviction of an innocent defendant versus the acquittal of a guilty one.

To stimulate jurors to have a common threshold probability and a high threshold probability in the .90s in accordance with the law, jurors can be instructed that it is considered ten times as undesirable to convict an innocent defendant as it is to acquit a guilty one (i.e., the 10-to-1 tradeoff instruction). Merely instructing them that the standard of guilt is "beyond a reasonable doubt" or that a conviction requires a .90 probability does not generate a common or high threshold probability. For example, male and female students at the University of Illinois were given diverse instructions on how to decide criminal cases, and then their threshold probabilities in rape cases were determined by asking them questions about their relative satisfaction or dissatisfaction from convicting a guilty defendant, convicting an innocent defendant, acquitting a guilty defendant, or acquitting an innocent defendant. The results were roughly as shown in Table 1.1.

Table 1.1

Type of Jury Instruction	Threshold Probabilities (in rape cases)	
	Males	Females
No Instruction	.65	.45
Beyond Reasonable Doubt	.75	.60
.90 Probability	.85	.75
10-to-1 Tradeoff	.90	.90

With no instruction, there is considerable divergence between the two groups and both groups are substantially below the desired .90 threshold probability. A verbal instruction increases both objectivity and conformity with the law, but not enough. A quantitative instruction makes for an improvement, but not as much as the 10-to-1 tradeoff instruction.

Although the optimum choice seems to be the 10-1 instruction, the empirical reality is generally no instruction. The difference between the empirical and the optimum here may possibly be caused by judges being aware that a 10-to-1, .90, or verbal instruction will make convictions more difficult to obtain, which they do not want to do. In other words, judges have decided on the no-instruction choice, and we assume they perceive that convictions will be more difficult to obtain by giving the recommended instructions. We thereby deduce that their values must generally be oriented toward keeping the conviction rate up, since there seems to be no other deduced value position capable of reconciling the decision reached with the assumed factual perception. This illustrates how optimizing analysis can often relate back to making deductions about decision-making behavior, just as deductions about decision-making behavior can often serve as the premises for an optimizing model.

SOME CONCLUSIONS

The two dimensions of deducing effects of policy changes and optimizing alternative public policies are two of the newest and most interesting aspects of policy analysis research. Although they have an element of newness to them, they both relate back to a traditional social philosophy concern for logical and normative analysis quite prevalent in the writings of such classical social philosophers as Aristotle, St. Thomas Aquinas, and other pre-twentieth-century thinkers. They also relate back to a more recent behavioral science concern for quantifying relationships, which has been quite prevalent in the post-World War II social science literature. Policy analysis research thus represents a kind of synthesis of classical social philosophy and modern behavioral science as applied to important policy problems.

Policy analysis also represents an interdisciplinary synthesis of methodological and conceptual contributions from such disciplines as economics, business administration, industrial engineering, and social psychology. Political science and public administration also contribute a perspective that emphasizes the need to consider problems of policy adoption, implementation, and political philosophy. The examples we have presented come from the substance of legal policy problems, but one can easily reason by analogy to policy problems from a broad variety of substantive fields. Both deductive modeling and optimization have wide potential applicability. What is especially needed now is even more researchers who are interested in developing that applicability for its theoretical and practical usefulness.

SUGGESTED READINGS

Gass, Saul I. and Roger L. Sisson. *A Guide to Models in Governmental Planning and Operations*. Washington, D.C.: Environmental Protection Agency, 1974.

Greenberger, Martin, Matthew A. Crenson, and Brian L. Crissey. *Models in the Policy Process: Public Decision Making in the Computer Era*. New York: Russell Sage, 1976.

Nagel, Stuart and Marian Neef. *The Legal Process: Modeling the System*. Beverly Hills: Sage, 1977.

　　　Policy Analysis: In Social Science Research. Beverly Hills: Sage, 1979.

Quade, Edward S. *Analysis for Public Decisions*. New York: American Elsevier, 1975.

Stokey, Elizabeth and Richard Zeckhauser. *A Primer for Policy Analysis*. New York: W. W. Norton, 1978.

2

SATISFICING, FEEDBACK, AND DECISION RULES IN GOVERNMENT

John E. Brandl

The most influential and elegantly developed insight of economic and political science in this country is that in some cases predictable social order can result from the apparent chaos of independent self-interested behavior by large numbers of individuals. Economists have derived a myriad of hypotheses to explain social interaction by applying powerful mathematical methods to the postulate that people act in self-aggrandizing fashion. This has been done by translating self-interest into a maximizing calculus. Neoclassical microeconomics, the branch of the discipline that deals with the decisions of individuals in the small, predicts the behavior of self-interested consumers and firms. In several strains of political theory, special interests are viewed as each acting in its own self-interest but competing in a political marketplace.

Turned upside down, this predictive theory becomes a normative theory of rational choice. Given an objective, the constrained maximization analytical method can be used to yield prescriptions for action instead of predictions. This has become the predominant theory of rational action. Much of policy analysis has consisted of iterative constrained maximization problem formulation and solution where the iterations occur as maximand and constraints change.

Competing explanations of behavior exist, of course, and some are associated with competing normative theories. The strongest of these competitors has developed in the past two decades under the generic title of organization theory. Herbert Simon has summarized the approach in an aphorism: "Man satisfices because he has not the wits to maximize."[1] Organization theorists and other critics see constrained maximization prescriptive theories as impractical counsels of perfection. They contend that whatever the value of optimization theories for prediction they are unrealistic for prescriptive purposes because omniscience is attributed to decision makers who are merely human.

In this chapter I begin an effort to provide the "wits to maximize" for a class of decisions. To the extent that this effort in prescriptive methodology development were to be successful and used, constrained maximization theories would become better predictors as well.

In rational choice theory it is generally assumed that the implications of a decision are known to the decider. If, unknown to the decider, implications of a decision are inconsistent with intentions and expectations, then, of course, neither the individual's nor society's interests are necessarily fostered. In this chapter it will be argued that for much governmental decision making, feedback to the decider is faulty. This conjecture is investigated by studying certain explicit decision rules used in government. The decision rules are revenue allocation formulas. Formulas are very widely used to distribute investment, revenue sharing, education and other monies from one level of government to another. Decision rules of this type have been selected for study because they appear explicitly, even algebraically, in legislation.

The central thesis of this chapter is as follows. In much governmental decision making, feedback to the decider is absent or distorted. In the absence of reliable feedback, an individual resorts to simplistic and faulty strategies and rules of thumb. Then *decisions have implications unintended by and unknown to the decider.* Such a situation will be termed an *incongruity.* The sheer complexity of the environment in which much governmental decision making takes place, the fact that a decision's effects may occur in diverse places separated by thousands of miles diluted by myriad other influences— these suggest that often in government what may be taken for inscrutable cleverness or even malice can be better explained by this notion of incongruity.

Section I is an overview of relevant aspects of rational choice theory. Section II reviews the ways in which explicit governmental decision rules have been studied by political scientists and economists. Section III develops a technique for constructing decision rules that reflect the intentions of governmental actors. Section IV is the conclusion.

I. AN OVERVIEW OF RATIONAL CHOICE THEORY

ECONOMICS AS A THEORY OF RATIONAL CHOICE

An individual consumer is assumed to make the best use of a limited budget, and his behavior traditionally has been described as the maximization of a utility function subject to a budget constraint. This utility function, incorporating the consumer's preferences, is recognized to be extremely complex, and difficult if not impossible to derive explicitly. In the past generation the theoretical study of the consumer has come to be dominated by revealed preference theory.[2] The latter was fostered by a desire to structure the study of the consumer in terms of operationally meaningful hypotheses, that is, hypotheses that are potentially refutable on the basis of empirical evidence. (These hypotheses predict, for example, changes in amounts of goods demanded when prices and/or income change.) The hypotheses themselves are derived axiomatically; to change the axioms or assumptions of the theory is, of course, to change the hypotheses. At the heart of the work is the assumption that a consumer's purchases reflect a preference ordering, a ranking of all possible combinations of goods in order of desirability. Different budget levels and different sets of prices yield different decisions; the observable data are, then, the actual amounts of each good bought at different budgets and prices. But the point to be made here and to which we shall return is that the preferences of the consumer are *defined* to be a preference ordering that is consistent with and derivable from the purchases he has made.

With similar logic, until recently economic theory has also generally assumed that firms maximize something—profits or perhaps sales.[3] From this and other assumptions are derived hypotheses about the behavior of firms.[4] In the 1940s a vigorous attack was made on the profit-maximizing assumption by people who produced evidence that, when asked, many firms do not claim profit maximization as their sole or even main objective.[5] The attackers clearly lost the battle if not the war, since their argument amounted to questioning an *assumption* (namely, conscious profit-maximization) of the theory of the firm. To disprove the theory, they were told, they would need to produce empirical evidence incompatible not with the assumptions but the *conclusions* (the theorems or hypotheses) of the theory.[6] Of course, some philosophers of science defend the quite obvious proposition that, after all, the assumptions of a theory must have some empirical basis or else theory building would be random and unaided by observation.[7] But the profit maximization theorists won the day. They were implicitly grateful to a chaotic universe for the favor of granting them hypotheses that could perceive and predict order. But they explicitly asserted that metaphysical questions of the relationship between the assumptions of their model and "reality" were simply not as interesting to them—if indeed meaningful at all—as was their criterion of the value of a theory, namely, that its hypotheses predict behavior.

So both branches of microeconomics posit an objective function or maximand; data collected on the behavior of the consumer or firm are presumed to reflect the respective actor's maximization of an objective subject to a posited set of constraints.[8]

CONSTRAINED MAXIMIZATION THEORY AND THE BEHAVIOR OF GOVERNMENTAL ACTORS

In recent years people have begun to apply this kind of theory to decision making in government. Attempts have been made to infer the preferences of governmental decision makers by attributing to the decision makers (in the manner of revealed preference theorists) preferences implicit in the distribution of resources brought about by a government decision or project.[9] Again, note the presumption that the implications of a decision can be construed to be the faithful reflection of the intentions of a purposive actor. Similarly, a full-fledged theory of supply of government goods and services has been developed, paralleling and following the same approach as the theory of the firm.[10] In it a bureaucrat is assumed to act so as to maximize the size of his budget or staff. A number of hypotheses have been derived, the most interesting and plausible of which is that bureaus are too large; that is, they produce more of their good or service at wastefully higher cost than would a firm operating in pure competition. Bureaucrats, like consumers and firms, are understood to be aware of what they want and to respond to changing circumstances so as to maximize those objectives within the limits of the conditions constraining them.

The foregoing are only the most obvious and formalized examples of social science positing and construing system from self-interested individual behavior. The science of politics, particularly as applied to designing government, has long made use of the notion that individuals and groups act in their own self-interest, and that conflicting interests could play off against each other to yield a harmonious, even desirable result. In 1705, fifteen years after the publication of Locke's *Treatise on Government,* Bernard Mandeville's *Fable of the Bees* foreshadowed both classical economics and Enlightenment political thought as later most eloquently expressed in *The Federalist Papers* of Madison, Hamilton, and Jay. Mandeville described a bee hive in which there were:

> Millions endeavoring to supply
> Each other's Lust and Vanity; . . .
> Thus every Part was full of Vice,
> Yet the whole Mass a Paradise.

That purposive self-interested behavior has its advantages was made clear after Jove responded to the entreaties of reformers by introducing honesty and checking avarice.

> But, Oh ye Gods! What Consternation,
> How vast and sudden was th' Alteration! . . .
> As pride and Luxury decrease,
> So by degrees they leave the Seas . . .
> All Arts and Crafts neglected lie;
> Content, the Bane of Industry,
> Makes 'em admire their homely Store,
> And neither seek nor covet more.
>
> THEN leave Complaints: Fools only strive
> To make a Great and Honest Hive

> T' enjoy the World's Conveniencies,
> Be fam'd in War, yet live in Ease
>
> Without great Vices, is a vain
> EUTOPIA seated in the Brain.
> Fraud, Luxury and Pride must live,
> While we the Benefits receive. . . .[11]

For nearly three centuries applied rational choice theory has posited purposive, informed self-interested behavior. The work has yielded hypotheses to be used for prediction; implications the operationalization of which could result in inferring the intentions of individual decision-makers; and normative judgments about political and economic organization.

THE ELEMENTS OF THEORIES OF RATIONAL CHOICE

The *Fable of the Bees* and *The Federalist Papers* contain in embryonic form the four elements of what has become the predominant strain of decision-making theory: a society composed of (1) self-interested individuals who (2) face options and who (3) act in accordance with their interests (4) toward the fortuitous result that not merely the individual but the whole society "the benefits receive." Differences exist among variations within the strain. By and large, and somewhat in contrast to the main stream of work in economics, the emphasis in political science has been more on defending the *procedure* of a free political marketplace as fair, as against predicting or gauging the desirability of the *results* of the process. Economists, though aware of the proceduralist case for pure competition (each individual is *free* to decide what is best for himself), have tended to concentrate on, and indeed to celebrate, the Pareto-optimality, i.e., efficiency, of the results of the competitive process.[12]

Of course, a great variety of attacks have been made on the prevailing approach. Mention of some of the objections to the four elements of the theory will bring others to the reader's mind. (1) For two hundred years people have puzzled over whether Adam Smith believed people to be the self-seekers of the *Wealth of Nations* or the altruists of the *Theory of the Moral Sentiments*. Is self interest a person's dominant motivation? (2) Organization theorists argue that individuals have limited intellectual capacities, are not omniscient calculators. Do people know their own preferences and the constraints on satisfying them? (3) Several strains of contemporary psychology question whether people act on the basis of conscious calculated motivations.[13] In what sense do people have preferences and motivations? Are these constructs as ephemeral and anachronistic as the phlogiston which eighteenth-century chemists needed to get their explanations to work? (4) Does self-interested behavior aggregate to societal advantage, or is that the rationalization of the bourgeoisie and the false consciousness of the oppressed?

It is difficult to conclude other than that the desire to perceive system in political and economic decision making has led a number of people in both disciplines to attribute all of the elements of a rational, even mechanical, system to some aspects of government when only certain of those elements were present. Newton's celestial mechanics were probably of more influence on the development of economic—and perhaps even political—thought than were the individualism of Locke and the proceduralism of Kant.

THE IMPORTANCE OF FEEDBACK IN RATIONAL CHOICE THEORY

In this chapter one aspect of the received theories of rational action is analyzed and questioned and a remedy of a sort is proposed. The chapter's purpose is not to devise an alternative predictive theory; it accepts the construct of a rational actor but seeks to bolster his ability to carry out his intentions. It is an exercise in the development of method. It seeks not better *predictors* of behavior, but rather *prescriptive* techniques to assist the less-than-omniscient actor.

Preferences are not automatically translated into actions consistent with those preferences. *In the absence of accurate feedback, maximization of objectives will not occur.* Traditionally, the assumption that behavior is self-interested has been taken to be sufficient to guarantee feedback of results. This is a characteristic common to the theory of the firm, that of the household, and the recent extensions of both of those theories to explain bureaucratic behavior and to infer governmental preferences. All of these as well as the generally less formally structured theories of liberal democracy take as given—in fact, as the very explanation of behavior—that the respective objectives are maximized. The theory of revealed preference is the embodiment of this idea. But as it is applied progressively from individual consumer to firm to bureaucrat to top-level government official, the argument that individuals know the implications of their actions becomes less and less credible.

Since individual consumers experience directly most of the goods and services they buy, the purchases can be said with some plausibility to reveal preferences. And the desire to make money, plus competition and the survival of the fittest could foster profit maximization at least by surviving firms. But the application to government of the idea of a feedback system powered by self-interest needs to be questioned. In a society which leaves some range of choice to the discretion of its public officials, there is no guarantee that they will maximize the attainment of their objectives. If the utility function of an individual is too complicated to be specified and maximized by an analyst, even with impressive mathematical and computational techniques, should it be expected that a politician or bureaucrat can accomplish this feat unaided by technical analytical tools? The answer to that question is "no," if he has neither the market signals experienced by a firm nor the introspectively perceived uneasiness of a consumer dissatisfied with the way last week's paycheck was squandered. Government officers do not experience directly the implications of many of their decisions. So, even if they wish to be maximizers, they may not know the extent to which what happens reflects their intentions.

II. THE USE OF DECISION RULES IN GOVERNMENT

A decision rule is a strategy stipulating an action, y, in terms of a number of other variables, x_1, x_2, . . . x_n. It is a decision maker's control over or, at any rate, knowledge of the values of some of the x's that suggests the term *decision* rule. Given values for the x's, y is determined. There is widespread use of such strategies or heuristics in government. Social scientists have perceived decision rules in two quite different fashions. Some have seen them as the optimal strategies of maximizing decision makers. Others view them as rules of thumb, habits, customs—more or less consistent coping actions but not optimizing procedures.

OPTIMAL DECISION RULES: THE STATE OF THE ART

The analytics of construing a decision rule as an optimizing strategy follow. The approach starts with a maximand

$$z = f(x,y,a). \tag{1}$$

x is a vector of variables the values of which a decision maker cannot influence. For purposes of analytical maximization it can be treated as a vector of constants. It is useful to distinguish x from a, which is a vector of parameters. In contrast with the predetermined x and a are the controlled or instrument variables, y, whose values can be manipulated by the decision maker. The maximand is subject to one or more constraints,

$$w = g(x,y,b) \tag{2}$$

where w and b are also vectors, of variables and parameters respectively.

From the maximand and constraints can be formed an expression

$$v = z + \lambda w. \tag{3}$$

Setting the partial derivatives of that expression, with respect (successively) to y and λ, equal to zero, yields a system of equations, the first-order conditions for a maximum or minimum:

$$\frac{\partial v}{\partial y} = 0.$$

$$\frac{\partial v}{\partial \lambda} = 0. \tag{4}$$

If second-order conditions are met, then solving the system of first-order conditions for y yields a set of optimum strategies, levels at which to set y in order to maximize z:

$$y = h(x,a,b). \tag{5}$$

These functions, h, are optimal decision rules; for given values of x (as well as a and b), they yield optimal values of y. That is, if a decision maker sets y at the levels stipulated by the decision rules, he will maximize z to the extent possible given the constraints. A demand function is a familiar example of a decision rule construed in this fashion.

People who have used the constrained maximization framework for studying decision rules in government have done so either by positing a maximand (and analytically deriving decision rules) or by estimating empirically decision rules presuming that the rules reflect and reveal decision makers' preferences.

For the past two decades explicit posited preference functions and, thus, inferentially, decision rules, have been a part of macroeconomic planning in several Western European nations. Henri Theil, Ragnar Frisch, and Jan Tinbergen were the main inventors of an approach for deriving optimal economic policy.[14] In its most ambitious form the approach posits a maximand for macroeconomic policy (containing such desiderata as employment, income, and price levels). This objective function is maximized subject to a set of constraints that constitute an econometric model of a national economy. Solving such a constrained maximization problem yields decision rules setting the levels of the arguments in the objective function. For example, a decision rule for employment states that variable as a function of variables that are either exogenous to the econometric model or are endogenously determined in the model. Inserting the values of those variables into the employment decision rule yields the optimal value for employment. Less use has been made of this approach in the United States, although it has appeared in the work of Gary Fromm, Ann Friedlander, Karl Fox, and others.[15] For computational reasons Tinbergen, Theil, and their followers have restricted themselves almost exclusively to using quadratic maximands and linear constraints, an implication of which is that the resultant decision rules are linear.

There are two limitations to the approach. The first is that maximands and constraints approaching real world complexity strain the powers of existing algorithms for solving such problems. The other is that in a pluralistic country any maximand posited for use in such analysis is somewhat arbitrary. In recent years Ragnar Frisch has begun to deal with these limitations by working on an interview approach for constructing a decision maker's preference function, one that presumably could be approximated by a simpler function.[16]

The other way in which governmental decision rules have been studied using a constrained maximization framework has been for estimating rules. The work of Burton Weisbrod and of G. C. Rausser and J. W. Freebairn is illustrative. Weisbrod posited a social welfare function that was a linear combination of the incomes of several groups in the society, then empirically estimated weights for the different groups. This was done by comparing several water resource projects. There is little reason to accept such a social welfare function; furthermore, Weisbrod's estimation technique was faulty. It involved solving four equations (for four water projects) in four unknowns (the weights associated with income benefits to four groups), thus begging the question whether a large series of decisions would reflect consistent weighting.

Rausser and Freebairn draw on the sophisticated work of Nijkamp,[17] who proposed to estimate a preference function from past governmental decisions, recognizing explicitly the constraints on a maximizing government. Again, the predictive value of work of this kind is problematic; group decision making probably does not reflect a consistent set of preferences. Rausser and Freebairn's work is the most ambitious attempt to infer what they term social preference functions from governmental actions. But they admit that the procedure is "naive" for several reasons; for example, their social preference functions regarding beef import quotas contain only two arguments.

HEURISTICS FOR MUDDLING THROUGH

The derivation of optimal decision rules makes explicit use of objective functions and constraints for the purpose of arriving at appropriate prescriptions for normative purposes. A second kind of work on decision rules is best understood as a reaction to the perception of decision making as rational. Apparently independently, persons in several disciplines have empirically derived relationships that describe actual decisions. The spirit of this inquiry has generally been atheoretical and descriptive.[18] A number of psychologists, following an approach suggested by the work of Egon Brunswick,[19] have estimated the relationship between a "judgment" or decision and a number of posited "cues," on which the judgment is expected to depend. In summarizing the results of this work, Paul Slovic and Sarah Lichtenstein assert that "judges have a very difficult time weighting and combining information—be it probabilistic or deterministic in nature. To reduce cognitive strain, they resort to simplified decision strategies, many of which lead them to ignore or misuse relevant information."[20] These "simplified decision strategies" sometimes have been captured in the form of linear regression equations—predictable, albeit mistaken relationships between judgment and cues. Recent evidence indicates that not only do many people not act in conformity with the predictions of the theory of maximizing self-interested behavior but also their actions contradict principles of decision making which they themselves espouse. Amos Tversky and David Kahneman have shown that often people make decisions by means of heuristics that "reduce the complex tasks of assessing probabilities and predicting values to simpler judgmental operations," and that this "sometimes [leads] to severe and systematic errors."[21] Their empirical work establishes the prevalence in actual decision making of such systematically mistaken notions as the gambler's fallacy (when flipping a coin, after a number of successive heads, tails is "due") and insensitivity to sample size in making inferences from a sample. This amounts to a severe challenge to, if not actual disconfirmation of, the axioms of rational decision making. That is not a fatal blow to the usefulness of the theory, since it could be argued that the ultimate test is the ability of the theory to predict behavior.

Those emphasizing the pervasiveness of the use of rules of thumb and simplifying heuristics in government have not proposed a normative framework of the richness of the theory of the rational actor. Empirical estimation of heuristics, as, for example, by Davis, Dempster, and Wildavsky has uncovered gross relationships between a given year's congressional appropriation, an agency's budget request for that year, and the previous year's appropriation and request.[22] But such knowledge is neither predictively nor normatively powerful. The linear decision rules they estimate were not derived from a set of axioms, e.g., postulated maximand and constraints. That is in part an aesthetic quibble, but it means, as Davis, Dempster, and Wildavsky graciously admit, that theirs are "explanatory," not predictive decision rules. The circumstances under which one might expect a given rule to apply—they estimated several—are not stated generally. In describing a particular agency's budget record, one is expected to try several rules to see which fits best. However, it is interesting (and promising for future empirical research) to realize that there is considerable regularity in governmental decision making.

For purposes of this chapter the main inadequacy of both strains of work on decision rules is that they are not of much value to individual bureaucrats or politicians who see themselves as decision makers. Individuals seem unable or at least unwilling to enunciate a preference function. Furthermore, the current state of the art in solving constrained maximization problems has limited almost all of the work of the Theil type to the maximization of quadratic maximands subject to linear constraints. Since there is little evidence to suggest that actual utility functions are as simple as to be quadratic, it yet remains to be seen whether that formulation of decision making will be of prescriptive usefulness. On the other hand, the prescriptive injunction to the public actor of the Davis et al. work appears to be "Don't rock the boat, except in special circumstances," which are not identified, or, even more discouragingly, "Don't even think of yourself as a decision maker; you are a cog in a process that is inexorable."

Is there a way out? The position taken here is that in the foreseeable future, neither of two conceptions of decision making will drive the other from the realm of respectable explanations of governmental activitiy—neither the individual as autonomous actor with control over certain phenomena and subjective criteria by which to distinguish relative merit nor the individual as cog in a process of which he is a witness.[23] The remainder of the chapter is an attempt to shore up the first of these conceptualizations. I propose to use the constrained maximization framework—not for deriving decision rules from more or less arbitrary posited preference functions, not for estimating preference functions as revealed in governmental decisions, and not for describing inconsistent and/or simplistic decision rules actually used in government. Rather, I accept the incrementalist explanation as descriptive of how harried public actors operate, often in ways inconsistent with their own intentions, but wish to use the analytics of constrained maximization to assist decision makers to derive decision rules that reflect their intentions.

DERIVING INTENTIONS FROM STATED DECISION RULES

Before moving to the construction of decision rules, it will be useful to consider what can be inferred about a decision maker's preferences from a decision rule when the decision rule is construed as the outcome of optimization. For example, think of the allocation formula for state aid to municipalities in Minnesota as an instance of one of the equations of system 5 above. As will be seen in the next section, a simplified version of the formula can be written as:[24]

$$G_{kj} = P_{kj}M_{kj}S_{kj}C_{kj},$$

where G_{kj} = grant to the kth municipality of county j

P_{kj} = population of the kth municipality of county j

M_{kj} = property tax mill rate of the kth municipality of county j

S_{kj} = an adjustment factor to account for differences in assessment practices; and

C_j = a normalizing term incorporating grants to all municipalities in county j

A partial derivative of the decision rule can be thought of as a rate of substitution or tradeoff between the two variables—the level of offsetting changes in the two that would leave the level of y unchanged.[25] It is of interest to take such derivatives and ask the creators of the decision rule—that is, the allocation formula—if the rates of substitution reflect their intentions. The conjecture of those who are skeptical of optimizing theories as explainers and predictors of behavior is that sometimes the rates of substitution will be rejected by the creators of a formula. That is what I mean by an instance of incongruity. In the case of the Minnesota municipal aid formula, the partial derivative of M with respect to P $\left(\dfrac{\partial M}{\partial P} = \dfrac{-M}{P} \right)$ is the rate of substitution, the implied tradeoff, between those two variables. The author has often observed creators of formulas reject their own handiwork when its implications are presented to them in the form of such tradeoffs.

Obviously, there exist many competing explanations why that happens. It could be argued that since an allocation formula typically results from political bargaining involving a number of competing groups, the result might not reflect the preferences of any single individual. Or it could be argued that the reaction of a creator of a formula to information on its implications cannot be accepted at face value, since for a politician openly admitting one's preferences can be counterproductive in bargaining. But if one takes the perspective of a political actor eager to insure that a formula he is proposing reflects his intentions, one can see there will be situations in which the rates of substitution derived from decision rules would be of genuine interest to decision makers. Thus, there would be cases in which political actors would cooperate with analysts attempting to discern their preferences.

III. CONSTRUCTING DECISION RULES

We seek now a way of insuring that the implications of a public actor's decisions are consistent with his intentions. The most direct way of doing this, especially for circumstances in which a succession of decisions must be made, in each case with the same set of relevant considerations, is to construct a maximand and solve it analytically subject to constraints. Whenever the maximand or a constraint changes, solve the problem anew. As we have seen, two difficulties in doing so are (1) it is difficult to determine whether a given stated maximand does in fact incorporate one's preferences, and (2) if it does, it is likely to be so complex as to defy analytical solution.

REVEALED PREFERENCE AND INTEGRABILITY

The economics and mathematics of integrability suggest a way of constructing decision rules which reflect an individual's preferences, thus obviating resort to distorting rules of thumb.

In 1950 Hendrich Houthakker proved that the so-called strong axiom of revealed preference implies the existence of a utility function. Houthakker proved the theorem in the context of the economic theory of the consumer. The strong axiom is that if q_2 (a certain quantity of a good) is revealed preferred to q_1, and q_3 is revealed preferred to q_2 . . . and q_n is revealed preferred to q_{n-1}, then q_1 cannot be revealed preferred to q_n. So the axiom is simply that preferences are consistent in the sense of being transitive. Analytically that means that a set of partial derivatives reflecting an individual's marginal preferences as between all combinations of goods yields a difference equation and that difference equation has a solution, the utility function. (Houthakker expressed his work in operational terms. The rates of substitution are knowable only as they are revealed through a pattern of consumption decisions in which an individual chooses different packages of goods at different prices.) Geometrically a purchase can be imagined as occurring at a point of tangency between an indifference hypersurface of a utility function and a budget constraint. The slope of the indifference surface at that point is the same as the slope of the budget constraint. So, for each purchase both a point on an indifference surface and the slope of the surface at that point are known empirically. Houthakker's accomplishment was to prove that if preferences are transitive in the sense that the strong axiom of revealed preference implies, these slopes can be "integrated" into a utility function. Integrability refers then to whether a differential equation implied by the set of points and slopes has a solution.[26]

AN APPROACH TO INFERRING DECISION RULES

In the present context Houthakker's theorem can be used to construct—or modify—a decision rule from a set of expressed rates of substitution. The rates of substitution would be determined by interviewing a decision maker (rather than by observing a succession of purchases in the marketplace), and the solution to the differential equation that is implied by the rates of substitution would be a revenue allocation formula (rather than a preference function). As will be shown, the actual calculation or "integration" of decision rules can be less burdensome than calculating utility functions. Some of the difficulties of calculation can be circumvented if there is active cooperation between a decision maker and an analyst assisting in constructing a decision rule. And, clearly, decision rules calculated in such a way as to insure compatibility with an individual's preferences could be of value in government. (To some extent this approach is an aberration from the point of view that has inspired work on integrability for the past several decades—namely, that actions speak louder than words, preferences are more dependably determined from observing actual behavior than from responses to hypothetical choices.)

From system 5 a single decision rule is of the form

$$y_j = h_j(x_1, x_2, \ldots, x_n, a_1, a_2, \ldots, a_m, b_1, b_2, \ldots, b_k.)$$

As we have seen, from a rule of this sort can be derived the set of partial derivatives relating each variable with each of the others. And, conversely, if the partial derivatives are known but the decision rule is not, the rule can be obtained from the derivatives by solving the differential equation which is implied by the set of derivatives. We seek now to discover or infer such a decision rule. (Hereafter for expository purposes all lower case letters with and without subscripts will denote scalars, not vectors.) Say that $x_1, x_2, \ldots, x_n$ consists of x_1, x_2, x_3.

(1) The approach involves first enunciating the rates of substitution of each of these variables for each of the others. In general,

each of the rates of substitution may be a function of all of the variables, or

$$\frac{\partial x_2}{\partial x_1} = g(x_1, x_2, x_3); \frac{\partial x_3}{\partial x_1} = h(x_1, x_2, x_3); \frac{\partial x_3}{\partial x_2} = k(x_1, x_2, x_3) = -\frac{h}{g}.$$

Each of the three partial derivatives in this last set denotes a tangent gradient to a point on the to-be-derived (hyper)surface, the decision rule or allocation formula.

(2) The set of tradeoffs or partial derivatives taken together constitutes or implies the total differential equation $Qdx_1 + Rdx_2 + dx_3 = 0$. This is a tangent (hyper)plane to the surface. It is this differential equation which must be integrable if the formula is to be constructed from the individual rates of substitution. Integrability conditions can be determined. That is, it can be determined whether a given total differential equation has a solution. Two kinds of difficulty could arise at this point. One is that the rates of substitution could simply be inconsistent with one another. In more complex cases tradeoffs between any two variables imply certain values for other tradeoffs. This is the integrability problem that Houthakker solved; that is, we know that if the partial derivatives are consistent with one another integrability is implied. Since we are developing a *normative* management tool, not a *positive* theory for explaining behavior, we will of course want to insure that consistency is a characteristic of the index. The other difficulty is that the total differential equation may be so complicated as to be integrable in principal but not practically. It is unlikely that that will be the case; if it does happen, some algorithms exist for approximating a solution.

(3) The desire then is to find an equation $f(x_1, x_2, x_3) = U$ which is the solution, the "integral" of the differential equation. At this point, holding U constant, this equation represents an isoquant hypersurface of the solution equation. Allowing all the arguments to vary in effect traces out the solution equation yielding a formula of $f(x_1, x_2, x_3) = U$ from $Qdx_1 + Rdx_2 + dx_3 = 0$.

AN EXAMPLE: THE MINNESOTA MUNICIPAL AID FORMULA

In 1976 the State of Minnesota allotted $42 per capita to each county (except for the Minneapolis-St. Paul seven-county metropolitan area which is treated as a single county). Within each county the $42 per person was allocated to local governments by means of the following formula:

> The balance of the distributions in 1976 pursuant to subdivision 1, shall be divided among the several cities and towns in the county's territory . . . in the proportion that the city or town's 1970 federal census population: times the sum of its average city or town mill rate for the three immediately preceding years divided by three: times its city or town 1974 aggregate sales ration as determined by the commissioner of revenue bears to the sum of the product of that calculation for all cities and towns in the territory.

> . . . If the amount distributed to a city or town pursuant to subdivision 4 is less than the aids the city or town received in 1975, before corrections for prior year aid payments, pursuant to Minnesota Statutes 1974, Section 477A.01, the amount distributed to it shall be raised to the amount the city or town received in 1975, before corrections for prior years aid payments, and the distributions to the other cities and towns within the county's territory shall be proportionately reduced as necessary to supply the difference.[27]

Translated into algebra, this becomes:

$$G_{kj} = \max (G_{1kj}, G_{2kj}),$$

where $\quad G_{kj}$ = grant to municipality k in county j in 1976,

$\quad G_{1kj}$ = is defined below,

$\quad G_{2kj}$ = 1975 aid to municipality k in county j.

$$G_{1kj} = \frac{P_{kj} M_{kj} S_{kj}}{\sum\limits_i P_{ij} M_{ij} S_{ij}} [42P_j - L_j],$$

where $\quad P_{kj}$ = population of municipality k in county j,

$\quad P_j$ = population of county j,

$\quad M_{kj}$ = property tax mill rate of municipality k in county j (averaged over the three previous years),

$\quad S_{kj}$ = an adjustment factor to account for differences in assessment practices,

$\quad L_j$ = state aid retained by county government j in 1975.

This program assists municipalities not merely on the basis of population, but rather on population weighted by "need" or tax "effort" as measured by the mill rate. (A municipality with a small property tax base requires a higher mill rate to raise a given sum than does a municipality of the same population but a larger property tax base.) But when written as

$$G_{1kj} = P_{kj}M_{kj}S_{kj}C_j \ \text{(where} \ C_j = \frac{42P_j - L_j}{\sum_i P_{ij}M_{ij}S_{ij}} \text{),}$$

it can be seen that the formula grossly violates simple horizontal equity. For since C_j can and does vary greatly by county, two municipalities identical as to their values of the supposedly relevant variables P, M, and S could receive considerably different grants. Since there are no two municipalities that are precisely identical, this violation of horizontal equity does not present itself from a mere inspection of the list of actual grants. (That is presumably because it is difficult to juggle mentally the several relevant variables to determine whether their weighting is appropriate.) But calculation of per capita grants to municipalities for given mill rates actually levied shows, for example, that *per capital grants to the set of municipalities which levied a mill rate of 15 ranged from $16 to $104*. Mill rates of municipalities receiving $40 per capita ranged from 4 to 40. Another way of making this point is to note that the changes in grant associated with a change in population or mill rate $\partial G/\partial P$, $\partial G/\partial M$ are not equal for municipalities with identical populations and mill rates. These incongruous implications of aiding municipalities using an intermediate county allotment reflect startling inequity.

Typically, formulas are evaluated by calculating and inspecting the allocations they yield. It is important to emphasize that the incongruitites noted here are not obvious from simple inspection of the formula or of the actual allocation of grant funds to municipalities.

To analyze this formula, start by calculating $\partial G_{1ij}/\partial P_{ij}$, the increment to a municipality's grant associated with an increase in population of one person for a number of communities. As the formula now stands, that quantity is $M_{ij}S_{ij}C_j$. Recall that the horizontal inequity results from the fact that C varies by county. An obvious way of removing that inequity is to fix C across the state, that is, to allocate all of the moneys from a single state fund rather than from separately determined funds for each county. Fixing C was considered and rejected in the 1975 legislative debate.[28]

Two observations on that fact are in order. First, the legislature was not aware of the degree of the inequity built into the formula it adopted, since mere inspection of allocation does not reveal the inequities. The second observation is that because of the difficulty of juggling four or five variables simultaneously, not only are inadvertent inequities not perceived, but compromise solutions incorporating some of the advantages of both the present formula and of one with a constant C term are difficult to conceptualize. Calculating the C terms for the several counties and the partial derivatives or tradeoffs between the variables in the formula not only would make explicit the inequities in the current formula but also would suggest alternative, presumably more acceptable, tradeoffs between the variables. Applying the three-step approach for constructing formulas to this case proceeds as follows.

(1) *Enunciate the rates of substitution.* For the Minnesota municipal aid formula these rates are:

$$\frac{\partial M}{\partial P} = -\frac{M}{P}, \frac{\partial C}{\partial P} = -\frac{C}{P}, \frac{\partial C}{\partial M} = -\frac{C}{M}.$$

As was indicated above, analysis of the formula suggests that other such tradeoffs might be more appropriate. A simple set of alternative tradeoffs would be to leave $\partial M/\partial P$ unchanged, but to set both $\partial C/\partial P$ and $\partial C/\partial M$ at zero. A change in population or mill rate would not be compensated for by a change in C. (This is a mathematically trivial example, and the reader may perceive at this point that setting $\partial C/\partial P$ and $\partial C/\partial M$ at zero is equivalent to holding C constant across the state.) The example will be used to outline the procedure to indicate how formulas involving more complex rates of substitution would be calculated.

(2) *Calculate the total differential equation implied by the partial derivations.* In our example this equation is:[29]

$$MdP + PdM + 0 = 0$$

(3) *Solve the differential equation.* We seek a solution of the form $f(P,M) = U$. Alternative pairs of values of P and M that satisfy this equation are alternative combinations of the three variables that could yield a municipality the same grant. Solving the equation in our example is straightforward.

$$MdP + PdM = 0$$

$$\int MdP + \int PdM = U$$

$$\text{or } MP = U.$$

We have the solution to the equation, a new index reflecting different weightings of the constituent variables. The value of U for each recipient municipality reflects the *relative* aggregate weighting of the several variables for that municipality. The grant for municipality k then becomes $[U_k / \sum_i U_i] A$, where A is the total sum of money to be allocated. So the new formula is $G_k = [P_k M_k / \sum_i P_i M_i] A = P_k M_k C$. Recall that the earlier version of the formula was:

$$G_{kj} = P_{kj} M_{kj} C_j,$$

where C varied by county, reflecting the two stage aid procedure—to counties, then to municipalities. The example is mathematically trivial, but the result is an interesting and practical alternative to the existing aid formula.

IV. CONCLUSION

A practical method for constructing allocation formulas has been presented in this chapter. It could assist both policymakers and the general public to know certain implications of governmental decisions. It rests on a conjecture that some inconsistencies in government decision rules are caused not only by disagreements among bargainers and not only by deviousness of political actors, but also by confusion arising from faulty feedback on the results of decisions.

The method is not yet developed in general form, and two important avenues for future research suggest themselves. It is important to determine the class of decision rules, partial derivatives of which equal the corresponding derivatives of the unknown underlying preference function. Second, work along the lines suggested by Frisch should be undertaken in order to be able to determine dependably the rates of substitution held by decision makers.

If and as the analytics of constrained maximization are applied prescriptively and the results used, the corresponding theories of rational choice will become better explanations and predictors of behavior.

NOTES

1. *Administrative Behavior,* 2nd ed. (New York: Macmillan, 1957) p xxiv.

2. Cf. Paul A. Samuelson, *The Foundations of Economic Analysis* (Cambridge, Mass.: Harvard Univ. Press, 1958).

3. Most influential in the development of the theory of the firm was Alfred Marshall's *Principles of Economics,* 8th ed. (New York: Macmillan, 1948). For a long while the discipline by and large ignored Marshall's own caveats concerning the appropriateness of assuming that firms maximize profits.

4. An example of a hypothesis of the theory of the firm: if an ad valorem tax of $† is levied on the product of a firm, then, given the (empirically derivable) demand function for the product and the (empirically derivable) cost function for the product, the price of the good will rise by $ $\triangle$p, the quantity demanded will fall by $\triangle$x units, and the profits of the firm will fall by $ $\triangle$r, where $\triangle$p, $\triangle$x and $\triangle$r are all potentially calculable.

5. This controversy is well summarized in Fritz Machlup, "Theories of the Firm: Marginalist, Behavioral, Managerial," *American Economic Review,* March 1967.

6. Milton Friedman has been the main proponent of the point of view that the appropriate and ultimate test of an economic theory is not the realism of its assumptions but its ability to predict behavior. See "The Methodology of Positive Economics," in Friedman, *Essays in Positive Economics,* (Chicago: Univ. of Chicago Press, 1953).

7. For example, see Ernest Nagel, "Assumptions in Economic Theory," *American Economic Review,* May 1963.

8. In the last two decades a new attack has been made on the received theories of the firm and household. This "behavioral" approach with its roots in organization theory argues that the calculations required of the entrepreneur or consumer in economic theory are superhuman. Real people "satisfice," muddle through. See J.G. March and H.A. Simon, *Organizations* (New York: John Wiley 1958), and R.M. Cyert and J.G. March, *A Behavioral Theory of the Firm* (Englewood Cliffs, N.J.: Prentice-Hall, 1963).

9. See Burton A. Weisbrod, "Income Redistribution Effects and Benefit-Cost Analysis," in Samuel B.Chase, ed., *Problems in Public Expenditure Analysis* (Washington, D.C.: Brookings Institution, 1968); and Gordon C. Rausser and J.W. Freebairn, "Estimation of Policy Preference Functions: An Application to U.S. Beef Import Quotas," *Review of Economics and Statistics,* November 1974.

10. Anthony Downs began this work in *Inside Bureaucracy* (Boston: Little, Brown, 1967). But rigorous development of the theory has been accomplished by William A. Niskanen, Jr., in *Bureaucracy and Representative Government* (Chicago: Aldine, 1971.)

11. *The Fable of the Bees or Private Vices, Publick Benefits,* (Oxford: Clarendon Press, 1924), pp. 17-37.

12. Milton Friedman is one economist who extols both the free procedure and the efficiency of competition. See *Capitalism and Freedom* (Chicago: Univ. of Chicago Press, 1962).

13. For example, see John Steinbruner, *The Cybernetic Theory of Decision* (Princeton, N.J.: Princeton Univ. Press, 1974).

14. Although others have contributed, the approach is due mainly to Jan Tinbergen and Henri Theil. See Jan Tinbergen, *On the Theory of Economic Policy,* rev. ed. (Amsterdam: North-Holland Publishing 1955); and Henri Theil, *Economic Forecasts and Policy* (Amsterdam: North-Holland Publishing Company, 1958), and *Optimal Decision Rules for Government and Industry* (Chicago: Rand McNally & Company, 1964).

15. See Fox, Jati K. Sengupta, and Erik Thorbecke, *The Theory of Quantitative Economic Policy with Applications to Economic Growth and Stabilization* (Chicago: Rand McNally, 1966); Friedlander, "Macro Policy Goals in the Postwar Period: A Study in Revealed Preference," *Q. J. of Economics,* Feb. 1973; and Fromm, "The Evolution of Economic Policies," in

T. H. Naylor, ed., *The Design of Computer Simulation Experiments* (Durham: Duke Univ. Press, 1969).

16. "Co-operation between Politicians and Econometricians on the Formalization of Political Preferences," in Frank Lang, ed., *Economic Planning Studies: A Collection of Essays by Ragnar Frisch* (Boston: D. Reidel, 1976).

17. See P. Nijkamp, "Determination of Implicit Social Preference Functions," Netherlands School of Economics, Rotterdam Report 7010 (1970).

18. There is a long and interesting history of laws of individual and social behavior inductively arrived at. Examples are the "laws" of Engel, Gossen, Weber-Fechner, del Vecchio, and Gini. These and numerous others are discussed in the author's Ph.D. dissertation, "The Early Development of Econometric Technique," Harvard University, 1963.

19. *The Conceptual Framework of Psychology* (Chicago: Univ. of Chicago Press, 1952) and *Perception and the Representative Design of Experiments* (Berkeley: Univ. of California Press, 1956).

20. "Comparison of Bayesian and Regression Approaches to the Study of Information Processing in Judgment," chapter 1 in Leon Rappoport and David A. Summers, *Human Judgment and Social Interaction* (Chicago: Holt, Rinehart and Winston, 1973).

21. Amos Tversky and Daniel Kahneman, "Judgment Under Uncertainty: Heuristics and Biases," *Science,* September 27, 1974, p. 1124.

22. Otto A. Davis, M.A.H. Dempster, and Aaron Wildavsky, "A Theory of the Budgetary Process," *Amer. Pol. Sci. Rev.,* Sept. 1966.

23. This distinction does not characterize the difference between the decision making as constrained maximization and the decision making as simplified heuristic approaches. Both of them are versions of the autonomous actor conceptualization.

24. The notation is further defined in Section III.

25. Professor Jose Encarnacion of the University of the Philippines has shown me that it is not always the case that the derivatives of a decision rule are rates of substitution of the underlying utility function. The total differentials (from which are determined the partial derivatives) can differ. I intend to investigate the conditions under which the partial derivatives of the two functions are equal.

26. Leonid Hurwicz has summarized his own and others' accomplishments regarding the integrability problem in the decades following Houthakker's important paper with the observation that integrability conditions are somewhat less restrictive than were those posited by Houthakker. See Hurwicz, "On the Problem of Integrability of Demand Functions," in J. S. Chipman et al., eds., *Preferences, Utility and Demand* (New York: Harcourt, Brace and Jovanovich, 1971), p. 183.

27. Laws of Minnesota for 1975, Chapter 437, Section 4, p. 1594. Also see R. Hackett, "Inter-City Equity and the Minnesota Municipal Aid Formula," School of Public Affairs, University of Minnesota, June 1976 (mimeo). The assistance and advice of Mr. Hackett for this section of this chapter is gratefully acknowledged.

28. Cf. James Carlson, "The 1975 Minnesota Local Government Aid Formula: A Case Study," School of Public Affairs, University of Minnesota, May 1976 (mimeo).

29. In general, the equation is easily derived from the stated rates of substitution by noting that $\partial M/\partial P = -Q/R$ and so forth.

3

POLICY ANALYSIS OF LEGAL POLICIES

Werner Z. Hirsch

How can economists address themselves to policy analysis of laws and of the legal system, and in what manner have they done so? These are the questions with which this chapter will be concerned. However, rather than trying to be all inclusive, we will concentrate on economic effect evaluation while giving short shrift to legal rule formulation, in my view a much less promising area. After a brief discussion of these two topics, some examples will be offered to show how in effect microeconomic theory and econometrics can be applied to a policy analysis of legal issues.

LEGAL RULE FORMULATION

Efforts of rule formulation are in the rational intellectual tradition of William Blackstone[1] on the legal side and Adam Smith[2] on the economic side. They can also be traced back to Jeremy Bentham's utilitarianism, "in its aspect as a positive theory of human behavior, . . . another name for economic theory."[3] A more recent proponent is Posner. His view of the world of economics, and to no

AUTHOR'S NOTE: *This chapter summarizes some ideas that will appear in the forthcoming* Law and Economics: An Introductory Analysis *(Academic Press).*

small extent of law, is "the assumption that man is a rational maximizer of his ends in life,"[4] an assumption, he correctly reminds us; "no stronger than that most people in most affairs of life are guided by what they conceive to be their self-interest and that they choose means reasonably (not perfectly) designed to promote it."[5] With this assumption as a base, three major fundamental economic concepts emerge.[6] The first is the inverse relation between price and quantity; the second is the economist's view of cost as opportunity cost, i.e., the price which the resources consumed in making (and selling) the seller's product would have commanded in their next best use—the alternative price; and the third is the tendency of resources to gravitate toward their highest value uses if exchange is permitted. If voluntarily exchanged, resources are shifted to those uses in which the value to the consumer, as measured by the consumer's willingness to pay, is highest. When resources are being used where their value is greatest, they are being employed efficiently; i.e., they produce the largest possible output.

This is not a new argument; it is found in most elementary textbooks of economics. Still, it is powerful and must be carefully understood and evaluated. Its basic propositions are not empirical but are based on assumptions about choice under scarcity and rational maximization. They are circular, arguing that since people are rationally self-interested, what they do shows what they value, and their willingness to pay for what they value is the ultimate proof of their rational self-interest. Some scholars have criticized the circularity of the argument (in the sense that it cannot be criticized); if human desire is made definitionally identical with certain human acts, then those human acts are also beyond criticism in normative or efficiency terms; everyone is doing as well as he can exactly what he set out to do, which, by definition, is "good" for him. In those terms, it is not at all surprising that economic analyses have "considerable power in predicting how people in fact behave."[7]

The question has also been asked whether value is indeed determined by people's willingness to pay or whether it is not determined rather by people's ability to pay for a good or service. Lester Thurow sees it thus: "A market economy that starts with an unjust distribution of economic resources will yield an unjust distribution of goods and services, regardless of its efficiency."[8]

Posner, for example, is convinced that, using microeconomic

arguments, "it may be possible to deduce the basic formal characteristics of law itself from economic theory."[9] Consequently, he argues
that "the ultimate question for decision in many lawsuits is, what
allocation of resources would maximize efficiency?"[10]

However, the application of microeconomic theory to legal rule
formulation poses a number of serious problems. One problem relates to the fact that while the theory is best equipped to deal with
resource allocation efficiency, justice and fairness, which relate to
distributional issues, must also be considered. Life would be so much
easier if efficiency could be rigorously defended as the only objective. Instead, we face two, all too often opposing, objectives—
efficiency and equity. The ultimate goal is social efficiency, which
requires trading off resource allocation efficiency against distribution
of income. Unfortunately, what is the most desirable distribution of
income is a highly subjective decision; nevertheless, legal rules must
be concerned about both efficiency and income distribution.

A further problem relates to the fact that even for the determination
of optimum allocative efficiency conditions, economists are forced to
make a number of restrictive assumptions. At least three such assumptions are made in relation to Pareto efficiency. They are zero
transaction costs, zero redistribution costs, and convexity. By transaction costs, economists mean real resources employed in bargaining, e.g., the costs which interfere with the working of competitive
markets.[11] Under this assumption all transactions are costless, including information about costs and prices.

The second assumption relates to the cost of redistributing incomes
among consumers. Given that the initial endowment is not appropriate and redistribution is undertaken, virtually every distribution
scheme is costly in that it distorts incentives and behavior and im-
poses political as well as administrative costs. Thus, redistribution of
income, e.g., through an income tax, changes consumers' budgets,
their spending habits, and their preferences for leisure.[12]

Finally, the economic implications of convexity circumscribe the
structure of consumers' preferences and of producers' technology. For
example, with respect to households, convexity means, in the words
of economist Kenneth Arrow, that: "If we consider two different
bundles of consumption, a third bundle defined by averaging the first
two commodity by commodity is not inferior in the household's preferences to both of the first two."[13] An example of nonconvexity

would be the renter who for years has lived in the downtown area and suddenly moves to the suburbs because of unchecked increases in downtown crime. After becoming a suburbanite, his interest in seeing crime combatted in the core city vanishes.[14] Nonconvexities are very common and lead to market failures, interfering with Pareto efficiency.

POLICY ANALYSIS FOR EFFECT EVALUATION

Major contributions can be made by economics through the application of economic theory and econometrics in order to specify and quantify economic effects—direct and indirect—of legal rules and rulings, and the distribution of these effects. At a time that rule formulation involves normative economics, effect evaluation is basically an exercise in positive economics.

For the purpose of effect evaluation, it is necessary to first build a microeconomic model that closely represents the environment of which the law is an important part and that links it to various outcome dimensions. One of the great challenges is to model the specific law and its effects on important outcomes in a manner that does not do too much violence to real life conditions. Yet the model cannot be too complex for fear that then it is unlikely to be implemented empirically. The single most significant implementation step involves econometric techniques. In cases in which the modeling and economic work is successful, quantitative statements about the probable effects of the law, i.e., statements within an inference setting, become possible.

But, more often than not, existing microeconomic theory, econometric methods, and the availability of data limit the degree to which definitive quantitative statements about side effects can be made. In such instances, the analyst will have to be satisfied with deductive inquiries which at times can yield qualitative conclusions of major policy value.

We will use *Crawford v. Board of Education* to illustrative how in particular an active court raises issues that demand policy analysis. Thus, for example, the California Supreme Court in *Crawford v. Board of Education* reconfirmed that "California School Boards bear a constitutional obligation to take reasonably feasible steps to alleviate school segregation, whether such segregation is *de jure* or *de facto* in nature,"[15] and required that "school districts take reasonable and feasible steps to eliminate *segregated* schools, i.e., schools in which the minority student enrollment is so disproportionate as realistically to isolate minority students from other students and thus deprive minority students of an integrated educational experience."[16]

Writing for a unanimous court, Justice Tobriner virtually spoke as a policy analyst when he said,

> A trial court can and should consider the potential costs, both in economic and educational terms, of the various proposals before it. Given the practical nature of the remedial issue, a trial court should take into account the long-range effects of the adoption of alternative proposals; a court may reject a particular approach if it finds that its implementation is likely to result in a one race or all minority school district and consequently in less ultimate opportunities for the benefit of a desegregated education.

> We do not mean, of course, that the threat of "white flight" may be used as a smoke screen to avoid constitutional obligations of a school district; instead, we simply recognize that in weighing the potential efficacy of alternative programs, a realistic evaluation of the ultimate consequences of a particular course of action cannot be ignored. . . . As with the numerous desegregation techniques adverted to above, in some circumstances busing will be an appropriate and useful element in a desegregation plan, while in other instances its costs, both in financial and educational terms, will render its use inadvisable.[17]

And Justice Tobriner concluded, "it is clear that the trial court's task in supervising the preparation and implementation of a school desegregation plan is an exceedingly difficult, sensitive and taxing one, requiring the balancing and reconciliation of many competing values."[18] It is in this connection that policy analysts can be of great value to the court, as two examples will show.

MALPRACTICE DETERMINATION

There has been a rapid increase in malpractice suits in recent years. Courts again and again have been faced with the need to determine whether a defendant had or had not met the standard of care required by law. Policy analysis is facilitated by the fact that in *United States v. Carroll Towing Company,* Judge Learned Hand offered the following algebraic formula: "If the probability be called P; the injury L; and the burden B; liability depends upon whether B is less than L multiplied by P; i.e., whether B is smaller than PL."[19] In short, in line with the Hand formula, the defendant is guilty of negligence if the loss caused by the accident multiplied by the probability of the accident's occurring exceeds the burden of the precautions that the defendant might have taken to avert the mishap. If a larger cost could have been avoided by incurring a smaller cost, Judge Hand would like to see the smaller cost incurred.

The philosophy underlying the Learned Hand formula can be summarized as follows: A reasonable man, before taking any action, weighs the cost and benefits of that action not only from his own personal perspective but also from the broader perspective of all the individuals within the possible scope of any resulting harm. From the economist's point of view, the Learned Hand formula seeks a tort system which maximizes social welfare over the action of all individuals involved in a given tortious act. When an individual's actions fall below the reasonable man standard, he is assessed liability for any resulting harm. Knowledge of this requirement creates incentives encouraging individuals to weight their actions from a social welfare point of view.

The Learned Hand formula can be placed into a benefit-cost framework, a framework which economists have developed with great care. Economists seek to measure the benefits and costs that are expected to be associated with different activities. The one that promises the largest difference between social benefits and costs is the preferred one.

We will apply the Hand formula to a Washington Supreme Court case, i.e., *Helling v. Carey.* The plaintiff Helling first consulted the defendant opthamologist in 1959 for myopia (near-sightedness) and was fitted for contact lenses.[20] She experienced a minimal amount of irritation during the next eight years, but in September of 1967 she consulted the defendants again, complaining of eye irritation. They diagnosed conjunctivitis (inflamation of the mucus membranes) and gave her a prescription. During several more visits in the course of the following month, the defendants decided Helling had corneal abrasions due to the contact lenses. In May of 1968, the plaintiff returned, again complaining about irritation. On October 1, 1968, the defendants tested for glaucoma and found it.

Glaucoma can result in blindness; but it can be treated and ameliorated if detected early enough. There are few symptoms until the harm is irreversible. It can be detected by a simple test, the major cost of which is the opthalmologist's time. The plaintiff's contention was that the defendants should have tested for glaucoma in 1967 and that they ignored their own training and advances in the profession in not doing so.

The defendants presented evidence that, although there were some opthalmologists who favored giving the glaucoma test to patients under forty years of age, the accepted national practice did not require giving glaucoma tests to patients under forty unless symptoms and complaints would indicate the presence of glaucoma. There was inconsistent evidence as to whether the defendants should have suspected glaucoma. It is also unclear whether testing in 1967 would have made any difference.

The Washington Supreme Court held that the defendants were negligent *as a mater of law* for not administering the glaucoma test. The court stated:

> Under the facts of this case reasonable prudence required the timely giving of the pressure test to this plaintiff. The precaution of giving this test to detect the incidence of glaucoma to patients under 40 years of age is so imperative that irrespective of its disregard by the standards of the opthamology profession, it is the duty of the courts to say what is required to protect patients under 40 from damaging results of glaucoma.

> . . . as a matter of law. . . the reasonable standard that should have been followed . . . was the timely giving of this simple, harmless pressure test. . . . In failing to do so, the defendants were negligent, which proximately resulted in the blindness sustained by the plaintiff.[21]

To support its decision, the court cited two nonmedical cases, including the *T.J. Hooper* decision,[22] in which Justice Learned Hand stated:

> In most cases reasonable prudence is in fact common prudence; but strictly it is never its measure; a whole calling may have unduly lagged in the adoption of new and available devices. It never may set its own tests, however persuasive be its usages. Courts must in the end say what is required: there are precautions so imperative that even their universal disregard will not excuse their omission.

In justifying its holding, the court emphasized that the glaucoma test is "simple, harmless, and inexpensive."

Empirical evidence of the incidence of glaucoma was recognized by the court; for those under forty, the expected incidence is 1 per 25,000 persons; among all those over forty, it is around 1 to 2 per 100 persons. The test is not totally without risk, since any time an instrument is placed on the eye there is a risk of scratching.

Standards for the test were evaluated by R. Crick, who concluded, "The prevalence of glaucoma is too low and the methods of detection such as to make population screening an uneconomic use of medical resources at present."[23] Crick, who is one important source of the incidence estimates given above, suggests that screening be limited to relatives of those known to have glaucoma, those over sixty, and motorists over forty.[24]

Since *Helling v. Carey* has the distinction of citing generally agreed-upon quantitative estimates on the probability of harm occurring, it is useful to place these estimates into the Hand formula. Judge Learned Hand, it will be recalled, defined the legal standard of liability applicable to most unintended acts of negligence as follows: The defendant is guilty of negligence if the loss caused by the event, e.g., accident (L) multiplied by the probability of the event occurring (P) exceeds the costs of the precautions that the defendant might have taken to avert it (C).

In relation to glaucoma in general and *Helling v. Carey* in particular, the following numbers might be illustrative. The medical profession indicates that (P) for persons below forty is 1/25,000 and for persons above forty, 2/100. C, the cost of preventing the occurrence of glaucoma is most likely about ten minutes of a doctor's time, e.g., $30. L, the loss associated with the occurrence of glaucoma, namely, blindness, is the most difficult parameter. Ideally, one would need to estimate the losses incurred by a person who goes blind, and do so year by year with each year reflecting the particular age. Since these losses constitute a flow over time, discounting would be necessary.

We can estimate for the two age groups at what L value the Hand formula would find the defendant liable for the ill effects of glaucoma, should he or she have omitted an examination. For persons under forty the defendant would be liable if the loss due to glaucoma is > $30/(.00004) or $750,000. For persons forty or older, the defendant would be liable if the loss due to glaucoma is > $30/(.02) or

$1,500. Thus, the critical loss figure for young people is about 500 times as large as for older people. Although younger people can look forward to a longer productive life than older persons, the income difference is unlikely to be more than 3 to 10 times greater on average. Although admittedly there are other than income losses to be considered, e.g., mental anguish, or any harm from unintended scratching of the eye by the testing procedure, they could hardly explain the 500-fold greater loss. It would, therefore, be interesting to contemplate whether the Washington Supreme Court would have ruled in favor of plaintiff Helling, had it placed its figures into the Hand formula.

HABITABILITY LAWS AND
THE WELFARE OF INDIGENT TENANTS

American laws pertaining to the relationship between landlord and tenant, like most of American property law, were adapted from the English common law, which historically favored landlords. The owner was not held to have a duty to repair or maintain residential premises leased to tenants.

In the postwar period, a significant realignment of rights and obligations occurred when most large American cities enacted housing codes. The landlord now is the party held ultimately reponsible for the condition of the building. In case he fails in his obligation, courts and legislatures have provided at least four types of remedy: (1) repair and deduct, (2) rent withholding, (3) receivership, and (4) retaliatory eviction laws.[25]

The repair-and-deduct remedy was available in nineteen states in 1974. It constitutes a self-help measure which allows the tenant, upon his own initiative, to repair his defective premises and deduct the repair charges from his rent, after the landlord has been notified of the defect and has failed to act within a reasonable time. This remedy is limited to minor defects and represents for the landlord the least costly code enforcement mechanism.

Rent withholding can rely on an escrow method or rent abatement. In the first case, the tenant pays rent into a court-created escrow account. Rental income is withheld from the landlord until violations are corrected. Three states (Illinois, Michigan, and New York) even authorize rent withholdings by the state welfare department or some other agency. An alternative is rent abatement, which permits a tenant to remain in possession of premises without paying rent, or paying a reduced amount until housing defects are remedied. The condition of the premises constitutes a defense either to an action of eviction or to an action for rent. Since the actual differences between withholding and abatement are very small, they will be treated together. There were twenty-five states with such laws in 1974.

Receivership involves appointment by the court of a receiver who takes control of buildings and who corrects hazardous defects, after a landlord has failed to act within a reasonable period. By 1974, this remedy had become available in twelve states. If large-scale repairs are needed which cannot be financed through rental payments, some statutes permit the receiver to seek additional loans. In so doing, old first liens are converted into new second liens, imposing particularly heavy costs on the lender and, therefore, ultimately on the landlord. Rent is deposited with the court-appointed receiver until the violation is corrected. As long as the tenant continues to pay rent into escrow, the landlord cannot evict for nonpayment.

Of these three remedies, receivership is the most potent for assuring habitable housing and at the same time the most costly to the landlord. All rental income to the landlord is stopped, since all tenants in the building, not only the aggrieved ones, pay rents into escrow. Moreover, the landlord loses control over his building to a receiver, who may be enthusiastic about fixing up the building, possible even above minimum standards established by housing codes. Finally, contrary to most repair-and-deduct and withholding laws, receivership is usually initiated by government with large legal resources behind it.

The three major remedies are often suppplemented by laws that can reinforce them—retaliatory eviction laws designed to protect tenants from being penalized by landlords for complaining against housing code violations. Such laws, which usually freeze rents for ninety days after compliance, existed in 1974 in twenty-four states.

From our analytic point of view, habitability laws, which have the overt purpose of assisting tenants, particularly low-income ones, shift from the previous doctrine of caveat emptor to one of caveat venditor. These laws can be viewed as rules that change the nature of the permissible contract. One simple interpretation is that the habitability law constrains actors to contracts in which the landlord bears the risks associated with repair and maintenance, while without that law the form of the contract is not constrained. If such an interpretation were correct, then a strong a priori case could be made for the inefficiency of habitability laws. However, it is equally likely that under caveat emptor the consumer is constrained from purchasing a desired bundle of housing services that includes warranties. Such would be the case if high transaction costs interfered with efficient reallocation of rights. The reasons are that deviations from a standard contract are costly and enforcement of any warranties purchased would be difficult under general application of caveat emptor. Finally, it may be that a contract that obligates the landlord to maintain the premises is efficient and has already evolved as the standard relationship between landlord and tenant, and that the habitability law merely provides legal recognition of this so as to reduce enforcement costs. Each of these alternative interpretations implies a different conclusion regarding the efficiency and distributional implications of habitability laws, and therefore provides the motivation for a theoretical-empirical inquiry.

For this purpose a microeconomic model of landlord-tenant relations, i.e., a demand-and-supply model reflecting rental housing markets of indigents, was built. Within this housing model it becomes possible to detect whether a specific habitability law affects the demands and therefore the welfare of indigent tenants as well as the supply of their landlords. Moreover, with the aid of econometric methods, it becomes possible to estimate the magnitude of these demand-and-supply effects, i.e., how much the demand-and-supply functions shift in a vertical direction. Should the vertical shift of the demand function resulting from the presence of a habitability law be significantly larger than that of the supply function, a clear-cut welfare conclusion can be reached. Specifically, under those circumstances the habitability laws increased indigent tenants' welfare more than the cost imposed by higher rents.

To implement this microeconomic model, demand-and-supply functions for seventy regions in the United States were estimated.[26] The econometric results can be summarized as follows. Of the three types of habitability laws, the one providing for receivership has a statistically significant increase in rental expenditures of indigent tenants, with expenditures outweighting benefits accruing to such tenants. Since of all three kinds of habitability laws receivership is by far the most potent one, we could have hypothesized that it is likely to be effective, although there is no theory to deduce whether the benefits accruing to indigent tenants would or would not exceed the cost imposed upon them.

The cost of providing habitable housing must be borne by someone. We found that the costs imposed by the most powerful habitability law, i.e., receivership law, is largely borne by tenants; they do not, however, receive fully compensating benefits. To the extent that habitability laws are mainly designed to improve the welfare of indigent tenants, they have failed, at least in the sample studied. Receivership laws may even have been counterproductive.

CONCLUSION

We have emphasized how economists can engage in legal policy analysis for effect evaluation. The efforts are promising on the basis of a few examples presented in this chapter. There are other promising areas for possible application of microeconomic theory and econometrics to the estimation of side effects. In relation to contract law one might want to estimate the side effects of consumer protection laws, e.g., those that reduce the rights of a seller under an installment plan to repossess cars, appliances, furniture, and the like. In relation to tort law, the potential for defensive medicine being practiced in the presence of res ipsa loquitur might be examined. And finally, in relation to criminal law the deterrence effect of incarceration as well as of the death penalty is of widespread concern. A few of these laws have already been modeled and empirically analysed. More remains to be done.

NOTES

1. W. Blackstone, Commentaries on the Laws of England (1765-1769), 4 vols.

2. A. Smith, An Inquiry into the Nature and Causes of the Wealth of Nations (1776).

3. J. Bentham, Theory of Legislation, ed., Ro Hildreth (1864), pp. 357, 325-326.

4. Posner, Economic Analysis of Law (1972), p. 1.

5. p. 5

6. p. 1

7. Leff, "Economic Analysis of Law: Some Realism About Nominalism," Virginia Law Review, 60 (1974), 451, 458.

8. Thurow, "Economic Justice and the Economist: A Reply," *Public Interest,* 33 (1973), 120.

9. Posner, p. 393.

10. p. 320

11. See W. Z. Hirsch, *Reducing Law's Uncertainty and Complexity,* UCLA Law Rev. 21 (1974), 1239; and K. Arrow, *The Organization of Economic Activity: Issues Pertinent to the Choice of Market Versus Nonmarket Allocation,* in Joint Economic Comm., 91st Cong., 1st Sess., The Analysis and Evaluation of Public Expenditures: The PPB System 47, 49 (Comm. Print 1969; hereinafter cited as Arrow).

12. T. Koopmans, *Three Essays on the State of Economic Science* (1957).

13. Arrow, p. 49, n. 3.

14. See M. Polinsky, "Economic Analysis as a Potentially Defective Product; A Buyer's Guide to Posner's *Economic Analysis of Law," Harvard Law Rev.,* 87 (1974), 1655.

15. *Crawford v. Board of Education* (1976) 17 C. 3d, 289.

16. *Crawford,* 303.

17. *Crawford,* 308-309.

18. *Crawford,* 310.

19. *United States v. Carroll Towing Co.* (1947) 159 F. 2d 169 2 Cir.

20. *Helling v. Carey* (1974) 83 WN. 2d 514, 519 P. 2d 981.

21. Helling, 519.

22. T.J. Hooper (1932) 60 F. 2d 740.

23. "Chronic Glaucoma: A Preventable Cause of Blindness," *Lancet,* Feb. 9, 1974, 207.

24. pp. 205-207.

25. W. Z. Hirsch et. al., "Regression Analysis of the Effects of Habitability Laws Upon Rent," *California Law Review,* 63 (1975), 1097-1142.

26. W.Z. Hirsch, *Law and Economics: An Introductory Analysis* (1979), pp. 44-71.

4

THE HUMANIZATION OF POLICY MODELS

Jack Byrd, Jr.

The term *policy analysis* often gives the impression that one is attempting to develop a totally rational approach to the issue of policy-making. Research efforts are often directed at improving the policy model by increasing the level of mathematical sophistication and comprehensiveness of the model. At the same time, the application of policy models has not reached the level of success promised or expected by either practitioners or organizations providing the financial support for the analysis.

The premise of this chapter is that the search for comprehensiveness and mathematical sophistication is a misdirected approach to making policy models more accepted. Models need to become more "humanized." The policy model should be able to incorporate the judgments, intuitions, and experiences of individuals in a significant manner. The remainder of this chapter will explore the philosophical and methodological underpinnings of humanized policy analysis.

POLICY ANALYSIS FROM THREE PERSPECTIVES

The usefulness of models in public sector areas has become a significant issue in the past several years. A survey of modeling efforts for government agencies points out:

> The survey data suggest that limited utilization of models is a major
> problem. The extent of use is hard to measure, and different questions
> yield different apparent utilization rates, but the most generous esti-
> mate would be that more than a third of those models intending policy
> use fail to achieve it, while a conservative estimate would put the
> failure rate as high as two-thirds.[1]

With such a limited utilization rate, it would be worthwhile to explore
the manner in which policy analysis is viewed by three different
groups involved in the policy process.

To the *technical expert,* policy analysis is a profession. From his
educational background, the policy analyst implicitly believes in the
proposition that policy decisions can be improved through the application of scientific, rational methods. The goal of the analyst is to
remove subjectivity from decision processes.

Although most policy analysts would give lip service to the notion of
intuition and informed judgments, their actions betray their true feelings. Extensive efforts are made to quantify objectives that are inherently qualitative. For some reason, the policy analyst cannot feel
comfortable in letting the experienced decision maker select the alternative that he believes intuitively to be the best. The analyst would
rather have the decision maker provide rankings for various objectives, which can then be given numerical scores to evaluate different
alternatives. When a decision maker's input is sought, it is typically
structured to make the process appear nonsubjective.

To the *administrative consumer,* the policy analysis process is hope-
fully looked upon as an aid to decision making. The administrator
looks to policy analysis more for its insights than for specific numer-
cial evaluations of alternatives. The administrator feels it is important
to know something about general trends but is not too concerned
about specifics since each alternative, he feels, must be evaluated on
many subjective factors.

The administrator probably cannot relate to requests for involved
sessions where he is to provide rankings for different criteria. He does
not appreciate the need for detailed schemes to solicit from him his
subjective feelings about different objectives. The administrator begins to view the policy analyst with suspicion, since it appears that the
analyst is attempting to overstep his authority.

To the *affected public,* the policy analysis process may seem to be another example of bureaucratic waste. The individual citizen has a personal objective which he wants satisfied. He cannot see the need to go through an expensive analysis to tell him what he already knows. The citizen views the analyst and the administrative decision maker as members of a bloated bureaucracy who are consuming vasts amounts of money to arrive at decisions that are obvious. In those cases where the citizen does not have as strong a personal view, the policy analysis effort may seem to be another step toward future shock. He cannot comprehend the analysis being performed and begins to give up hope of being an informed citizen on the issue. In both types of cases, the citizen loses respect for the policy analysis effort.

A NEEDS ASSESSMENT
FOR POLICY ANALYSIS

To make the policy analysis effort more effective, the analyst often looks for methods of improving the technical process. Significant research is performed in such areas as multiobjective decision making, fuzzy sets, and utility theory. As these increasingly sophisticated methodologies are applied in policy studies, the resultant acceptance of the study has often been diminished rather than enhanced. The analyst looks upon the nonacceptance of the study as a failure in the methodology, and proceeds to advance the model's level of sophistication. The analyst in this case has failed to conduct a needs assessment of what the policy model should really do.

A generalized needs assessment for policy analysis should include the following, as paraphrased from an article by Little:[2]

> (1) The analysis should be *simple.* The failure of many models seems to be that they include levels of detail which are insignificant to the intended purpose of the model. Following Pareto's Law, 80 percent of the total value of a model to an administrator can be achieved from 20 percent of the details which could be incorporated into a model. As the analyst considers the addition of another level of detail to be incorporated into the model, an informal assessment should be made as to where that increased detail will place the value of the model.

(2) The model should be *robust*. The model should not give absurd
answers. Audit features need to be built into the model to check for
abnormal data input. The structure of the model should constrain
the results to be within reasonable ranges of values. The validity of
a model is often called into question when the user attempts to get
an answer to a question for which the model was not explicitly
designed. For example, a policy model of U.S. housing trends to
the year 2000 could very easily give ridiculous results if the trends
of the 60s and 70s were projected to 2050. A feature of the housing
policy model must accommodate the extensions of the model in
unexpected directions.

(3) The model must be *easy to control*. The user of the model should
be able to get any results he wants from the model. The customary
approach to policy analysis has been to structure the model to
accept input conditions and to project the consequences of these
conditions. A more useful role for a policy model would be to have
the user to specify a desired result and the model to generate the
input conditions that are necessary to achieve this result. The ability to control a model often represents a difference in operation
between the policy analyst and user. The analyst, through accumu-
lated levels of technical training, is accustomed to an investigation
procedure that begins with input conditions. The intent of the analysis is to hypothesize the effect these conditions will have on any
number of output factors. The administrator, on the other hand,
begins with a goal to be achieved and must determine the mix of
input conditions necessary to meet the goal. A model developed to
evaluate the consequences of different input conditions is not as
useful as a model that allows a user to specify a desired goal and
work backward to identify the input necessary to achieve that goal.
For example, an input-oriented housing model would take relevant
data and, from these, project housing patterns for the future. A
goal-oriented housing model would ask the user to specify the
housing patterns desired and would then generate the conditions
necessary to achieve the specified goals. A frequent criticism of
this approach is that the user can manipulate the model to get any
preconceived result. The scientific community is suspicious of the
unscrupulous user who will subvert the model for some personal
gain. The fallacy in this reasoning is that decisions must be made by
those in decision-making roles. They are evaluated on their ability
to make decisions. To circumvent the results of a valid model
would only lead to misguided policies, and the consequent danger

would ultimately outweigh any short-term personal gain that might be achieved with the improper use of the model.

(4) The model should be *adaptive*. Policy decisions are not static. As new situations arise, new decisions must be made. If the policy model is to be of use, it must be able to be updated with minimum effort. This criteria complements the simplicity feature mentioned earlier. An extremely complex model which is "data bound" may be so unwieldy as to make it virtually impossible to use on a continuing basis.

(5) The model should be *complete on important issues*. In nearly every policy issue, there is a full range of difficult-to-measure parameters which must be accommodated. For these parameters, the model should use the subjective judgments of the decision makers as an alternative to elaborate and often imprecise measurement schemes. More will be said later about some potential schemes for involving subjective judgments in the modeling process.

(6) The model should be *easy to communicate with*. Closely related to criteria one and four, this objective relates to the ability to use the model independent of the developer. Requests for data should be in the user's language. Whenever possible, the model should be interactive. The user should be able to use the system with a minimum of computer red tape. Output should also be in the language of the user, not the analyst.

As a result of the needs assessment, the policy analyst is guided to a new kind of model—one that is less sophisticated than before. The new model will have several sources of subjectivity. It will not be normative. The model will be heavily oriented toward the user and will have as its goal *the improvement of the decision maker's intuition*. The focus of the model will be insights, not numbers. This type of model will be referred to as the *humanized policy model* in the remainder of this paper.

The idea of a humanized policy model is not a new concept. Dror speaks of extrarational subphases in his policy analysis model. "There are perhaps enough indications so far to make some sort of prima facie case for the claim that extrarational processes are sometimes a better method for policymaking (and have a higher net output) than pure rationality, even if the latter is possible."[3] Little describes this type of model as a "decision calculus": "a model-based set of procedures for processing data and judgments to assist a manager in his decision making."[4]

Peter Drucker views the interrelationship between models and managers with the following commentary: "Insight, understanding, ranking of priorities, and a "feel" for the complexity of an area are as important as precise, beautifully elegant mathematical models—and in fact usually infinitely more useful and indeed even more "scientific." They reflect the reality of the manager's universe and tasks."[5]

Although the idea of a humanized policy model is not new, specific means for achieving this end are often not discussed in the literature. Two areas where the humanized policy model can make an impact in the overall modeling process are the generation of alternative policies and evaluation of multiple-objective decision situations.

GENERATION OF ALTERNATIVES
FROM INTUITIVE PROCESSES

The generation of alternative policies is an area where traditional policy models can be helped by the intuition of the policymaker. Consider the case of a policy model in a situation which has literally thousands of possible solutions. Traditional models are very efficient at scanning the solution set for the one solution that optimizes a particular objective. However, there is not a single objective. As additional objectives are added, the scanning process loses its efficiency and completely fails to identify appropriate solutions for objectives that are qualitative.

A humanized policy model would approach this situation from one of several directions. In the first case, the policymaker has a model which he uses in his decision-making effort. The model is established on an interactive computer system which asks for inputs in a question-and-answer format. Since the system is interactive, the results are generally printed within seconds of the data input.

Something about the results goes against the policymaker's intuition. While still at the terminal, he begins to analyze the problem. Maybe a preconceived notion about the policy was wrong. Maybe a constraint needs to be altered. Maybe more of a compromise is desired between two of the objectives. In any event, the model is changed and new results are obtained.

This trial-and-error investigative process continues until the policymaker has generated a solution or set of solutions which appears satisfactory. What has been the role of the model in this case? Certainly the results of the original model were not accepted as gospel. Instead the model played a role in improving the manager's understanding of the problem by giving him a means of relating inputs to outputs, thus updating his intuition about the problem.

A system of this general type has been used by the Institute on Man and Science in a community development project for Dunbar, a small southwestern Pennsylvania town. The community, beset with significant socioeconomic problems, was selected as a model for testing participatory approaches to the resolution of community problems.

A community development impacts model was established to view the interrelationships among housing, industrial development, demographic characteristics, income distribution, and municipal services. Two task forces were established from Dunbar's citizenry to look at options in housing and industrial development.

The housing task force initially approached the policy model as a means of giving support to decisions it had already made. As the study progressed, the use of the model as an aid to decision making became more accepted. Gradually the model began to play an interactive role in the policy process. As the authors state, "The interactive process helped the group at the outset identify and articulate pressing uncertainties in potential development impacts, and answered quantitative questions regarding taxation, demographics, etc. In the final discussion, however, the group relied on unquantifiable value judgments to arrive at a consensus."[6]

After similar success followed with the local economy task force, the model became a participant in the policy making process. In this particular illustration, the role of the model was to generate a solution from the given problem statement. The role of intuition was to evaluate the solutions generated and make problem formulation changes as deemed necessary.

In other cases, the system under analysis is so complex and unpredictable that human judgement remains the only effective method of managing the activity. For example, a public service commission must make hundreds of complex rate-setting decisions, each of which would require extensive and time-consuming modeling to examine. Can modeling be of any value in a case such as this when the decision time and complexity would seem to be a deterrent to effective analysis.

Modeling in a situation such as this still has its value. Models of smaller components of the rate-setting system can be structured to be used as training exercises. The role of the model in this case is to present the policymaker with general concepts through a simulated exercise. As the decision maker participates in the rate-setting exercise, he begins to assimilate the concepts presented and in turn, it is hoped, is a better decision maker when confronted with the full system.

The simulation game which has become a very popular instructional vehicle in recent years is an example of this type of approach. The CITY MODEL developed by EPA has as its goal "to build a laboratory where social scientists could test their theories on political, economic and social relationships in urban areas."[7] While the developer of the CITY MODEL acknowledges a lack of use of the simulation game in a policy mode, House points to this use for the future when he states, "A remaining frontier for gamers is the use of games for policy purposes; that is, the application of games in real problem-solving areas with real issues and real actors."[8]

There have been few actual applications of the simulation gaming approach as a vehicle for improving governmental policy making, but its use in business and the military is more common. As such, the use of simulation gaming offers another approach to the humanization of policy models.

The third application of intuition in modeling involves those problems for which an optimum solution is difficult to obtain. This situation particularly is evident where complex decisions are involved and it takes too long or is too expensive to generate a computer solution. For example, the problem of apportioning voting districts involves a model which is established to determine how to assign precincts to various districts. So far, almost all the optimization procedures developed either require too much computer time to be effective or ignore key qualitative factors.

A more effective use of a model in this case is to generate feasible but nonoptimal solutions and then let intuition take over to see if a better solution can be achieved. Intuition in these cases can often improve on the solution or make an assessment if the solution is good enough for implementation. In this regard, intuition plays an evaluative as well as a contributing role in the development of solutions for which formal optimization routines are impractical.

Easingwood has developed an interesting approach to this problem as applied to sales force assignments.[9] An "evenness" index was prepared to evaluate different assignment alternatives. Sales managers were then asked to intuitively make assignments. The evenness measure was then calculated and evaluated by management. If the assignment was considered sufficiently uneven, the assignment process was repeated. After six trials, the variation in assignments was considered acceptable.

Again, management made the decisions intuitively, and the model provided an evaluative aid. The end result was a successful assignment scheme brought about by the effective integration of model and manager.

Although the examples illustrated in this approach could be considered less than policy level, they influence policies to a great extent. For example, the policy of one-man-one-vote can be subverted without an effective method of implementing the policy.

In general, intuition appears to be a valuable aid in a number of "combinatorial-style" problems for which acceptable computer solutions are difficult to obtain. In many of these cases, a model spends considerable time in generating a good feasible solution as a starting point based upon intuition. Angel et al. illustrate how this may be done in computerizing school bus scheduling.[10] Again, the policy of busing to fulfill racial balances can be difficult to achieve without an effective model of balancing the various school districts. Although a model could be developed to make the necessary allocations, a much more effective approach would have the intuitive decision maker develop an initial solution based upon his experience and let the model then generate an improved solution.

Finally, there may be problem areas for which no tractable relationship can be identified. Although policymakers may have been involved in this area for some time, attempts to describe the system's behavior have not been successful. An alternative in this case is to model the policymakers. The premise of this approach is that the policymaker has some intuitive feel for the problem area and a model of that process can be a first step to an improved understanding of the overall process.

If a model can be developed to replicate, in part, the policymaker's intuitive processes, the model could then be extended to investigate other options and perform sensitivity analysis. Of the approaches listed, this one is by far the most difficult to accomplish. Where it has been attempted, it has been moderately successful in subpolicy areas as medical diagnosis and manpower scheduling. Whether such an approach could work in more complex policy analyses is debatable.

Table 4.1 summarizes several approaches for including policymaker in the modeling process. While these approaches can be effective methodological tools, they also serve a very useful purpose in getting the policymaker involved in the model. As a recent survey[11] of federally supported mathematical models has shown, the "distance" between the model developer and user is a major correlate of model usefulness. The approaches discussed here are means for shortening the distance between the model and policymaker.

Table 4.1   Approaches for Involving the Policymaker
in the Generation of Alternatives

Approach	Role of the Model	Role of Intuition
1	Generate solutions from problem statements	Evaluate solutions, make necessary problem formulation changes
2	Train decision maker to improve intuition	Generate solutions
3	Generate initial solution	Improve upon initial solution
4	Refine initial solution	Provide initial solution
5	Develop solution procedure after observing intuition	Provide basis for modeling

Once the policymaker has become an integral part of the generation of alternatives, the next area where the humanization approach can be effective is in the evaluation of those alternatives.

THE EVALUATION OF ALTERNATIVES

The development of policy models in situations involving multiple objectives has led to frequent difficulties with respect to how these objectives are resolved. One common approach has been an attempt to quantify each objective and then translate the consequent measurements into a single value. Cost effectiveness ratios are typical of this type of approach.

In many cases, the selection of a preferred alternative based upon a single valued criteria has led to significant problems. The management for which the analysis is being performed may not be able to relate to the measurement criteria being used. Since the measurement criteria were developed by the analyst, the weighting of the various objectives may not comply with the policymaker's value system.

For those models which are descriptive in nature, the resolution of the multiple objectives should be accommodated outside the model. The model should not be designed to identify a preferred alternative since this would presume that the various objectives can each be measured quantitatively according to some common measure. The role of the model should be instead to characterize the alternatives in terms of the various measures of effectiveness. The selection of the preferred alternative must be left to the decisionmaker, who uses the characteristics of the alternatives identified by the model, imparts his value judgments to the conficting measures of effectiveness, and decides upon the preferred alternative.

In the decision on a gasoline tax, the measures of different alternatives (economic impact, conservation effect) can be identified through the use of a model. To combine these into one common measure (e.g., dollars) is an inappropriate role for the model. Since the political and societal objectives cannot be developed in the model, an optimizing model would consider only a limited aspect of the problem.

In general, the best approach to decision-making situations involving multiple objectives is to have the decision maker apply his own judgment to the resolution of the tradeoffs among the various alternatives. Although this approach works well for those models which do not require a specific objective function, formulation models such as linear programming which require a specific formulation of an objective function must be approached differently. Consequently, optimizing models require some mechanism for dealing with multiple objectives. There are several approaches to doing this.

Perhaps the most obvious approach is to rank or weight the various alternatives. For example, a model may be set up to indicate which programs should be supported in a statewide recreation commission. The objective is to accommodate as many visitors as possible, but therein lies the problem. The different programs each contributed differently to the commission's objectives. Program 1 gives the

greatest number of out-of-state visitors, whereas program 2 provides
the greatest benefits for state residents. The ranking or weighting
approach says that the policies should be assigned numerical constants which reflect their respective importance. For example the
objective function

$$\text{Max } P_t = 2P_1 + 3P_2 \ 4P_3 + P_4$$

essentially makes program 3 four times as important as program 4
and twice as important as program 2.

Of course, the major weakness in this approach is how to rank or
weight the various options. Much as been written about this problem,
but little has been done to actually resolve the issue. Most researchers
seem to agree that the policymaker should be the one to provide the
ranks or weights. The problem lies in how to get the decision maker to
provide a valid estimate. The various approaches to this estimation
process are primarily concerned with the consistency of the estimates; that is the weights should all be in proper proportion to each
other. Although consistency is certainly a desirable attribute, the real
problem concerns whether the manager can make reasonable estimates in the first place without fully comprehending how those
weights will influence the final solution. For example, does a weight
of four for program 3 mean that four times as many visitors will be
accommodated as compared with program 4? The answer is, probably not. In fact, without really understanding the model in great detail, it is hard to say what effects the weights will have. For this
reason it is unrealistic to believe the weights provided by the policymaker will be at all valid. It is doubtful if any intelligent decision
maker would even participate in the entire process.

Another approach to this problem of resolving multiple objectives
is to simply optimize the model for each objective taken separately.
For example, a recreation program may have three distinct objectives:
maximize tourist dollars, maximize in-state participation, and minimize the cost per participant. The model could be run for each objective and a set of solutions generated. The difficulty with this approach
is that each solution represents an all-or-nothing condition. No compromise among the objectives is really achieved. Although this approach is invalid when considered alone, it does represent a useful
first step for two other approaches.

The third approach would take the solution values from the separate optimization runs and use these as the basis of performance standards. For example, the maximum tourist dollars may have been found to be $1,000,000; the minimum cost/participant, $10/year; and the maximum in-state participation, 3 visits/year. One of the objectives is designated as the primary objective, and the others are then established as constraints. For example, the primary objective may be to maximize tourist dollars while constraints are added which would reflect the upper limit on costs and lower limits on in-state visitors. For example, the commission may decide that it is willing to go 10 percent above the minimum cost and 20 percent below the maximum in-state visitors. These percentages are referred to as the performance standards.

While this process involves subjectivity in deciding on the performance standards, it involves asking the policymaker to make estimates on quantities that he can relate to and visualize. He has experience with costs and participation rates, and he has a reasonable idea on what the range of these values should be.

A fourth approach combines the separate objective function approach with the weighting approach. In this case each objective is assigned a weight which is varied over a given range. Solutions for various combinations of the weights are then given, and the policymaker can decide which combination gives what he considers to be the proper solution. In this case no attempt is made to be precise about what specific weights are used. Rather, the function of the weights is to generate the various compromise solutions. The policymaker then decides which solution is best without any explicit knowledge of the weights used to generate the solution. Again, the subjectivity involved relates to something tangible making this approach more acceptable.

In summarizing these approaches, the key element is the way in which subjectivity is used in resolving the multiple objectives. When subjectivity pertains to something tangible, decision makers can relate to the process and will be more receptive to the decision effort.

As was the case with the generation of alternatives, the involvement of decision makers in the evaluation of alternatives has two general advantages. It makes use of the vast experience of the policymaker and consequently expands the number of factors that can be incorporated in the modeling process. While the model may be able to handle effectively a limited set of quantitative factors, the integration of the model and decision maker has a synergistic effect.

The approaches for both the generation of alternatives and their evaluation require significant input from the policy maker. The next section of this chapter will be devoted to mechanisms for gaining the interest of the policymaker.

GAINING THE INTEREST OF THE POLICYMAKER IN THE MODELING PROCESS

There are perhaps hundreds of rules of thumb which can be suggested for gaining the interest of a policymaker in the development and use of a decision maker. The suggestions offered here are largely a reflection of the author's experience in modeling.

The use of a *pilot study* can be a significant tool for involving the policymaker in the analysis. A pilot study in this case is a small, simplified model used to demonstrate the type of input and output to be expected from the model. It will have approximate calculations in many cases. It may contain completely hypothetical data.

The advantages of the pilot model are numerous. It gives the policymaker a very early look at what can be expected from the model. The enthusiasm for a project generally wanes quickly after its initiation. A pilot study, since it is a simplification of the eventual model, can generally be completed very quickly. The level of enthusiasm can be kept at a rather high level since the policymaker can see very quickly some tangible results.

The pilot study also has the advantage of being a vehicle for discussing such issues as data requirements, output formats, and computational assumptions. Although these discussions could have taken place without a pilot study, the existence of a system that can be seen adds more meaning and interest to the discussion. It is not uncommon for significant data modifications and output changes to result from such sessions.

A recent study[12] which was performed for an industrial organization is equally applicable to a public sector organization. The organization in this case wanted a policy model that would look at product mix issues. The analysts prepared a pilot model that illustrated the basic principles to be developed eventually in the full model. The pilot study achieved several important objectives. It gave the task force which sponsored the model a chance to see what the model would eventually look like. The task force chairman became so excited with the model that he requested several additional runs, even though the model was hypothetical. The analysts presented the pilot study to other task force members to make it more compatible with their wishes. Refinements were also made regarding the model's assumptions and data requirements. The enthusiasm that developed from the pilot model carried through the entire study and greatly aided in its eventual implementation.

Once the pilot study has been demonstrated and future directions agreed upon, the next step is the development of the full model. In this regard, a *user-directed step-by-step approach* can facilitate the implementation of the model. This approach involves the policy-maker in a directing capacity. The analyst begins with a very simple model which is demonstrated to the policy maker. Additions to the model are made at the suggestion of the policymaker not the analyst.

This approach accomplishes several objectives. It builds the policymaker's trust in the model, since he has provided the major direction for it. Although the initial model may be an oversimplification; it does give the policymaker a chance to use the model at its most elementary level and gain confidence in its use. As the model complexity grows, the policymaker can adjust more easily to the higher levels of detail.

The step-by-step modeling approach also allows the policymaker to eliminate unnecessary detail from the model. Since the policymaker has been involved with the model on a continuing basis, he is a better judge of when the modeling effort has reached a point of diminishing returns.

Continuing with the example presented earlier, the analysts developed the model on an incremental basis. As each new feature was added to the model, the results were presented to the policymakers. At each step in the process, the analysts solicited advice of future directions to take. The task force requested several additional features in the process, including an expansion in the number of products in the model and an addition of another processing step.

Collecting data for modeling effort can often be a difficult process. Policymakers may not see the need to provide all the data requested. In this regard, the approach to take is to *develop the model with limited data* at first. If the step-by-step approach works, the policymaker will be increasingly more and more interested in the modeling effort. As successive stages of the model are developed, the policymaker will be more receptive to seeing that the additional data is provided.

In the study mentioned earlier, the task force chairman had his staff work up the data for 29 products. Since these products made up 75 percent of the company's profits, this data was considered sufficient. However, once the results of this study became known, the task force was anxious to have the full 98-product line added to the model. The step-by-step approach in this case made additional data collection much easier.

A final approach in the process of gaining interest in the modeling effort is to adopt a *no-fault revision policy*. Revisions are inevitable in a policy modeling effort. Sometimes they will result from misunderstandings between the policymaker and analyst; in other cases they may just be requests for additional detail. Analysts may become defensive about any necessary revisions, whereas the policymaker may view the necessity for revisions as a lack of insight on the part of the analyst. Since the assessment of blame for revisions does not contribute to the success of any project, an attitude of no-fault revisions can make a substantial contribution to the eventual implementation of the policy model. The acceptance of revisions as a fact of life can help in adopting a no-fault attitude.

In the policy study mentioned earlier, revisions were necessary in several cases. Some of the original data was incorrect, and the processing configuration as originally presented was in error. In each case, the analysts and policymakers accepted the model changes without recriminations. This spirit of cooperation was another contributing factor to the model's success.

There are many other approaches that could be suggested for gaining the interest of the policymaker in the modeling process. The suggestions discussed here have been tried and found effective on several modeling projects. They serve as a prime ingredient in the development of a humanized policy model.

SUMMARY

Humanized policy models are nothing new, but they do represent an approach to narrowing the gap between the policymaker and model. In particular, the policymaker should be built into the model as much as possible. The humanized policy model places stricter requirements on the relationship between the policymaker and analyst than is typical in many policy modeling efforts.

NOTES

1. G. Fromm, W. Hamilton, and D. Hamilton, *Federally Supported Mathematical Models: Survey and Analysis* (Washington, D.C.: Government Printing Office, 1974), p. 27.

2. John D.C. Little, "Models and Managers: The Concept of a Decision Calculus," *Management Sci.*, 16 (1970), B466-B485.

3. Yehezkel Dror, *Public Policymaking Reexamined* (Scranton: Chandler, 1968), pp.152-153.

4. P. B470.

5. *Management, Tasks, Responsibilities, Practices* (New York, Harper & Row, 1973), p. 56.

6. R. Cohen, S. Awerbuch, and W.A. Wallace "A Test of an Interactive Community Development Impacts Model in a Rural Environment," *Interfaces*, 7 (1976), 56.

7. Richard Laska, "City Models Challenge Urban Managers," *Computer Decisions*, 1972, p. 7.

8. Peter House, "Building Games—Retrospection," *Simulation & Games*, 3 (1972), 286.

9. C. Easingwood, "A Heuristic Approach to Selecting Sales Regions and Territories," *Operational Research Q.*, 24, (1973) 527-534.

10. R.D. Angel, W.L. Caudle, R. Nooman, and A. Whinston, "Computerized Assisted School Bus Scheduling," *Management Sci.*, 18 (1972), B279-B288.

11. Fromm et al.

12. L. Ted Moore and Jack Byrd, "For Practitioners Only: A Case Study in Selling an OR/MS Project to a Nameless Company," *Interfaces*, 8, (1977), 96-104.

5

POLITICAL SCIENCE AND PUBLIC ADMINISTRATION AS KEY ELEMENTS IN POLICY ANALYSIS

Stuart S. Nagel

Many people consider economics, especially benefit-cost analysis, to be the most important type of study to prepare one for evaluating alternative public policies. That methodology may be quite important, but there may also be a need to give strong recognition to the importance of public administration and political science in the growing field of policy analysis, public policy, or policy studies. The purpose of this chapter is not to play down economic modeling, the pretest-posttest models of social psychology, or any other approaches to analyzing alternative policies. Rather, the purpose is to show how essential public administration and political science often are.[1]

The relevance of these two disciplines partly depends on how policy analysis is defined. If the field is defined in a rather general way as the study of the nature, causes, and effects of alternative public policies, then almost by definition PA and PS are quite relevant. Political science is then clearly relevant by virtue of the fact that the essence of political science is the study of how government policy is made or formed, which fits well into determining the policy causes. Public administration is also then clearly relevant by virtue of the fact that its essence is the study of how government policy is or should be administered or implemented, which fits well into determining policy effects. In this chapter, political science will generally be referred to before public administration because PS tends to emphasize the earlier stage of policy formation, and PA tends to emphasize the later stage of policy administration, although there is plenty of overlap between the disciplines and the processes.[2]

Showing the relevance of public administration and political science is more difficult if policy analysis is more narrowly, but perhaps more meaningfully, defined as the study of how to determine what policies will maximize or achieve given goals. Political science is then also clearly relevant because without an understanding of the political aspects and constraints of policy formation, one is likely to recommend politically unfeasible solutions to policy problems. Public administration is then also clearly relevant because without an understanding of the effects of alternative administrative systems, one is likely to recommend administratively unfeasible or nonoptimum solutions. At least a few examples can be given of policies that economists have often recommended without adequately considering either political or administrative constraints.[3]

EXAMPLES OF POLICY RECOMMENDATIONS
THAT LACKED POLITICAL FEASIBILITY

In the field of environmental policy, economists often recommend some form of pollution tax, discharge fee, or effluent charge in order to minimize pollution. Such a tax in the water pollution field might involve requiring all firms on a given river segment to be taxed in accordance with the amount of pollution generated by each firm. Before levying the tax, engineers could determine the total cost of keeping the river segment at a given quality level by building a downstream filtration plant. If that total cost is $10 million a year and firm X contributes 5 percent of the pollution in the river segment, then it should pay 5 percent of the $10 million. Under such a system, each firm would have an incentive to reduce its pollution in order to reduce its assessment. If reducing its pollution is more expensive than the assessment, the firm can pay the assessment, which will then be used to clean up the river segment before the pollutants damage downstream communities.

The main advantage of such a system is that it internalizes the cost of the external damage that business firms are doing by polluting rivers or other water systems. In the absence of such a system, the costs are absorbed by the general public in the form of waterborne diseases and general taxes, and potential deterrent effect of a pollution tax is thereby lost. That economic advantage, however, is the main political disadvantage of such a system. Making the business firms so explicitly bear the costs of their expensive pollution would arouse them to exert great efforts to prevent such legislation from being adopted. If the sky over Washington was supposedly dark with Lear jets when the Carter administration sought to deregulate natural gas, one can imagine how black the sky would be if the Carter administration were to propose a pollution tax which would affect virtually all industries, not just the natural gas industry. The political unfeasibility of such a solution to the pollution problem under present circumstances is illustrated by the fact that when Congress established the National Water Quality Commission, the Commission was prohibited from even investigating the pollution tax as an alternative to the regulatory antipollution system, which is part of the 1972 water pollution legislation and the 1970 air pollution legislation.

What may therefore be needed as a politically feasible antipollution policy is more indirect and selective approaches. These include federal government subsidies to municipalities and tax rewards to business firms. In other words, legislation that subsidizes is generally more politically feasible than legislation that taxes, especially legislation that taxes business firms. Politically feasible antipollution policies also include ones that emphasize case-by-case litigation through the courts rather than an expensive blanket requirement for a given industry. Thus, business interests do not seem to be as opposed to allowing rare or occasional damage suits, injunctions, or even fines as they are to prohibiting automobiles or cigarettes that exceed strict pollution thresholds. An optimum antipollution policy could therefore be defined as one that minimizes pollution within the political constraints of present adoptability.[4]

Tariff reduction is another example of a policy almost universally endorsed by economists. The endorsement, however, is generally made without adequately considering whose ox is going to be gored and how to minimize that perceived damage. In 1930, thousands of economists signed petitions calling upon the Hoover administration to reduce tariffs in order to facilitate international trades. The Hoover administration, however, raised tariffs in order to satisfy the political demands of the numerous business firms that felt they needed such protection from foreign competition. Instead of simply cutting tariffs, it would have been more politically feasible to provide substitutes along with the tariff reductions, as was learned subsequent to World War II. Those tariff offsetting sweeteners have included negotiating reciprocal tariff reductions, offering government credit and aid to facilitate foreign purchases of American goods, and providing government subsidies or tax benefits to industries and firms hurt by tariff reductions.[5]

Farm support policy provides another example of economics advocacy lacking adequate concern for adoption problems. A favorite solution of many economists is to determine which farm families have less than a minimum level of annual income and then have the government subsidize those families enough to bring them up to that minimum level. Such a solution has the advantages of (1) making clear the costs of boosting farm income and thereby facilitating a benefit-cost analysis, (2) excluding farmers who do not need government support in order to achieve a minimum income level, and (3) allowing the prices of farm products to fall to a natural unsupported level to the benefit of consumers and the free market. All those economic advantages represent political disadvantages. The farmers receiving such direct support resent that type of program because it sounds like a welfare program. The well-off and politically powerful farmers not receiving support under that type of program might resent having their present support withdrawn. In the past, farmers in general have preferred and obtained indirect supports that increase demand, decrease supply, and thus increase prices. What may ultimately enable the economic optimum and the politically feasible to come together is the reduction in the power of farm interests as a result of the decreased quantity of farmers.[6]

EXAMPLES OF POLICY RECOMMENDATIONS
THAT LACKED ADMINISTRATIVE AWARENESS

In the field of housing policy, economists in the late 1960s often recommended government programs designed to convert poor people from tenants into homeowners. In theory, the idea sounds fine. By becoming homeowners, poor people would have a greater stake in their dwelling units, and thereby take better care of them. They would be especially unlikely to burn them down as they were sometimes doing during the 1960s. By becoming homeowners, poor people might acquire a more positive self-image and a more favorable attitude toward society, thereby becoming better citizens in ways other than just taking better care of their homes.

Partly in reliance on that kind of economic analysis, the Nixon administration pushed a home-ownership program for the poor that would involve government-guaranteed mortgages with low payments per month, comparable with what the Federal Housing Authority had for years been providing for middle-class people. The program turned out to be a rather dismal failure. Homes were sold to poor people at inflated assessments, often as a result of sellers bribing government assessors to exaggerate the value of the homes in order to increase the government guarantee. Homes were also sold to poor people without adequately informing them of the expensive maintenance costs and defects in the plumbing, heating, or electrical systems. As a result, maintenance and repair costs were often too high for poor people to handle, and they used the mortgage payments for repairs, thereby incurring foreclosures. Some of these foreclosed houses exchanged hands more times than a repossessed used car, since houses are normally more durable than cars. The program was wracked with the same kind of supplier fraud as the medicaid and medicare programs with doctors, dentists, pharmacists, optometrists, nursing home owners, and others overcharging for services rendered and not rendered.

What may have been needed in designing the program is more concern for the effects of alternative administrative systems. Perhaps a big mistake of the Nixon home-ownership program was that it involved government funding through the private-sector real estate system. An alternative way of administering or delivering the program would be for salaried government employees to sell homes to the poor that the government would have previously obtained by tax foreclosures, government purchases, or government construction. Salaried government employees selling government-owned housing to poor people would have no incentive to inflate the assessed valuation of the property or to withhold information on likely maintenance or repair costs.

An analogous government program is the Legal Services Corporation, which consists of salaried government attorneys providing legal services to the poor. No attorney from the Legal Services Corporation nor its predecessor, the OEO Legal Services Agency, has been involved in any scandal related to overcharging the poor for actual or fictitious services. Such a system would be adminstratively feasible for selling houses or supplying medical services to the poor. The system might, however, not be politically feasible for medical services, given the fear of the American Medical Association that such a system would lead to socialized government medicine for the total population. There is no likelihood that the government is going to go into the real estate business for the total population, and thus having salaried government home finders for the poor might be politically feasible.[7]

The negative income tax experiments represent another related example where economic modeling may have missed some important insights by not adequately considering alternative administrative systems. More specifically, over $10,000,000 was spent in New Jersey to test such relations as the effects on job getting of being given alternative amounts of money. Families were randomly assigned to various income-receiving groups. One group may have received enough money to satisfy only about 33 percent of minimum needs, as is done under the Mississippi welfare system; a second group may have received income at the 66 percent level, which corresponds roughly to the Texas welfare system; and a third group may have received income at the 100 percent level, which is what most northeastern states provide. Conservatives hypothesize that as welfare payments go up, ambition to get a job goes down, because the welfare recipient has less need for a job. Liberals hypothesize that as low welfare payments go up, ambition to get a job may also go up, because the welfare recipient may have his appetite whetted and his expectations raised. The true relation might involve job getting going up to a point and then going down. The expensive experiment, however, shows a nearly flat relation between job getting and welfare payments within the monetary range of the experiment.

Perhaps, however, a much steeper relation might have been observed if the families had been randomly assigned alternative delivery systems as well as, or instead of, alternative welfare amounts. The basic alternative delivery systems consists of (1) the compulsory caseworker, as exists under the present aid to dependent children system, or (2) the check in the mail, which is associated with the negative income tax system that seeks to minimize administrative interference in the lives of the poor. Maybe the compulsory caseworker stimulates job getting by informing the welfare recipient about available jobs or by harrassing the welfare recipient into taking a job on his own. On the other hand, maybe the compulsory caseworker lowers the self-esteem of the welfare recipient and makes him more dependent than he would be in the absence of a caseworker. Unfortunately, that kind of alternative administrative hypothesis was never tested, possibly because of a lack of participation by public administration people in the negative income tax experiments.[8]

SOME CONCLUSIONS

In light of the above examples, one can readily conclude that political feasibility and administrative awareness are important factors to consider in recommending policies for maximizing or achieving given goals. In light of that conclusion, perhaps policy formation and policy administration should play a more important role in the curricula of interdisciplinary policy programs and in the articles and book chapters of the public policy literature. To develop more fully the potential contributions of political science and public administration to policy analysis, perhaps people from those two disciplines should also become more aware of the policy analysis literature so that they can better contribute to it. In that sense, there are reciprocal arrows or mutually beneficial relations between political science and policy analysis, and between public administration and policy analysis. Those relations are also helping to build closer relations between political science and public administration to their mutual benefit.[9]

NOTES

1. Books that emphasize the importance of economic reasoning in policy analysis include Edith Stokey and Richard Zeckhauser, *A Primer for Policy Analysis* (New York: Norton, 1978);

Edward Quade, *Analysis for Public Decisions* (New York: Elsevier, North-Holland, 1975); and Stuart Nagel and Marian Neef, *Policy Analysis: In Social Science Research* (Beverly Hills: Sage, 1979).

2. Books defining the field of policy analysis, public policy, policy studies, or policy sciences include Harold Lasswell, *A Pre-View of Policy Sciences* (New York: Elsevier North-Holland, 1971); Yehezkel Dror, *Design for Policy Sciences* (New York: Elsevier North-Holland, 1971); and Stuart Nagel, ed., *Policy Studies Review Annual* (Beverly Hills: Sage, 1977).

3. Books emphasizing the role of public administration in policy studies include George Frederickson and Charles Wise, *Public Administration and Public Policy* (Lexington, Mass.: Lexington-Heath, 1977); Francis Rourke, *Bureaucracy, Politics, and Public Policy* (New York: Little, Brown, 1976); and Robert Golembiewski, *Public Administration as a Developing Discipline* (New York: Dekker, 1977). Books emphasizing the role of political science in policy studies include Austin Ranney, ed., *Political Science and Public Policy* (Chicago: Markham, 1968); Robert Spadaro, et al., *The Policy Vacuum: Toward a More Professional Political Science* (Lexington, Mass.: Lexington-Heath, 1975); and Ira Sharkansky (ed.), *Policy Analysis in Political Science* (Chicago: Markham, 1970).

4. On the economics of pollution taxes and antipollution policies, see Allen Kneese and Charles Schultze, *Pollution, Prices, and Public Policy* (Washington, D.C.: Brookings Institution, 1975), and William Baumol and Wallace Oates, *The Theory of Environmental Policy* (New York: Prentice-Hall, 1975). On the political science, see Walter Rosenbaum, *The Politics of Environmental Concern* (New York: Praeger, 1977), and Clarence Davies, *The Politics of Pollution* (Indianapolis: Pegasus, 1975).

5. On the economics of the tariff, see Donald Snider, *Introduction to International Economics* (Homewood, Ill.: Irwin, 1975), and Jan Pen, *A Primer on International Trade* (New York: Random House, 1967). On the political science, see Raymond Bauer, Ithiel Pool, and Lewis Dexter, *American Business and Public Policy; the Politics of Foreign Trade* (Atherton, 1963), and E.E. Schattschneider, *Politics, Pressures, and the Tariff* (New York: Prentice-Hall, 1935.)

6. On the economics of farm support policy, see Charles Schultze, *The Distribution of Farm Subsidies: "Who Gets the Benefits?" (Washington, D.C.: Brookings Institution, 1971), and John Galbraith, "Economic Preconceptions and Farm Policy," Amer. Econ. Rev. 44 (1954), 40-52. On the political science, see Ross Talbot and Don Hadwiger, The Policy Process in American Agriculture* (New York: ITT, 1968), and Charles Hardin, *The Politics of Agriculture* (Glencoe, Ill.: Free Press, 1952.)

7. On the economics of housing the poor, see Henry Aaron, *Shelters and Subsidies* (Washington, D.C.: Brookings Institution, 1972), and Anthony Downs, *Federal Housing Subsidies: Their Nature and Effectiveness and What We Should Do About Them* (NAHB and Real Estate Research, 1972). On the public administration, see Carter McFarland, *Federal Government and Urban Problems: HUD, Successes, Failures, and the Fate of Our Cities* (Boulder, Colo.: Westview, 1978), and Jon Pynoos, Robert Schaefer, and Chester Hartman, eds., *Housing Urban America* (Chicago: Aldine, 1973). The more successfully administered legal services program is described in Harry Stumpf, *Lawyers and the Poor* (Beverly Hills: Sage, 1973).

8. On the economics of welfare and the negative income tax idea, see Harold Watts and Albert Rees, eds., *The New Jersey Income Maintenance Experiment: Labor Supply Responses* (New York: Academic Press, 1977), and Peter Rossi and Catherine Lyall, *Reforming Public Welfare: A Critique of the Negative Income Tax Experiment* (New York: Russell Sage, 1976). On the public administration, see Gilbert Steinger, *Social Insecurity: The Politics of Welfare* (Skokie, Ill.: Rand McNally, 1966), and Frances Piven and Richard Cloward, *Regulating the Poor* (New York: Pantheon, 1971).

9. Books describing interdisciplinary policy studies teaching and research programs that

recognize the need for combining public administration and political science along with economics, social psychology, planning, and other disciplines include William Coplin, ed., *Teaching Policy Studies: What and How* (Lexington, Mass.: Lexington-Heath, 1978); Harold Lasswell, *A Pre-View of Policy Sciences* (New York: Elsevier North-Holland, 1971); Yehezkel Dror, *Design for Policy Sciences* (New York: Elsevier North-Holland, 1971); and Stuart Nagel, ed., *Policy Studies and the Social Sciences* (Lexington, Mass.: Lexington-Heath, 1975).

6

MOTIVES AND METHODS IN POLICY ANALYSIS

Barbara A. Bardes
Melvin J. Dubnick

INTRODUCTION

The flurry of activity termed "public policy analysis" is a recent development within the social sciences. Its newness is characterized by Dwight Waldo as resembling a situation where a young person has found a first job and is now seeking a career. Yet, in its period of relative youth the study of public policy has achieved a great deal and continues to demonstrate considerable promise. Shaped by events from the Great Depression to campus rebellions of the late 1960s and early 1970s, public policy analysis recently began to provide form and direction to the very disciplines which created it. In the process it is changing not only university curricula but the methodology and content of certain disciplines and career opportunities for many social scientists.

The degree to which this revolution succeeds and its implications for the study of social, economic, and political behavior are matters for study by those concerned with the intellectual development of the "soft" sciences.[1] Our concern is the nature of public policy analy-

AUTHOR'S NOTE: *This is an extended and substantially revised version of an article originally published as "The Why and How of Public Policy Analysis" in the September/ October issue of* Society *Magazine.*

sis as a field of inquiry rather than speculation on its impact or future. The questions most central to our investigation are, *why* do social scientists and others engage in policy analysis and *how* do they accomplish their respective tasks? We suggest that the motivation for doing policy analysis is linked closely to the methods chosen; that is, knowing why can tell us a great deal about how. However, before considering the breadth of public policy analysis, we need to answer a more fundamental question: what qualities are central to the many approaches of policy analysis? After describing those common elements, we shall examine the differences which have emerged among analytic approaches and discuss the relationship between those differences and the motivations behind public policy research.

THE COMMON ELEMENTS

In attempting to approach the phenomenon called public policy analysis, we face the fundamental fact that there is no widely accepted definition of public policy which acts as a substantive link among policy analysts. For some scholars public policy is only government action, whereas for others it includes stated intentions and symbolic acts of public officials. The debate over a definition for public policy could itself fill a volume. For present purposes we assume that in very general terms public policies are government actions or statements, although we acknowledge the lack of a definitive boundary or substantive core for the field.

The lack of a clearly defined subject matter has produced a diversity of endeavors, each taking up the label of policy analysis but in fact being quite distinct from one another. As we demonstrate below, each undertaking is based on a different set of motivations which, in turn, produces unique approaches to the study of public policy. But are these different approaches completely unrelated? Is there nothing tying them together and justifying their sharing the title "public policy analysis"?

One link is that all forms of *public policy analysis* involve *the application of problem-solving techniques to questions concerning the expressed intentions of governments and those actions it takes or avoids in attaining those objectives*. This broad definition is based on several qualities common to most policy analysis efforts.

Public policy analysis is applied. The task of the public policy analyst goes beyond merely "knowing the facts" about a government statement or action. One can have an extensive knowledge of policy and still not *understand* it. One can know, for instance, that 8,750,000 Americans served in Vietnam as members of the armed forces between August 1964 and January 1973; one can know that between 1961 and 1977, U.S. casualties directly related to the Vietnam conflict numbered more than 304,000; and one can know that of that number, 46,000 were battle-related deaths. But awareness of those facts does not provide meaning to what the U.S. policy in Vietnam entailed; nor does it give us insight into why those forces were there or what factors contributed to the high casualty figures; consequently, knowledge of basic facts cannot provide us with the discernment needed to determine what impact the Vietnam conflict had (and continues to have) upon American society or its foreign relations. Such things come not from a simple knowledge of facts; rather, they develop from a self-conscious *application* of appropriate tools, techniques, and conceptualizations to those facts. Understanding, in short, involves the processing of known facts. In this sense, all public policy analysis is applied.

Consider the difference between knowing about "stagflation" and understanding it. Popularly defined, stagflation is a condition of the economy existing when there are inflated prices during a period of stagnant growth patterns. It was a term often used to describe the economic situation of the United States between 1973 and 1975. During that period the consumer price index rose from 133.1 to 161.2, while the wholesale price index climbed from 134.7 to 174.9 (in both cases, 1967=100). During that same period, the number of unemployed in the civilian labor force increased from 4,304,000 to 7,830,000, and this increase was reflected in an unemployment rate jump from 4.9 percent to 8.5 percent. Despite the old cliche, such figures did not "speak for themselves." They had to be given meaning, and the concept of stagflation accomplished just that—although not to everyone's satisfaction. In a similar fashion, public policies— whether dealing with problems of the domestic economy or foreign relations—must be given meaning. This, in turn, implies that someone (e.g., an analyst) must take steps to convert the knowledge of basic facts into an understandable bit of information.

The distinction stressed here is an important one, especially in the study of public policy where many writers tend to ignore the implications of the word "analysis" and its role in changing "knowing" into "understanding".[2] Analysis is a process by which "known transformation processes" (i.e., problem-solving techniques) are applied to information "so as to make transparent the obscure or hidden."[3] Economists *know* about unemployment, but they *understand* it through the *application* of macroeconomic-analysis techniques. Sociologists *know* about discrimination, but they *comprehend* its consequences through the *application* of analytic methods used throughout the social sciences. Political scientists *know* that voters are predisposed to identify with the political party of their parents, but they are *able to explain* such behavior only through the *application* of various theories adapted from psychology and sociology. So it is with all public policy analysts, for they undertake the *application* of information-processing techniques in order to *understand* policies, *comprehend* their consequences, or *explain* their existence.

Public policy analysis uses problem-solving techniques. Problem solving, according to engineer and systems theorist Moshe F. Rubinstein, "is a matter of a process leading to a desired explicitly stated goal."[4] It is, in other words, a matter of choosing (or even creating) the appropriate tools and methods to be applied in order to answer given questions raised by problematic situations. Like other problem solvers, policy analysts have a standard bag of tricks at their disposal—an inventory of readily available tools and techniques useful for many of the problems they confront.[5] This collection of commonly applied techniques and modes of analysis includes many economic and political models as well as frameworks derived from theories of management, psychology, and organization development. Taken together, these techniques range from conservative pluralist to the radical Marxist, with the one point in common that they are all tools useful in attempts to approach public policies as problems to be solved. In addition, policy analysts are not unknown for their creativeness when it comes to developing new models or adapting old ones to new uses. This, too, reflects the fact that what is primary for the study of public policy is not necessarily adherence to a particular model or approach (although this does happen) but rather the search for problem-solving techniques which are useful for answering the questions facing the analyst.

This perspective has implications for what makes a good analyst of public policy. Any person who applies current and widely used problem-solving techniques to questions of public policy can claim to be a policy analyst, but not necessarily a good one. What makes an analyst good is not the efficiency of his or her application of a given technique to a problem but rather the effectiveness and usefulness of the answer arrived at.

For example, the analysis of foreign policy and international relations has tended to concentrate on simple and basic explanations of world politics. For a period of time it was popular to use a framework of analysis which attributed the behavior of nations to a driving desire to accomplish some goal which was in their "national interest." At other times it was the striving for economic or military power which determined (according to most analysts) international relations. The various explanations of foreign policy and world politics which have proliferated over the years fill up many volumes and constitute an interesting collection of analytic techniques which any analyst can use. The problem is that many analysts have a tendency to apply only one or two of those techniques and ignore the rest. These analysts may be extremely knowledgeable and highly adept at using these specific frameworks; however, that does not make them successful policy analysts. The measure of success is not in the application of the techniques alone; ultimately, it is the understanding obtained from their analysis which counts.

In this sense the policy analyst is not merely a technician; nor is a good policy analyst one who knows only the current tools of the trade. The key to problem solving—and thus the key to policy analysis—is the development of one's ability to make *appropriate* selections of problem solving techniques.

Public policy analysis deals with a variety of questions. What policy analysts do depends on what questions or problems they seek to solve. This is as true for the lay analysts as it is for highly trained experts. Analysis begins with a problem, and the nature of that problem is a crucial determinant of the entire analysis enterprise.

The range of policy questions and problems susceptible to analysis is very broad. "Which national health insurance plan is best?" "What would be the impact of a $25 billion tax cut on inflation without an equal cut in government spending?" "Under current wage base and coverage rules, what will per capita cost of Social Security and related programs be in the year 2050?" "What is the most efficient

means for reducing traffic fatalities?" These and similar queries,
covering topics ranging from the mundane ("How many snow plows
should the city purchase?") to the critical ("Should we control oil
supply by a preemptive attack on Saudi Arabia?"), not only cover a
variety of situations and substantive issues but also reflect the different types of questions which arise. Policy analysis problems encompass questions ranging from the descriptive ("What is Carter's economic policy?") and explanatory ("Why did Congress vote for a tax
reduction this year?") to the evaluative ("How successful was Nixon's
Vietnamization policy?") and the prescriptive ("Which weapons systems would deliver the most offensive capability for the least cost?").
This variety is basic to the richness and diversity we see in the policy
studies field.

Even more significant is the characteristic shifting nature of policy
analysis problems, for the questions which need to be answered vary
over time and from one situation to another. There is no fixed agenda
for policy analysts.

*Public policy analysts deal with expressions of government inten-
tions or actions taken (or avoided) to achieve policy objectives.* Despite debate over an exact substantive definition of public policy,
there are certain types of statements or events analysts seem to focus
upon. First, they tend to be concerned with expression of government
intentions. Second, they concentrate on what governments actually
do.

Expressions of what government intends to do about a public
problem come in many forms, formal or informal, official or unofficial. Government policy statements are always official when issued
as formal documents. Legislatures issue *statutes* or *resolutions* which
are "laws" in the most legitimate sense; mayors, governors, and
presidents disseminate *executive orders,* which are enforceable as
law; and courts provide written *judicial decisions,* which have the
impact of law. Informally, policy statements can range from the
official speech to the unofficial "leak." On an official level, informal
policy statements have played an important role in American foreign
policy, from the Monroe Doctrine asserting the interest of the United
States in preserving hegemony in the Western Hemisphere to President Ford's Pacific Doctrine speech, which expressed a commitment
to the "preservation of the sovereignty and the independence of our
Asian friends and allies." Such statements differ substantially, how-

ever, from the unofficial comment attributed to a "high level spokes-person" which expresses the government's intention to take certain action, e.g., to cut off military sales or other aid to Israel unless it adjusts its stand on settlements in the Sinai.

Regardless of the specific form of policy statements, what government says it will do is analytically important for two reasons. First, those statements may be *indicative* of what government actually intends to do. Thus, such statements could provide some insight into the questions of what a policy is, why it is, and what its intended consequences are. For example, if we assume that U.S. policy statements regarding the Vietnam conflict were valid reflections of the government's intentions, then the analyst's task of answering descriptive, explanatory, and evaluative questions about U.S. involvement in Southeast Asia can be facilitated. The policy analyst would be able to go directly to policy statements to find out what the official or unofficial U.S. policy in Vietnam was, what reasons were given for that policy, and whether those intentions were carried out to the fullest.

A second reason for studying what government says about a public problem is that such statements may be significant in and of themselves—that is, as *symbolic* expressions of intent which do not reflect contemplated government actions but rather function as solutions to the policy situation. Policy statements, in other words, may be used as a substitute for policy actions. Talk is a powerful policy tool. "Through language," notes Murray Edelman, "a group can not only achieve an immediate result but also win the acquiescence of those whose lasting support is needed." He also notes:

> That talk is powerful is not due to any potency in words but to needs and emotions in men. In subtle and obvious ways cultures shape vocabulary and meaning, and men respond to verbal cues. People who share the same role learn to respond in common fashion to particular signs. Specify a role and a political speech, and you can also specify a response with a high measure of confidence.[6]

It follows that a policy statement may be sufficient to satisfy a particular portion of the public concerned with a given problem. For example, during the first year of his administration, President Carter found himself under critical attack from the leadership of the National Urban League. Vernon Jordan, head of the league, accused Carter of not doing enough to fulfill his campaign pledges about jobs for black Americans. Although not completely placating League members, Carter did satisfy many of them when he reasserted his pledge in a speech before a meeting of the Urban League. His words soothed many of the disenchanted—at least temporarily. In that instance as in many others, the expression on intent—a statement of policy objectives and purpose—was as much an instrument of policy as governmental actions.

In hindsight, many people believe that policy statements made by the U.S. government during the Vietnam conflict were merely symbolic rhetoric and did not represent actual government intentions. If such is the case, then the task of the policy analyst might be to examine not only the content of the statement but also the reason for its use. For example, who were targets of these statements? What was the impact of the policy statements; e.g., was the target public sufficiently satisfied? Did the statement have any impact on other publics? If so, was their response positive or negative? These and related queries could produce some very interesting insights into many facets of the policymaking systems as well as the policy issue involved.

Regardless of whether analysts approach formal or informal, official or unofficial policy statements, and no matter if they examine those words as what government actually intends or merely as symbolic expressions, the focus on what government says is a critical and common topic for analysis.

What government does about public problems—its "performance" in David Easton's terms[7]—has also received a great deal of attention from policy analysts. For example, Ira Sharkansky, a prolific writer who has done a good deal of work in this area, considers public policy as representing "actions taken by government";[8] whereas Heinz Eulau and Kenneth Prewitt see policy as a "standing decision" manifest in the "consistent and repetitive" behavior of "those who make it and those who abide by it."[9] Of course, although the consideration of government actions has been increasing, not all analysts have focused on similar phenomena. Some are concerned with *discrete events,* i.e., acts and behaviors which can be pinpointed and analyzed as singular manifestations of some policy statement or objective. Usually accomplished through case studies,[10] these have attracted a considerable amount of analytic attention. Other analysts have turned to policy actions as *clusters* of discrete events related to each other through some common theme, target group, or subject matter.[11] For example, one can study the USSR's policy in Africa, Jimmy Carter's "fiscal" policy, Lyndon Johnson's "urban" policies; or short-term policies related to health care, education, welfare, or transportation.[12] What links these actions together is not related policy objectives or policy instruments but rather some shared point of organization, some common location, some basic policy statement, some historical or cultural tie. Still others focus on what James N. Rosenau terms *undertakings,* which he defines as a course of action that duly constituted officials of government pursue in order to preserve or alter a situation in the social system in such a way that the results are consistent with a goal or goals decided upon by them or their predecessors.

> An undertaking begins when a situation arises . . . that officials seek to maintain or change. It is sustained as long as the resources of the society mobilized and directed by the officials continue to apply to the situation. It terminates either when the situation comes to an end and obviates the need for further action or when officials conclude that their action cannot alter or preserve the situation and abandon their efforts.[13]

As an example of the difference between these views of policy action, consider how one might approach the study of U.S. policy with regard to Fidel Castro's Cuba. At the discrete-event level, one may study a specific occurrence such as the Bay of Pigs invasion, the missile crisis of October 1962, or the negotiation of an antihighjacking agreement between Cuba and the United States. At the level of clusters of policy actions, the concern would be for the relations between the two countries under some specific administration (e.g., Kennedy, Johnson, Nixon, Ford, or Carter); or it would focus on some specific matter over a period of time (e.g., trade relations). On the level of undertaking, one can study policy as those actions taken by the United States and its representatives to isolate the Castro regime from the rest of the Western Hemisphere.

Distinctions between discrete events, action clusters, and undertakings are sometimes arbitrary, and they frequently overlap. Similarly, choosing to focus on statements and/or actions is extremely significant in providing direction to analysts. What is consistent, however, is the general concern with actions and statements which permeates all public policy analysis. Such concerns are central to those who study public policy. However, it is obvious that the linkages among policy studies we have described here are quite loose. In fact, what ties many types of public policy analysis together (i.e., application, problem-solving techniques, and a responsiveness to questions about public policies) is probably less important for an understanding of the field as it now stands than the differences separating the multitude of approaches.

WHY POLICY ANALYSES DIFFER

Among social scientists in general and political scientists in particular, the focus on analysis has traditionally been the institutions and processes of pubic policymaking rather than public policies themselves. Studies which actually focused on public policies—that is, which regarded them as the primary subject of concern—evolved slowly within the social sciences as reactions to several major developments over the past fifty years. The most important of these forces were the Keynesian Revolution in economics during the 1930s and 1940s, the development of what Harold Lasswell has labeled "policy sciences" during and immediately after World War II, the adoption of quantitatively sophisticated budgeting techniques by the federal government during the 1960s, and the impact of the campus rebellions of the late 1960s and early 1970s on academic social science.

The Keynesian Revolution was instrumental not only in justifying public sector intervention in the economy but also in establishing a "foothold" in government for the first professional analysts of public policy. In the U.S. these economic analysts were eventually institutionalized as the Council of Economic Advisors in an attempt to put specialized advice "at the President's elbow."[14]

The creation of the council in 1946 also drew on the acceptance policy analysts achieved during World War II. Many psychologists, sociologists, and public administrators had been mobilized during the war to put the theories of their respective disciplines to work for the war effort. Some of these research directions in the "policy sciences" continued after the war and became institutionalized in private "think tanks" such as Rand and in public sector research and development agencies established in a number of departments.[15]

The work of the policy sciences together with some innovations in private corporate management techniques brought new budgeting approaches to the federal government in the 1960s. The programming-planning-budgeting process introduced by Robert McNamara to the Department of Defense (and mandated in 1965 for all agencies) shifted the focus of most government organizations from operational and personnel concerns to decisions about agency goals and objectives. Public budgeting, in short, went from the realm of the accountant to that of the policy analyst.[16]

A fourth major force producing the current interest in public policy analysis emerged from the turmoil of American university campuses during the 1960s and 1970s. Cries of "irrelevance" and accusations that scholars were serving only the "establishment" led to a renewed interest in the real impact of government policies, particularly from a critical, if not radical, viewpoint.[17]

All of these influences plus various improvements in scientific and rational decision-making techniques led to the adoption of policy analysis in many sectors of public life—for many different reasons. As a direct consequence of these developments, the number of individuals calling themselves public policy analysts grew in number, until today we have what can be best described as a diverse and growing corps of social scientists who identify with the field. But historical events and intellectual trends are not clearly associated with the variety of approaches which has emerged. In fact, considering the multiple "roots" of policy analysis, no one factor can be identified as primary nor can any causal relationship be established between historical developments and specific analytic approaches.

Lacking any such historical connection, we adopt the thesis that motivation determines methodology. We suggest that how a given policy analyst goes about his or her work depends on why the task is being undertaken. If this is the case, then the primary questions are: What motivates individuals who do policy analysis? What are they trying to accomplish or achieve?

In 1968 political scientist Austin Ranny provided a partial response to that question when he took note of three fundamental reasons for studying public policy: scientific, professional, and political.[18] Here we examine those three as motivational perspectives and add two more such motivating viewpoints to round out Ranney's study.[19] From this classification of analytic roles, we can speak to the question of what makes one policy analyst use one approach while another uses a different methodology.

Scientific reasons. According to Ranney, there are policy analysts who believe their studies "will add significantly to the breadth, significance, and reliability of . . . a special body of knowledge."[20] From this point of view, the prototypical analyst is a scientist, i.e., a person involved in "basic research" who is "restrained, dispassionate, conservative, and willing to suspend belief, pending more evidence."[21] Such an individual is a "policy analyst" in Thomas R. Dye's sense of that title: one engaged in a search for the *causes* and *consequences* of polices who has a concern for "explanation rather than prescription," who undertakes with "scientific rigor" the analysis of policies, and who makes an "effort to develop and test general propositions . . . and to accumulate reliable research findings of general relevance." Thus, scientific policy analysis is accomplished to discover what policies are and why they are, but not what they "ought to be." In short, policy analysis for the scientist is not policy advocacy.[22]

What are the implications of this approach? For the policymaker they are significant, since the study of public policy for scientific reasons can prove a frustration to decision makers. In his critique of policy analysis, Dye discusses several basic conflicts between "decision-oriented" policymakers and "theory-oriented" (i.e., scientific) policy analysts. Underlying these differences is the belief that whereas the policy maker seeks "guides for effective government action" the policy analyst (as scientist) "seeks to test and develop theories about the causes and consequences of public policy."[23]

For those who teach policy studies, this scientific approach would mean stressing the importance of social science methodologies and other techniques related to systematic research. The student would learn the logic of empirical inquiry, its capabilities, its limits, and how it is applied. In addition, the scientific study of public policies would mean training in the proficient use of theory-building research methods and the analytic frameworks associated with them. In short, to be a policy scientist is to learn the discipline of basic research. It is to seek the accumulation of knowledge for knowledge's sake. For some, the task of scientific investigation also includes critical analysis.[24] In either case the curriculum developed with such purposes in mind would reflect an emphasis on scientific methodology, with substantive concerns playing a secondary role.

Professional reasons. Some individuals study public policy in order to improve it. As one author puts it, although the scientific approach represents the study *of* public policy, there are those concerned with studies *in* public policy.[25] Professor Ranney describes this approach as the study of public policy which seeks the application of "scientific knowledge to the solution of practical problems."[26] Policy improvement is the end, and the application of expert "policy knowledge" is the means. In the post-World War II period, Lasswell called for development of "policy science," believing that from relevant studies in certain fields there will emerge an approach which "will bring about a series of 'special' sciences within the field of the social sciences, much as the desire to cure has developed a science of medicine . . . distinct from, though connected with, the general science of biology."[27]

The need for (and design of) a policy science profession has received a great deal of attention in recent years.[28] Even more significant is the fact that "applied" policy research has become a major component of government programs at all levels in the United States. This occurred through what economist Alice M. Rivlin has termed a "quiet revolution" wherein policy analysis became "part of the decision process" and the policy analyst an accepted "participant at the decision table."[29] One indication of the impact of this revolution is found in a 1974 survey of federal agencies conducted by the General Accounting Office, which uncovered a 500 percent increase in expenditures for professional policy research (specifically program evaluations) between 1969 and 1974.[30] A similar expansion in the use of professional analysts is evident at the state and local levels, where policy analyses are used extensively to assess program effectiveness and improve administrative productivity.[31]

The ever-increasing role of professional policy analysts in government has neither gone unnoticed,[32] nor lacked critics.[33] Nevertheless, one can approach the study of public policies from the professional perspective, and a curriculum structured along these lines would seek to provide students with the background necessary to develop "policy science" skills. Here, as in the scientific approach to policy analysis, there would be a strong concern for methods of scientific investigation. However, the tools and techniques of "professionals" will differ from the basic research of the "scientists." The stress is increasingly on "applied" research. Thus, from the professional perspective, policy analysts should be able to specify their goals and the values sought. It is also crucial that they be capable of (a) effectively defining and diagnosing policy problems, (b) proposing policy alternatives, (c) developing models which can aid in the achievement of desired ends and methods for testing those models, (d) establishing intermediate goals, and (e) estimating the feasibility of various policy programs.[34]

The overall objective of the professional policy analyst is to serve the policy-making system with either "policy-issue knowledge" (i.e., information about a substantive policy matter, such as defense or health care) or "policy-making knowledge" (i.e., dealing with the organization and operation of the structures and processes for formulating, implementing, and evaluating public policies). In summary, a basic introduction to public policy analysis for the professional would necessarily emphasize the evaluative and instrumental functions of policy studies and focus on how analysis could be used to improve public policies or the policymaking system.[36]

Political reasons. For others the function of public policy analysis is to provide a basis for advocating a particular policy position which is perceived as "right" and politically warranted. Ranney and Dye are critical of this perspective, regarding such political work as unscholarly since it is seemingly highly subjective and (as they see it) a misapplication of the social scientist's role.[37] There are others, of course, who believe that policy analysts have fulfilled such political functions in the past, and have done it well. This is a point made by Daniel Patrick Moynihan, who points out that until recently the task of social scientists who were asked for advice on policy matters was to justify a given position. Policy analysis was frequently political, not professional. Its task was giving credence to certain policy positions, not challenging them.

> Advocates of social change, especially to the degree that they base their advocacy on normative grounds, are naturally disposed to be impatient, to ask that remedies be as near as possible immediate. So long as social science was essentially asked to certify that the normative grounds were justifiable, its task was relatively simple, and it could be sure to be invited back for the next round of certification. But once it was asked actually to implement—forthwith—the normative imperative, it is up against a very different matter indeed.[38]

Despite controversy over the value of undertaking policy studies for political reasons, an argument can be made that the contemporary study of politics and policies has its roots in the teaching of rhetoric,[39] and that political policy analysis follows in a long tradition of political rhetoric which develops supportive evidence on behalf of specific policy positions.

Teaching policy analysis for political reasons would involve the development of fundamental research skills and instruction in the rhetorician's methods of rationalization and argumentation. Work and training based on this approach would focus on substantive issues and their effective presentation; and since there is often "no better offense than a good defense," the student of political policy analysis would also be adept at critical thinking and capable of responding to those who oppose a preferred position. At the heart of this approach is the primary objective of neither discovering nor applying policy-relevant knowledge, but rather convincing others of the correctness of one's position on an issue.

Although Ranney's survey of reasons for undertaking public policy analysis touched upon three major motivations of academics, there were at least two other reasons which he failed to mention but which deserve attention here. For one thing, there are a significant number of individuals involved in the design and application of policy implementation procedures who do policy analysis for *administrative* reasons.

Administrative reasons. It is taken for granted that those who are called upon to carry out a policy ought to comprehend it. Ideally, they should try to understand the policy, the intent of those who passed it, and the various means available for implementing it. Their objective should be to administer the policy both efficiently and with the greatest effectiveness. To do so, they should become policy analysts.

Administrative theorist and nobel laureate Herbert A. Simon has taken this point even further by noting that "administrative processes are decisional processes: they consist in segregating certain elements in the decisions of members of the organization, and establishing regular organizational procedures to select and determine these elements and to communicate them to the members concerned." Following this line of thought, "correct" administrative decision exists when the "appropriate means" are used "to reach designated ends. The rational administrator is concerned with the selection of these effective ends."[40] In other words, the effective implementation of public policy or any other set of goals given to administrators depends upon the policy analytic capabilities of the administrator. Understanding a policy, being able to "break it up" into its component parts, and developing appropriate strategies to achieving the ends as stated— these are the keys to rationality in administrative decision making and the source of concern among implementors for the task of public policy analysis. In their attempt to achieve higher levels of rationality, many administrators do, in fact, undertake policy analyses.

By the early 1960s, government agencies throughout the United States were incorporating basic benefit-cost policy analysis into many of their administrative decisions to help the bureaucracy meet its objectives at the lowest possible cost. In the years that followed, systems analysis and PPB came to the foreground as a means for fitting the policy objective to "suit available resources." We entered the period of "program budgeting," where the administrative analyst began to determine both the "ends and means" of policy, i.e., the "best" objectives and the appropriate combination of resources to be used in their achievement. Political scientist Aaron Wildavsky traces this development in an essay highly critical of the administrative analyst. According to Wildavsky, the administrator moved quietly from technician (benefit-cost analysis) to analyst (systems analysis) to policymaker (program budgeting) during this period, and in the process many "political" aspects of policymaking became irrelevant and thus ignored.[41]

Regardless of the implications, administrative policy analysis has become quite sophisticated in recent years, especially as incorporated into budget and management techniques. A course on policy analysis for administrators would focus almost exclusively on the latest tools available for improving the efficiency of policy implementation, from OR (operations research) and PERT (performance evaluation and review technique) to critical path method and PPB. It would stress the application of microeconomic analysis to questions of policy choice, and promote the use of simulation, gaming, and automatic data processing where possible in the implementation process. In short, administrative policy analysts would be well trained in contemporary management science,[42] and the curriculum written for them would be in that field.

Personal reasons. One does not need to be reminded of the pervasiveness of government in our lives—"from cradle to grave" and more. We can always add to that cliche by pointing out that in purely economic terms, the public sector has an immense influence upon us, economically amounting to over 22 percent of our current gross national product. Leaving economics aside for a moment, consider the incredible size (and growth) of public sector regulations which intervene in our work-a-day lives. As some indication of this, Table 6.1 shows the growth of regulatory agencies from 1970 to 1975. "Economic" regulators such as the Interstate Commerce Commission and the Securities and Exchange Commission (which concentrate on market access, rates, and obligations to provide service) have increased by one-quarter during that period, while "social" regulators such as the Environmental Protection Agency and the Occupational Safety and Health Administration (which determine conditions of production and production characteristics) have increased by one-half. Meanwhile, expenditures for these agencies have risen 157 percent and 193 percent respectively, while the total number of regulations proposed and added to the federal code have increased substantially. The point is that people ignore government and its activities only out of ignorance, foolishness, or alienation. Just the impact of public policy on our lives should be sufficient reason for being interested in learning and doing public policy analysis.

Educating persons with the intention of making them "better citizens" and more aware individuals is anything but new. "Civics education" had just that purpose, and it received considerable attention in the United States at the turn of the century. At that time, the function of such instruction was to socialize and indoctrinate a large immigrant population into an American "culture." Although such socialization can be criticized for creating a homogenous and mostly apolitical population,[43] it can also create citizens who look at government policies with a critical eye. In recent years there has been a renewed concern for instruction which aims at instilling in students the ability to understand and contend with problems of the contemporary world. Present efforts are inherently more critical than the civics education of earlier years. Consider, for example, the purpose of political education expressed in the following statement by political scientists Vernon Van Dyke and Lane Davis:

> We take it for granted that students in our course are, or are likely to be, participants in politics, if only as voters; at the very least, they are interested observers of politics. As participants or observers, they

necessarily face political conditions and practices, and confront issues, that call for some sort of decision on their part: an appraisal, a
judgment, a choice. As we see it, the major general objective of
teaching should be to help students make better decisions.[44]

From this view, one studies public policy to learn what questions to
ask about public (hence political) decisions and how to find (and
evaluate) some possible answers.

The personal policy analysis endeavor differs from the scientific in
seeking available information and clarification rather than new
"truths" and in having as its objective the facilitation of personal
choices rather than the accumulation of knowledge. Like professional policy analysis, this personal approach makes use of many
techniques and whatever knowledge is available; yet however much
the end products of both professional and personal types of analysis
may resemble each other, the objectives differ substantially. Professionals are technicians who work to solve the problems of their clients. The utility of policy analysis for citizens is found in the capacity
it gives them to reach tentative solutions to some of the basic problems discussed in the previous chapter. Where the professional seeks
to find and apply appropriate knowledge (knowledge which is scientifically credible and technically reliable), citizens seek insight and
some comprehension which allows them to understand and reflect
upon (and perhaps even participate in) ongoing policy debates.

Nor is the personal approach the same as the political. Politicos
study and apply policy analysis to maximize the possibility that the
values and priorities they support or represent will be accepted. What
they look for are methods by which to rationalize and obtain the
adoption of particular policy positions. But, although those undertaking policy analysis for personal reasons may value one policy
position over another, their primary objective is *to understand* the
problems policies confront and the value of alternative courses of
action being considered. Policy analysis for personal reasons is not
policy advocacy; i.e., it is not necessarily political, although it may
become a factor in political acts like voting.

And obviously it is not the same as administrative policy analysis,
at least not unless the citizen is specifically concerned with the efficiency of policy implementation and is seeking to understand the
policy execution process. The techniques of administrative policy

Table 6.1 Growth of Federal Regulation, 1970–1975

Year	Number of Major "Economic" Regulatory Agencies	Number of Major "Social" Regulatory Agencies	Expenditures of Major "Economic" Regulatory Agencies (in Millions)	Expenditures of Major "Social" Regulatory Agencies (in Millions)	Number of Pages in Federal Register	Number of Pages in Code of Federal Regulations
1970	8	12	$166.1	$1,449.3	20,036	54,105
1971	8	14	$196.8	$1,882.2	25,447	54,487
1972	8	14	$246.3	$2,247.5	28,924	61,035
1973	8	17	$198.7	$2,773.7	35,592	64,852
1974	9	17	$304.8	$3,860.1	42,422	69,270
1975	10	17	$427.6	$4,251.4	60,221	72,200
Per Cent Increase 1970–1975	25	42	157	193	201	33

SOURCE: William Lilley III and James C. Miller III, "The New 'Social Regulation'," *Public Interest*, 47 (Spring 1977), p.50.

analysis are often very sophisticated, and to apply methods such as benefit-cost analysis is difficult enough for the public administrator, let alone the concerned citizen. Nevertheless, individuals who undertake policy analysis for personal reasons ought to familiarize themselves with the concepts underlying the policy analysis of management science, if for no other reason than to know its capabilities and limitations.

Of course, just as there is no single approach to policy analysis, there is no single reason for studying the topic. The goals and methods of the scientist, professional, administrator, politician, and citizen can be described as distinctive. However, much of the time the activities of those who hold such roles are hard to distinguish. Scientists may find themselves providing "professional" advice on how to accomplish a policy goal. They may, particularly in technical issues like nuclear engineering, supply politicians with a rationalization for a particular viewpoint. Similarly, administrators may add to the knowledge of the scientific estate, and citizens may use the skills of politicians to persuade their friends and neighbors.

Yet, despite the propensity to "mix" one's motivations, the analyst generally remains methodologically linked to the primary motivation of the study at hand. This tendency to rely on a set of methodological approaches is reinforced by the training of the analyst, and that reinforcement is an important ingredient in the formula which makes one analyst choose one direction while another travels a different road. But the crucial factor is something much different—one which goes much deeper than mere training, i.e., the problematic foundations.

THE PROBLEMATIC FOUNDATIONS

The irony of public policies is that they are simultaneously sources of solutions and causes of problems. Public policies are responses to human needs which have become public issues. In that sense they are solutions to problems—reactions to some particular dilemma faced by government officials. Yet public policies are themselves generators of dilemmas, and not only for government decision makers. Put briefly, if there is a quality which pervades all public policy, it is its problematic nature.

This quality has its impact on public policy analysis. For, from each perspective we have discussed thus far, public policy takes on a problematic character which is distinctive to its approach. Scientists, for example, regard policies as *theoretic problems*. That is, scientists view public policy, its causes and consequences, as a challenge to the accumulation of knowledge and the development of a scientifically credible and empirically warrantable theory of that phenomenon. Their objective is to predict consistent patterns of public policy with some certainty. For scientific analysts it is the unexplained and unpredictable which is at the heart of the problem of public policy. It is a "gap" in social science knowledge which they seek to fill, and the creation of a credible theory is their primary objective.

For professional analysts—i.e., those who seek to apply the scientific approach to public problems—policies are *design problems*. They want to apply the credible theoretic knowledge at their disposal to the improvement of current or future policies. Thus, they are often involved in the dissemination of relevant information used to facilitate improved policy choices; but even more crucial are their attempts at helping to reorganize the structures and procedures through which public sector decisions are made. For professionals the problems of public policy design are twofold: deciding which policies are "best" (i.e., optimal for the task at hand), and determining which policy-making mechanism will result in the selection of the optimal choice from among several alternatives. In either case the problems they contend with ultimately stress the development and organization of a better policymaking system, one which applies rational and empirically warranted knowledge to the making of public sector decisions.

The political policy analyst considers policy statements and actions as *problems of value maximization*. Politicos seek, for either themselves or others, the adoption and institutionalization of a specific set of priorities. At times this means seeking changes in current policy priorities; at other times it calls for a defense of the status quo. In this view public policies pose problems as either objectives to be achieved or barriers to be overcome. It is a set of values which the political analyst fights for, and the analysis undertaken for this purpose reflects that goal.

Administrative policy analysts face problems of a different sort, for, as policy implementors, their objective is to carry out the designs and priorities given them by legislators or other key decision makers.

While in practice these analysts deal with design and value maximization problems, their primary focus is on public policies as *problems
of application*. Ideally, their objective is to carry out efficiently and
effectively the programs of government which have been authorized,
to carry these out in accord with the intentions of the policymakers,
and to enforce relevant sanctions and incentives where necessary.
Developing the right organization and procedures for accomplishing
these tasks is at the center of the administrative analyst's concern.

Although all of these perspectives on public policy problems are
important, they are the concern of relatively few individuals. Of
greater importance is the fact that public policies statements must be
"lived with"—that each and every one of us must contend with public
policy statements and actions on a personal-level every day of our
lives. Thus, public policies are *problems of contention* for the general
public, and we all deal with these problems differently. Some of us
contend with a given public policy by obeying its directives whether
they be positive or negative, or whether they take the form of rewards
or punishments for certain behaviors. Others contend by disobeying a
policy whenever convenient and possible (as many do when exceed-
ing a posted speed limit on an interstate highway or in a residential
area) or challenging its legitimacy if they believe it necessary to do so
(e.g., the NAACP's challenge of school segregation policies through
litigation eventually led to *Brown v. Board of Education* in 1954).
Still others contend by finding and using "loopholes" in the policy
which are to their advantage (e.g., think of the time and financial
resources put into investigating and taking tax breaks as a means of
avoiding paying personal income taxes), or attempting to get the
policy changed by joining with others to lobby for adjustments in a
law. Whatever the course of action we choose, we do live (and must
deal) with public policies. Who we are makes a difference. However,
public policies are part of our lives whether we are black or white,
Christian or Jew, laborer or banker, scientist or administrator, professional or politico.

Table 6.2 summarizes the relationship between these problem
orientations and the various approaches to public policy analysis. In
each case, the perceived problem follows from the analyst's motivation, and this in turn conditions the approaches taken and the training
received. What are the implications of this view? It is evident that the
field we call public policy analysis is so diverse that it would be

Table 6.2

Type of Policy Analyst	Public Policy Problem	Motivation	Approach	Relevant training
1. Scientist	Theoretic	Search for theory, regularities, "truth"	Scientific method, objectivity, pure analytics	Basic research methods, canons of social science research
2. Professional	Design	Improvement of policy and policymaking	Utilization of knowledge, strategic	Strategic; benefit-cost analysis; queuing, simulation, decision analysis
3. Political	Value maximization	Advocacy of policy position	Rhetoric	Gathering "useful" evidence; "effective" presentation
4. Administrative	Application	Effective and efficient policy implementation	Strategic, managerial	Strategic; same as professional with stress on those talents useful in implementation
5. Personal	Contention	Concern for policy impacts on life	Mixed	Use of many models and techniques from other approaches; less sophisticated

impossible to summarize in any single curriculum, text, symposium, or lecture. Yet, for all its diversity there is a common definable thread which runs through public policy analysis, namely, its existence as problem solving applied to policy-relevant problems.

Thus, although it is impossible to cover all of policy analysis in its variety of forms, it can be viewed through the lens of the problem-solving approach as it is applied to diverse policy problems. This perspective makes it possible to suggest what policy analysis is, why it is carried out, and the almost unlimited potential for new and creative work which the the field offers to those who accept the challenge.

NOTES

1. For a discussion of those implications, see James C. Charlesworth, ed., *Integration of the Social Sciences Through Policy Analysis* (Philadelphia, Pa: American Academy of Political and Social Science, 1977).

2. The distinction made here owes much to the work of John Dewey. See his *Experience and Nature* (New York: Dover, 1929/1958), ch. 4; also Dewey and Arthur F. Bentley, *Knowing and the Known* (Boston: Beacon, 1949).

3. Moshe F. Rubinstein, *Patterns of Problem Solving* (Englewood Cliffs, N.J.: Prentice-Hall, 1975), p. 7

4. pp. 6-7

5. There are, for example, certain "models" familiar to many students of political life which can be used to describe, explain, or evaluate certain sets of policies: the group-theory model, the single-elite or pluralist models, incrementalist models, and others. In analyzing foreign policies, commentators and political candidates may use models of international relations, such as balance of power, detente, or tripolar world. See Thomas R. Dye, *Understanding Public Policy,* 3rd ed. (Englewood CLiffs, N.J.: Prentice-Hall, 1978); also Peter Woll, *Public Policy* (Cambridge, Mass.: Winthrop, 1974), especially ch. 2.

6. *The Symbolic Uses of Politics* (Urbana; Univ. of Illinois Press, 1964), pp. 114-115. Also see Edelman's *Political Language: Words That Succeed and Policies That Fail* (New York: Academic Press, 1977).

7. *A Systems Analysis of Political Life* (New York: John Wiley, 1965), p. 353.

8. "Environment, Policy, Output and Impact: Problems of Theory and Method in the Analysis of Public Policy," in Ira Sharkansky, ed., *Policy Analysis in Political Science* (Chicago, Ill.: Markham, 1970), p. 63.

9. *Labyrinths of Democracy: Adaptations, Linkages, Representation, and Policies in Urban Politics* (Indianapolis; Bobbs Merrill, 1973), pp. 464-481.

10. See Raymond A. Bauer and Kenneth J. Gergen, eds., *The Study of Policy Formation* (New York: Free Press, 1968), especially Bauer's introductory chapter: "The Study of Policy Formation: An Introduction," pp. 1-26; also Graham T. Allison, *Essence of Decision: Explaining the Cuban Missile Crisis* (Boston, Mass.: Little, Brown, 1971); A. Lee Fritschler, *Smoking and Politics: Policymaking and the Federal Bureaucracy,* 2nd ed. (Englewood Cliffs, N.J.: Prentice-Hall, 1975); and Theodore J. Lowi et al., *Poliscide* (New York: Macmillan, 1976).

11. See the discussion on decision cluster studies in James A. Robinson and R. Roger Majak, "The Theory of Decision-Making," in James C. Charlesworth, ed., *Contemporary Political Analysis* (New York: Free Press, 1976).

12. Consider the chapter titles given in Fred I.Greenstein and Nelson W.Polsby, eds., *Handbook of Political Science, Vol 6: Policies and Policy-making* (Reading, Mass.: Addison-Wesley, 1975): "Making Economic Policy . . ."; "Science Policy"; "Welfare Policy"; "Race Policy"; "Comparative Urban Policy . . ."; "Foreign Policy."

13. Rosenau, "Moral Fervor, Systematic Analysis, and Scientific Consciousness in Foreign Policy Research," in Austin Ranney, ed., *Political Science and Public Policy* (Chicago: Markham, 1968), p. 222.

14. Walter W. Heller, *New Dimensions of Political Economy* (New York: Norton, 1967), ch. 1.

15. Harold D. Lasswell, "The Policy Orientation," in Daniel Lerner and Harold D. Lasswell (eds.), *The Policy Sciences* (Stanford, Ca.: Stanford University Press, 1951), p. 4 also see Irving Louis Horowitz and James Everett Katz, *Social Science and Public Policy in the United States* (New York: Praeger Publishers, 1975), esp. Chapter 2.

16. For background, see Leonard Merewitz and Stephen H.Sosnick, *The Budget's New Clothes: A Critique of Planning-Programming-Budgeting and Benefit-Cost Analysis* (Chicago: Rand-McNally College Publishing, 1971); Ida R. Hoos, *Systems Analysis in Public Policy: A Critique* (Berkeley, Calif.: Univ. of California Press, 1972); and Robert H.Haveman and Julius Margolis, eds., *Public Expenditures and Policy Analysis* (Chicago: Markham, 1970), esp. parts four and five; Fred S. Hoffman, "Policy Expenditure Analysis and the Institutions of the Executive Branch," in Haveman and Margolis, p. 424; and Alice M.Rivlin, *Systematic Thinking for Social Action* (Washington, D.C.: Brookings Institution, 1971), esp. ch. 1.

17. For instance, see the work of the Union for Radical Political Economics, which was established in 1968. Specifically, see Richard C. Edwards, Michael Riech, and Thomas E. Weisskopf, eds., The Capitalist System: A Radical Analysis of American Society, 2nd ed. (Englewood Cliffs, N.J.: Prentice-Hall, 1978); also see Alvin W. Gouldner, *The Coming Crisis of Western Sociology* (New York: Avon, 1970); Charles A. McCoy and John Playford, eds. *Apolitical Politics: A Critique of Behavioralism* (New York: Harper & Row, 1967); Marvin Surkin and Alan Wolfe, eds., *An End to Political Science: The Causcus Papers* (New York: Basic Books, 1970); Philip Green and Sanford Levinson, eds., *Power and Community: Dissenting Essays in Political Science* (New York: Vintage Books, 1970); and George J. Graham and George W. Carey, eds., *The Post-Behavioral Era: Perspectives on Political Science* (New York: David McKay, 1972).

18. "The Study of Policy Content: A Framework for Choice," In Austin Ranney, ed., *Political Science and Public Policy,* pp. 3-21. In his categorization of reasons, Ranney is using Don K. Price's "four estates" classification originally presented in *The Scientific Estate* (Cambridge, Mass.: Belknap, 1965), pp. 122-135. Ranney's scheme has been used by others to explain the reasons for studying public policy. For example, see Thomas R. Dye, *Understanding Public Policy* (New York: Prentice-Hall, 1975, *Public Policy-Making* (New York: Praeger, pp. 5-7; also James E. Anderson, 1975), pp. 6-8.

19. As will become evident as we consider each of these reasons, the categories applied here are far from exhaustive. In fact, there are several important reasons not even mentioned. For example, some policy analysts are coerced into their tasks, as is the student who must complete an assignment involving policy analysis under threat of receiving a poor grade if it is not done or not done well. There are other analysts who do it "for the money" or some similar reward. Although these reasons are related to those briefly discussed under the category of "personal," they are quite different and, therefore, do not receive specific consideration.

20. "The Study of Policy Content," p. 13.

21. Martin Rein and Sheldon H. White, "Can Policy Research Help Policy?" *Public Interest*, 49 (Fall 1977), p. 135.

22. Dye, *Understanding Public Policy*, pp. 5-8, A related point is expressed by Elliot Feldman: "Analysis is the product of science, and science is not and cannot be prescriptive." See his "An Antidote for Apology, Service, and Witchcraft in Policy Analysis," in Phillip M. Gregg, ed., *Problems of Theory in Policy Analysis* (Lexington, Mass.: Lexington Books, 1976), p. 19. Some scholars hold that even if policy analysis could have prescriptive value, it ought not to take on such a role. See Kenneth M.Dolbeare, "Public Policy Analysis and the Coming Struggle for the Soul of the Postbehavioral Revolution," in Green and Levinson, eds., *Power and Community*, pp. 85-111; also Theodore J.Lowi, "The Politics of Higher Education: Political Science as a Case Study," in Graham and Carey, eds., *The Post-Behavioral Era*, pp. 11-36.

23. The source for much of this discussion is Dye, *Policy Analysis: What Governments Do, Why They Do It, And What Difference It Makes* (University, Ala.: Univ. of Alabama Press, 1976), pp. 15-19.

24. Although Feldman, Dolbeare, and Lowi (see n. 22) regard the scientific, nonprescriptive endeavor of policy analysts as primary, they would argue against an approach which did not involve critical analysis of current policies, proposed solutions to policy problems, or social conditions which are incorrectly approached by government. In this sense they are not quite as "objectively" scientific as Dye seems to advocate.

25. Jacob B. Ukeles, "Policy Analysis: Myth or Reality?" *Public Administration Rev.*, 37 (May/June 1977), p. 224.

26. "The Study of Policy Content," p. 15.

27. "The Policy Orientation," pp. 8-10.

28. Lasswell continues to write on behalf of this idea; see *A Pre-View of Policy Sciences* (New York; American Elsevier, 1971). Also see the work of Yehezkel Dror, especially *Public Policymaking Reexamined* (Scranton, Pa.: Chandler, 1968) and *Design for Policy Sciences* (New York; American Elsevier, 1971).

29. *Systematic Thinking for Social Action* (Washington, D.C.: Brookings Institution, 1971) pp. 3-4. Since writing those words, analyst Rivlin has been appointed to head the new Congressional Budget Office, where she plays a major role in the decision process.

30. Cited in Rien and White, "Can policy research help policy?" p. 119.

31. See Selman J. Mushkin, "Policy Analysis in State and Community," *Public Administration Review*, 37 (May/June 1977), pp. 245-253.

32. Nor unstudied. See Arnold J. Meltsner, *Policy Analysts in the Bureaucracy* (Berkeley, Calif.: Univ. of California Press, 1976).

33. See Rein and White, "Can policy research help policy?"; Feldman, "An Antidote for Apology, Service, and Witchcraft in Policy Analysis"; and Dolbeare, "Public Policy Analysis and the Coming Struggle for the Soul of the Post-behavioral Revolution." Also interesting in this regard are comments in Ukeles, "Policy Analysis: Myth or Reality?" and Rivlin, *Systematic Thinking for Social Action*.

34. These suggestions for training objectives are drawn from Duncan MacRae, Jr., "Policy Analysis: An Applied Social Science Discipline." *Administration & Society*, 6 (1975), especially pp. 376-380.

35. This distinction is drawn from Dror, *Public Policymaking Reexamined*, pp. 7-9.

36. Dror, *Design for Policy Sciences*, p. 102; details of the suggested curriculum are found in that work on pp. 103-111. Also see Lasswell, *A Pre-View of Policy Sciences*, ch. 8.

37. See Ranney, "The Study of Policy Content." p. 18; and Dye, *Understanding Public Policy*, pp. 7-8.

38. "Liberalism and Knowledge," in Daniel P. Moynihan, *Coping: On the Practice of*

Government (New York: Vintage Books, 1973), p. 263. Moynihan's views on policy analysis and the role of social science in policy arenas are discussed by Marvin Surkin in "Sense and Non-Sense in Politics," in Surkin and Wolfe, eds., *An End to Political Science,* pp. 18-21.

39. See J. Peter Euben, "Politics, Piety, and Profession: The Ethics of Teaching Political Science," paper presented at annual meeting of American Political Science Association, Washington, D.C., September 1977.

40. Herbert A. Simon, *Administrative Behavior: A Study of Decision-Making Processes in Administrative Organization,* 2nd ed. (New York: Free Press, 1975), pp. 8, 61.

41. Aaron Wildavsky, "The Political Economy of Efficiency: Cost-Benefit Analysis, Systems Analysis, and Program Budgeting," in Ranney, ed., *Political Science and Public Policy,* pp. 55-82.

42. For a discussion on this point, see Nicholas Henry, *Public Administration and Public Affairs* (Englewood Cliffs, N.J.: Prentice-Hall, 1975), ch. 6.

43. See G. David Garson, *Power and Politics in the United States* (Lexington, Mass.: D.C. Heath, 1977), ch. 8, for a brief historical and critical survey of civics education during that period.

44. "Values and Evaluation in Teaching Political Science," paper presented at Conference on Political Science: The Teacher and the Policy, Iowa City, Iowa, October 1974. For still another view, see Michael Oakeshott, "Political Education," in Peter Laslett, ed., *Philosophy, Politics and Society,* 1st Series (Oxford: Basil Blackwell, 1956/1967), pp. 1-21.

7

POLICY ANALYSIS METHODS
AND GOVERNMENTAL FUNCTIONS

Duncan MacRae, Jr.

The field of policy analysis combines valuative judgments, technical calculations, and politically oriented action. Practitioners often learn these ingredients through combinations of material from various disciplines and professions, together with experience on the job. A more systematic definition of the field is needed, however, both to fill gaps in practitioners' preparation and to establish a solid basis for instruction in the field. Major intellectual contributions to policy analysis have been made by economics, operations research, and applied statistics; but I shall argue here that a broader alternative framework may be preferable.

As this field develops, it must regulate its relations with the political system in which policy choices are made and the academic system in which the quality of recommendations is controlled. Such a field, if it exists within a democratic polity, must avoid contributing to an increased domination of decisions by experts. It must not be an occult administrative science, but must frame its recommendations in terms intelligible to citizens and public leaders. Its princi-

AUTHOR'S NOTE: *This is a revised version of a paper published in* Society *as "Concepts and Methods of Policy Analysis." An earlier version was presented at the annual meeting of the American Political Science Association, New York, N.Y., September 3, 1978. I am indebted to Robert P. Strauss for a helpful suggestion.*

ples and procedures must be widely disseminated among citizens rather than restricted to the staff of government and powerful private organizations.

A tension exists between the requirements of such a field for citizens and those for staff analysts. Citizens must be concerned with broad questions of value and political philosophy; staff analysts must often take their superiors' values as given. Citizens must be concerned with what government *is* as well as with what it *does;* thus, their education must deal with constitutional and institutional change. On the other hand, the acceptance of this new field by academics as well as employers can be fostered by stress on technical and quantitative skills in which expertise can more easily be demonstrated and quality more easily reviewed by expert peers.

I shall center my discussion on the methods or methodology of policy analysis, as a collection of procedures that can be taught and reviewed so as to establish an academic definition for the field. We must recognize, however, that methods potentially encompass much more than procedures for the gathering and statistical manipulation of data. They extend to procedures of logical criticism that may be directed at theories or at systems of valuation. They include the systematic component of "soft" aspects of policy analysis, such as the assessment of political feasibility. They extend, in fact, to any systematic procedure shared by members of an expert community in their published work and in their critical judgment of one another's work.[1]

Taking this broad view of methods, I shall ask whether the discourse of policy analysis can eventually resemble that of an academic discipline or subdiscipline, so that its quality can be monitored by a group of trained experts.[2] This question, concentrating on the community of experts, is distinct from that of the relation of policy analysis to *political* communities; questions concerning the interests, privileges, and power of analysts must also be examined if we propose that the field be a discipline. I shall deal here with the internal intellectual relations of such a discipline, not its external or political relations; but by defining *methods* broadly, I am advocating the instruction of citizens and not merely of government officials.

I shall present a general classification of methods in relation to a systematic view of the elements constituting policy analysis.

Within this general classification I present two approaches to the classification of one of these elements, models of causation: a more conventional one based on their form and procedure, and another related to the functions of government. This last classification suggests the possibility of a distinctive field of policy analysis with close connections to political science.

THE ELEMENTS OF POLICY ANALYSIS

Policy analysis may be defined as the choice of the best policy from among a set of alternatives with the aid of reason and evidence. Its methods may be organized about a set of elements or parts:

(1) *Definition of the problem.* We need to learn how the various preexisting definitions of our problem may be transformed into our "analyst's problem"[3] which is rephrased in precise enough terms to permit analysis, is related to a system of values providing criteria for choice, and yet can be introduced into the processes of enactment and implementation of a particular political community.

(2) *Criteria for choice.* Whether we use "objective functions" of operations research or systematic ethical criteria such as those of equity or cost-benefit analysis, we must formulate and use clear valuative criteria for comparison of results of policies. Precise valuative discourse such as that of philosophy and economics can reshape the ambiguous values of citizens' discourse, but eventually the results of this technical discussion of values must be reintroduced into the discourse of citizens and understood by them.

(3) *Alternatives, models, and decisions.* Policy analysis involves comparison among possible alternative policies. The expected consequences of these policies are compared after being predicted by models of causation, and are expressed in terms of the valuative criteria we have previously specified.[4] On the basis of the values or disvalues of the alternatives, we then choose among them. One model of particular importance is the economic model of the free, competitive market, including possible departures from this model and means of coping with them. Numerous other relevant models exist, drawing on knowledge from various natural and social sciences and combinations of them. These models differ in their form, in the procedures used for testing them, and in their relation to governmental functions; I shall classify them below in these respects.

(4) *Political feasibility*. Analysis of the prospects for enactment and implementation of a chosen policy is an essential feature of the larger analytic process. This topic draws on both political science and sociology, but also involves much information that is specific to particular political situations as well as skills of nonacademic practitioners.

Each of these elements of policy analysis, as we shall show, involves some aspects that can be criticized as part of an academic literature; other aspects, however, vary with the particular problem at hand and with the analyst's role and are less easily subjected to reasoned public criticism.

DEFINITION OF THE PROBLEM

The choice of the analyst's problem illustrates an aspect of analysis in which skill or art predominates over formal methodology. Even in scientific research, the art of choosing problems that are theoretically significant and feasible to investigate is largely a matter of experience and talent rather than of formal procedure. In policy analysis there is even greater room for individual judgment, since the significance of an analysis depends on the feasibility not only of processing information but also of action on the recommendation that is made—not to mention significance for a particular system of values. There may be checklists that will provide some guidance in the choice of problems for analysis, but we cannot easily speak of a methodology for this purpose.

The definition and redefinition of a policy problem depend on the analyst's learning at the start the various definitions of the "problem situation" that are held by significant participants. The analyst must learn to inquire directly and indirectly, to listen, and to read between the lines. He must judge what elements of a group's position are unalterable, and which are possibly subject to bargaining or compromise. His choice is not only whether to work in a given problem area but how to reshape its definition in a way that is consistent with his capacities for analysis and with the expected response of the relevant actors to his proposals. The definition of the problem thus overlaps with the assessment of political feasibility, to which we return below.

FORMULATING AND MEASURING VALUATIVE CRITERIA

The first element of policy analysis for which we may consider a methodology is the development of criteria for choice. Although in a positivist perspective our basic values are mere givens, insusceptible to debate or reasoned discussion, I have proposed[5] that we can follow a systematic method in putting forward and comparing the values on which policy analysis is based. This method involves first rendering any proposed system of values clear, consistent, and general, and then comparing two or more such systems in terms of particular moral convictions shared by the participants in the discussion. Valuative discourse of this sort is not easy to carry out; but the value system developed in welfare economics stands as an example challenging the proponents of other values to formulate theirs with equal precision. It is conceivable that academically public discourse of this sort could be extended to include other value systems concerned with the general welfare, and mutual criticism among them.

Not every policy decision will involve value systems of this degree of systemization. In actuality, analysis may be based on multiple values that have not been rendered consistent. It may involve very specific values specified by an employer, the law, or community consensus. But insofar as a methodology of valuative discourse is possible, it is likely to involve not only careful verbal logic but also mathematics or formal logic, such as we see increasingly in the valuative discussions of philosophy, economics, and public choice.[6]

The methodology of valuative discourse may be extended from the conceptual and logical definition of the values used to their measurement. The specification of a procedure for measuring a valuative criterion is one way of defining it clearly. In economics the principal methods of measurement have been introduced in benefit-cost analysis or applied welfare economics. Conventions have been introduced for defining and measuring costs; for avoiding double counting of benefits; for comparing increments of change under resource constraints in terms of benefit-cost ratios; and for choosing among alternatives given their streams of benefits and costs over time.[7] Survey methods may also be adaptable to the measurement of demand for publicly supplied goods and services.[8]

Measurement cannot, however, be separated from the more basic question of whether the things measured are really the values we wish to achieve. Economic values, for example, rest on the assumption of fixed preferences, the satisfaction of which is by definition equivalent to an increase in welfare; but the mere fact that this assumption has been formalized elegantly does not require us to accept it.

An alternative methodology for the measurement of well-being, relevant to this discussion even though it is not widely used in policy choice, is being developed in the field of "subjective social indicators."[9] Here the satisfaction or happiness of individuals is measured directly by questioning them. Such measurements then allow us to raise the question whether the possession of goods and services does indeed lead people to say they are happier or more satisfied—a question that cannot be answered in the economic perspective where preference satisfaction is tautologically equivalent to welfare.

The comparison of these two methods of measuring welfare is of special interest as regards the valuation of human life. If policies are to be judged in terms of their effects on human beings, their consequences must be compared in terms of their effects on human welfare. Insofar as welfare is viewed as extending over time, then an extreme case of difference in welfare is that in which various policies lead to differences in the expected length and quality of human lives. Cost-benefit analysis typically assesses the value of human life in terms of a stream of earnings, discounted over time. Some studies of health policy have made use of the notion of "quality-adjusted life-years,"[10] based in part on comparisons that individuals make of the quality of life under different circumstances and partly on a notion of discounting. In addition, individuals may be questioned after experiencing various life conditions, and their reported levels of satisfaction or happiness may be compared. Comparison of these methods may give rise to fruitful discussions of the philosophical notions on which these measurements rest.

When particular outcomes of decisions may be assigned numerical values, and when they are expected to occur with known probabilities, methods for computation of statistical expected values may be used. For discrete alternatives, these methods of choice may be expressed in the form of decision trees.[11] This procedure includes the calculation of the numerical value of a criterion function, but the probabilities and the form of the tree also express the causal model involved; we return below to the relation between decision trees and models.

The maximization of a value such as net monetary benefit or happiness is one form that a consistent ethical system may take. Often, however, such maximization is constrained by unconditional or nonteleological values that correspond to moral prohibitions, laws, rules, or contractual agreements. A set of methods exists for choosing the best alternative under conditions of constrained maximization; they include linear programming.[12] These methods in effect provide an operational definition of the consistent valuative system that combines the variable to be maximized and the constraints. They also involve models of causation, which may be involved in the equations that define the value at a point in terms of the spatial coordinates.

The combination of two or more valuative criteria entertained by a particular decision maker has also been approached through multiattribute decision analysis.[13] A partial reconciliation of two incommensurable criteria is also made in cost-effectiveness analysis. This method is used for comparison of a set of alternatives (e.g., policies expected to produce certain amounts of change in health or knowledge) each of which is characterized by a value of "effectiveness" and a disvalue of "cost." When effectiveness cannot be translated into monetary terms, these pairs of numbers have no simple ordering. Nevertheless, procedures exist for ordering them to some extent.[14]

Specific and distinct criterion variables are also often measured without an explicit formal method for reconciling them. Such a disparity of criteria often arises when various public programs (e.g., health, education, social services) are being compared. For any one such program we may attempt to measure the need for it,[15] its effectiveness,[16] or citizens' satisfaction with it.[17] "Methodologies" exist for measurements of this sort even though the underlying values are not parts of general ethical systems. These methodologies lead, in turn, to diverse notions of how the resulting analyses should be related to the political systems in which they function. The reconciliation of various specific values, corresponding to particular measures, may take place through pluralistic political decisions;[18] or through assignment of numerical values by a group to possible outcomes of policy alternatives, producing a "social welfare function" for the particular problem at hand.[19]

So far we have considered the formulation and measurement of values that exemplify shared concepts such as the public interest or the general welfare. Such formulations may be compared and discussed publicly in terms of their adequacy. Some approaches to policy analysis, however, include in the criteria for choice aspects of the chooser's personal welfare.[20] In this case the values of various choosers differ in part because they include a diversity of "tastes," and public discussion to reconcile them seems pointless.

MODELS: FORM AND PROCEDURE

The best-known and most extensive domain of methods in policy analysis concerns models of causation, relating policies to their expected consequences.[21] Two main bases of classification of these models are available: (1) their form, and the procedures for testing them; and (2) their relation to functions carried out by governments. The first sort of classification, treated in this section, is not specific to *public* policy; it is found in fields such as operations research and management science or, as regards procedures, in evaluation research or applied statistics. The second, which we shall discuss in the following section, is more specific to analyses of public policies and has some affinity with political science.

We first set aside the possibility that knowledge generated by pre-existing academic disciplines is automatically optimal for policy analysis, needing only to be "applied." Knowledge generated by basic natural science is indeed often appropriate for policy choices, being applied by engineering and health sciences. Even in natural science, however, there are models that derive directly from an effort to predict valuative variables, rather than to seek knowledge for its own sake. This approach has been proposed for biological research in agriculture.[22]

For policy choices relating to social processes it is all the more necessary to seek the relevant models directly rather than to expect them to develop from basic science. Much basic research, at least in sociology and political science, deals with variables over which policymakers have no control, unrelated to explicit valuative concerns. The generalizations that arise from this research are far less precisely verified than those of natural science,[23] and parameters in them may even change over the years. As Foote maintains, "Sociological generalizations do not cumulate; they obsolesce."[24] This difficulty may well hold for other social sciences.

Many of these models of causation are subject to quality control and review through publication for expert scrutiny. Some, however, are not; the models used in concrete policy choices always involve some degree of conjecture or subjective assessment. Policy choices are made with a finite time horizon, in contrast to the indefinite time horizon of pure science. Unless the decision maker is extremely fortunate, he must always engage in probability judgments, and even the necessary probabilities cannot be known with certainty by the use of standard methods. He must conjecture not only about probabilities but also about the form of the model (what variables are really relevant?) and its applicability to the concrete case at hand. The concern of decision theorists with Bayesian prior probabilities [25] is thus a manifestation of an essential and unavoidable feature of policy analysis. The subjective character of these probabilities has contributed to the reluctance of many statisticians to accept the Bayesian approach; their concern with the objective bases of their scientifically public discourse leads to this position. Nevertheless, when the necessity of making public decisions is considered, we have no choice but to admit these judgments.

Classification by form. Some bases for classifying models by form concern whether they are simple or complex; represented explicitly or by simulation; discrete or continuous in the alternatives presented; based on adversary assumptions like games; homeostatic or not.

The *complexity* of a model concerns the number of variables it contains, or the related question of whether it encompasses a segment of a system or a larger system. Procedurally, we here distinguish between models that may be formulated in explicit mathematical terms and those whose complexity requires simulation.

The distinction between *discrete* and *continuous* alternatives may be illustrated by the types of models related to decision trees, on the one hand, and maximization problems using calculus, on the other. Continuous alternatives are also involved in linear programming. Problems of optimal allocation of resources may involve alternatives of either type; for example, choice of paths of travel can involve discrete alternatives, and choice of amounts of factors of production can involve continuous ones.

Models in which we face an opponent require that we take into account his possible anticipation of our choices. This anticipation leads to *games;* to human simulation as in war games; and in decision trees, to assignment of probabilities that take the opponent's tactics into account.

Homeostatic models are those that return to a desired equilibrium when disturbed. Some undisturbed ecological systems have this property. The model of a perfect competitive market has an analogous property; a change in the exogenous variables of supply, technology, or taste leads to a new equilibirum but one that is again Pareto efficient.[26] Some models of political systems—two-party competition or pluralistic interaction of groups—have been alleged to have similar properties, but these models have been formulated more often verbally then mathematically. The implicit policy prescription, when a homeostatic model is claimed to apply to a segment of reality, is to do nothing; thus, free-market and pluralistic models have been associated with conservatism.

A wide variety of nonhomeostatic models have also been proposed: Keynes' general theory, the Richardson arms-race model,[27] and contemporary models of future world population growth and energy shortage are among them. Simulations of river basins, weapons systems, and urban development are also usually nonhomeostatic. Such models are complex; insofar as they predict extreme and undesirable results, they may be used as calls for innovative interventions—provided that they include relevant manipulable variables.

Classification by testing procedure. The methods discussed so far, in connection with models, concern the combination of presumably known information and relationships so as to predict the consequences of policies. Many methods, however, deal with the ascertainment of relationships or the testing of models.

The *procedures* used for testing or verifying models distinguish such approaches as the true experiment, the quasi experiment, and nonexperimental inferences of causation. Related to this classification is the question whether we "verify" assessments of feasibility at the same time as we verify models or separately; Braybrooke and

Lindblom have proposed an incremental procedure that combines both testing processes.[28]

The most general approach to testing procedures is that which regards the gathering of information as itself a decision, made so as to further a value or values. In this perspective, our choice whether or not to engage in analysis, including the gathering of information, is weighed in terms of its expected benefits and costs, estimated in terms of prior probabilities. Vaupel has used a decision tree to derive the criterion for analysis $pd > c$, where

p = the probability that analysis will make a difference,
d = the difference it will make if successful, and
c = the cost of analysis.[29]

If the inequality is satisfied, analysis is worth the cost. Raiffa introduces the notion of the value of information, assessed in terms of outcome-values for a given decision tree.[30] This notion may also be applied to the choice of optimal sampling designs when various elements in the design have different benefits or contributions to reduction of variance in an estimate,[31] or different costs.[32]

The gathering of information to test models is most rigorously done by means of experiments; in the social sciences, these normally require randomized controls.[33] Techniques of experimentation, including their organizational and professional sources of support, are analyzed in Riecken and Boruch.[34] The relation between experimental and quasi-experimental designs is discussed in detail in Campbell and Stanley.[35]

Two important nonexperimental procedures are those of path analysis (structural equation models) and time series analysis. Path analysis has been developed extensively by sociologists, with contributions from econometrics.[36] It permits a systematic test of linear causal models, some of which involve dozens of variables. The results of such tests need to be cross-checked, however, by experiments and actual policy interventions.

The analysis of time series interrupted by policy interventions provides another opportunity for testing models in a way that goes beyond cross-sectional path analysis. Even when these interventions do not involve randomized controls, time series provide useful information, including information about delayed effects, gradually disappearing effects, and other time-dependencies. A comparison between empirical time series analysis and structural equation models has been presented by Hibbs.[37]

MODELS AND GOVERNMENTAL FUNCTIONS

Another major basis for classification of models concerns the *functions* that governments perform. *Public* policy analysis is concerned with governmental actions—conditions under which they should be undertaken, conditions for their efficiency, conditions for their implementation, and the possible establishment of structures that will facilitate the proper choice and implementation of policies. We thus consider the relation of policy-analysis methods to the substantive functions of government. This sort of classification may allow us to organize models of effects of policies in a way that will help to distinguish policy analysis from other fields, while drawing its component parts together.

We shall classify the functions of government in relation to the models necessary to analyse them. We conceive of government as performing seven types of functions that correspond roughly to different types of models: (a) direct monetary transactions including taxes and subsidies; (b) production and delivery of goods; (c) delivery of services; (d) regulation; (e) monitoring and enforcement; (f) persuasion and socialization; and (g) meta-policy. We shall discuss each of these in turn, defining it and indicating the types of models that seem appropriate to it.

(a) Direct monetary transactions including taxes and subsidies. The other functions that government performs are supported by taxes (if not by direct participation as in the case of the military draft). A particular type of expenditure together with an earmarked tax can bring about redistribution of income, but that redistribution appears in its purest form if tax receipts are given to lower-income persons or families as direct monetary payments. One form of such redistribution is a negative income tax, which may be evaluated in terms of both vertical equity and efficiency. Experimental studies of the negative income tax have focused on its efficiency in providing work incentives, however;[38] consideration of vertical equity has not been analyzed directly as an ingredient of optimum policy but has simply been taken to be limited by political feasibility.

The design of tax systems has been a major concern of the field of public finance.[39] This concern has been directed largely at efficiency in relation to production possibilities and consumer demand, but much less systematically at vertical equity, which is seen as involving arbitrary valuative judgments or social welfare functions.

Taxes or subsidies that are conditional on certain activities by payer or recipient are considered below as means of regulation.

Horizontal equity in the collection of taxes has also been the subject of systematic research, as in the case of real property taxation.[40] Analytic methods have also been used to assess horizontal equity in the distribution of municipal aid to Minnesota counties. This type of study of equity has analogies in the distribution of goods and services.

(b) Production and delivery of goods. The first question that must be asked about governmental production of a good (or service) is whether and how much the government should be involved. The question whether government should be involved at all is paramount in the analysis of "market failure," centering in a model of the free, competitive market. Departures from this model create a prima facie case for government intervention. The development of public-choice models of government behavior, however, has led some to question whether governments may not themselves be susceptible to "failure," i.e., to less-than-efficient production.[41]

There are other grounds than economic efficiency, however, on which government production or supply of goods has been justified, notably equity, rights, and needs. Justification in terms of rights or needs makes it difficult to allocate scarce resources among different programs at the margin, since various rights or needs constitute incommensurable criteria. Considerations of equity may be included in a general "social welfare function," either by assigning priority to certain persons or groups or by weighting the consequences to them more heavily, in terms of specific operational definitions of equity.

If we can demonstrate that government should produce or supply a good (or service), we next face the question of how much should be produced. One way to estimate the proper scale of production is to compare demand with cost, if these functions can be estimated accurately.[42] Such comparisons are further complicated if the basis for justifying governmental production is a criterion other than

economic efficiency, for in that case the economic method of calculation is less well developed. Equity adjustments, for example,
involve equity not only among those receiving the good but also
among taxpayers.

Problems of spatial and temporal distribution of supply lead to a
number of models that have been studied in the application of operations research to public systems: degree of decentralization; optimum location; allocation of supply and consumption over time;
speed of response; and problems of congestion and queuing.[43]

Delivery or availability of goods involves the closely related
question of who should receive them and how this distribution is to
be implemented. A special problem arising for government supply
of goods or services is that of determining eligibility. Goods may be
made available on the market with a user charge and subsidy (the
amount of which must be chosen), or given free to all as a right, in
which case these problems do not arise. But if given to some and not
all, they have to be distributed through a process that determines
eligibility, leading to problems of monitoring and enforcement such
as we mention below.

The distribution of goods, when only some receive them, also
leads to problems of vertical and horizontal equity. If the poor are
provided with food or housing, for example, then the measure of
poverty that determines eligibility may be scrutinized in terms of its
relation to the needs of family units. Not only income but family
size and composition and sometimes savings are considered.
These considerations of equity and need are over and above the
problems of disincentives to earn that exist when goods are made
available only below a threshold value of income.

So far, in speaking of "goods," we have referred to problems that
exist for the furnishing of services as well. We have nevertheless
distinguished goods from services in order to distinguish those
methods appropriate to technologies of material production from
those involving human relationships. "Goods," in this connection,
refer to transportation, utilities, weapons, health technology, and
other things requiring organization and technology to produce;
many of the corresponding models lie in operations research and
engineering. Analyses of such processes for the private sector are
largely adaptable to the public sector, provided that we substitute
some measure of the general welfare for private profit as a criterion

or objective function.

As we move to the more labor-intensive production of services such as fire protection or the removal of solid waste, the necessary models are less technical and more social in nature. Each of these examples, however, involves some technology; we must stress, therefore, that our distinction between goods and services is in some respects a continuum.

(c) Delivery of services. Here we are concerned with the delivery by a government agency of a service, often including personal interaction between the deliverer and the client or beneficiary. Estimating the consequences of policies involving services includes sociological studies of the ways in which professionals act.[44] It may also involve studies of the ways in which clients, individually or in groups, participate in service delivery.[45] These models are thus more likely to involve other contributions from the social sciences than operations research or management science in a narrow sense. Problems of equity, availability, and distribution of services also arise that are similar to those mentioned above for delivery of goods. An example of statistical analysis to estimate degrees of equity in the delivery of police services is given by Bloch.[46]

(d) Regulation. In contrast to the provision of goods or services, we see regulation models as involving prediction of the functioning of a larger system including the regulated person or organization. Regulation ordinarily involves the provision of a "bad," rather than a good, to the persons whose activities are affected. They are assumed to take steps to reduce the undesirable consequences of this "bad" if possible, e.g., by shifting taxes to consumers or renters, by changing production technology to reduce concentrations of specific effluents, or by changing modes of transportation when regulation makes one mode more expensive. Effects analogous to those of conditional taxation can also be brought about by subsidies; family allowances have been introduced to stimulate fertility, and industries may be encouraged by subsidies. Tariffs, or the taxation of competitors, can have a similar effect.

The general type of model that seems appropriate for the study of consequences of regulatory policy is then one of a system that may be altered by the reactions of those affected. We assume that they comply with the legal requirement but adjust some of their other activities as a result; in the next section "Monitoring and enforcement," we consider the possibility that those potentially affected may not comply. In addition to the desired effects of compliance, regulatory policies have also involved costs in their implementation.[47]

System models or simulations are also relevant to prediction of the results of plans that are to be put into effect over time. Here again, even if there is compliance, the functioning of a larger system may affect the results. A plan for attaining a given spatial allocation of functions in a city or for furnishing a supply of manpower over a decade may well be affected by other variables that change during that period, such as changes in population composition and location, demand, and alternative sources of supply. To anticipate these changes, a "social indicator model"[48] may be desirable, provided that it takes into account the manipulable variables through which policies work. Analogous models of expected changes in natural systems are also useful, e.g., in projecting quantities and compositions of waste water in a watershed system. Models of this sort have broader application than to regulatory policies; they are relevant, for example, to forecasting need or demand for given types of governmental production—e.g., waste removal or purification, social services, or schools.

(e) Monitoring and enforcement. We classify as a separate function the assurance that those who are regulated actually comply with a policy once it is enacted. This compliance may be either implementation by government employees,[49] or obedience to laws or regulations by citizens. This category of government functions resembles regulation, in that a "bad" is being delivered; but we are dealing here with possible deviance from an instruction or law rather than with legally permitted avoidance or shifting of costs. Simulation models related to regulatory policies typically assume that the regulation is successful (at least to a specified extent) in obtaining legal compliance—that speed limits are obeyed, that taxes are collected, that agricultural production or airport noise is reduced to within a prescribed limit. Models of monitoring and enforcement, however, deal with the possibility that some of those affected do not comply, and with policies to increase compliance.

There is a superficial similarity between these types of models and the statistics of quality control, which provides guidance as to how many items emerging from a productive process should be inspected and how they should be chosen in order to maintain given quality standards. The problem is complicated, however, by the fact that sanctions are involved, e.g., for health conditions in restaurants or for the safety of buildings. The result is in part a game-type situation in which those affected seek to avoid inspection, anticipate it, or circumvent the results (e.g., by modifying the indicators that measure compliance). Modeling such processes is more complex than modeling industrial processes for quality control; in addition, it involves political elements in that the person inspected or monitored is a citizen of a free society who claims rights against unannounced government searches, electronic eavesdropping, and the like.

A general abstract model for estimating the optimal level of such policy variables as severity and certainty of punishment has been proposed by Becker;[50] but many problems are involved in translating it into practice. A related question concerns how "finely tuned" sanctions should be, in view of their cost and complexity. In addition, a factor neglected by economic models is the degree to which norms are internalized by the public, leading to compliance without sanctions; this possibility leads us to the following type of governmental function, persuasion and socialization.

(f) Persuasion and socialization. In a free society, as well as in economic models, we tend to assume that government does not persuade citizens or change their preferences. Such activities are associated with totalitarian regimes and are seen as incursions on citizens' freedom. Yet one reason that has been advanced for having a public school system, aside from its provision of job opportunities, is its contribution to citizenship. Citizenship does not consist merely in political skills or capacity to seek one's self-interest through the political process, but involves civic obligation, devotion to the general welfare, and willingness to abide by procedural rules that govern collective decisions. Whether schools actually produce these values is an empirical question; possibly the study of political socialization could throw light on the effectiveness of various public policies in this respect.

Some governments go farther in socializing and persuading their citizens, in the service of goals that may be argued to be in the general interest. Instruction centered about a particular notion of human development or perfection may be of this sort, though it cannot easily be undertaken by public policy in a pluralistic society and may be more appropriate to religiously based states. Some governments have urged their citizens to curtail their reproduction rates, and public exhortation is also a possible means for reduction of demand for energy as the supply dwindles. If models of these social processes were available, they would deal with the formation of social norms[51] as well as with the persuasion of individuals.

(g) *Meta-policy.* Not only do governments tax, subsidize, provide specific goods and services, regulate, enforce, and persuade; they also make policies that affect the making of decisions themselves. It is in this aspect of policy analysis that the traditional concerns of political science are most relevant. The assessment of regimes, constitutions, political party systems, legislative procedures, electoral laws, jury procedures, and other procedural policy alternatives is a major concern of applied political science, and was so before the "behavioral revolution." The general values that are discussed in normative political theory, as well as more specific values of interest to political science, are often most relevant to choices of this sort: do these meta-policies provide for innovation, consensus, support, participation? Do they protect against tyranny, or encourage the development of character and personality? Changes in decision systems may also be assessed in material or economic terms; Dye's efforts to relate state welfare expenditures to party competition show, however, that this relation is not always easy to demonstrate.[52]

Other meta-policies involve altering the structure of the organizations that supply goods and services, but that also make decisions; creation of a Department of Energy, for example, involves a structural decision as well as a substantive one of allocation of goods and services. Organizational change often makes available a new "bundle of products" that may be provided more or less efficiently, in greater or lesser quantity, under the new organizational form than under the old. Conceivably such changes can be evaluated in terms of outputs and their costs.

Prediction of the consequences of changing political institutions or organizational forms seems considerably less certain than operations research on management problems. Abstract models have been developed for assessing constitutional arrangements in terms of preference satisfaction,[53] but such models seem somewhat removed from the concrete detail of specific choices among political institutions.

The seven types of governmental functions we have distinguished correspond roughly to types of policy-related models. Our typology of government functions corresponds at some points to a typology advanced by Lowi.[54] Our categories (b) and (c), corresponding to the provisions of goods and services, correspond roughly to his "distributive" policies; (d) and (e) correspond to aspects of his "regulative" policies; and (f) and (g) to his "constituent" policies (in which he includes "propaganda"). His category of "redistributive" policies relates primarily to our category (a), but also enters somewhat into the delivery of goods and services to particular groups, (b) and (c). There seems to be a lack of systematic methods for dealing with redistribution. We may need to supplement analytic methods developed for the private sector by specific concern for the redistribution function of government.

FEASIBILITY

We now return from our discussion of models of the effects of policies to methods for estimating whether the policies will be enacted and implemented. We have dealt in part with feasibility of implementation above, in connection with monitoring and enforcement. But for most of our analyses of feasibility, precise and systematic models are hard to find. Indeed, much of our discourse about feasibility is relatively inaccessible to the criticism of an expert community, because of its links to highly specific situations that are of limited general and theoretical interest.

A major effort to predict the type of politics that will be associated with a policy proposal has been that of Lowi. His approach "begins with the assumption that *policies determine politics*."[55] Even if this determination is subject to the influence to other variables and only approximate, insofar as it exists it can help us to chart our course toward feasibility. In proposing a systematic classification of policy processes, Lowi asserts that this procedure "converts ordinary case studies into chronicles and teaching instruments into data."[56] To the degree that this claim can be sustained, it may move case studies of policy analysis into the domain of analysis and criticism by experts in general terms.

The enterprise, however, is not an easy one. Much of the literature on feasibility and implementation consists of accounts relatively unilluminated by predictive theory. Other useful approaches
consist of checklists or characteristic patterns for guidance in our
quest for feasibility.[57] They cannot thus easily enter the scientific
discourse that consists of verified general propositions. In one
sense, it is a challenge to political science to find generalizations
about feasibility; but the very fact that such generalizations, once
found, would be known to opponents as well as proponents of a
policy would lead to counter-strategies and perhaps change the
character of the generalizations themselves. A "methodology" for
feasibility will not be easy to find.

CONCLUSION

This discussion, ranging across various disciplines and fields,
has been directed at the formation of a domain of discourse concerning policy analysis, monitored and criticized by a community of
experts. But in putting forward the ingredients of this domain, I
have also tried to distinguish between those that are most fully
developed and those least developed.

Methodology as we know it pertains best to models of production
and distribution. These models have been developed in economics,
operations research, and applied statistics. There are nevertheless
numerous other ingredients of policy analysis that are essential to its
conduct, whether they can be rendered as precise as economics or
not. These include the assessment and reformulation of problems as
presented; the development of consistent and operational ethical
criteria for choice (for which welfare economics provides only one
type); the choice among political institutions and organizations; and
the assessment of feasibility. If the field of public policy analysis is
to be directly applicable to concrete policy choices, than all these
considerations must be combined. Just as in basic social research,
quantitative methods must be combined with qualitative,
participant-observer, and historical analyses, in the methodology of
policy analysis we need to combine a variety of methods aimed at
our substantive goal of successful analysis.

NOTES

1. John Ziman, *Public Knowledge,* (London: Cambridge Univ. Press, 1968).

2. Duncan MacRae, Jr., *The Social Function of Social Science* (New Haven, Conn.: Yale Univ. Press, 1976), ch. 9; and MacRae, "Technical Communities and Political Choice," *Minerva,* 14 (1976), 169-190.

3. Duncan MacRae, Jr., and James A. Wilde, *Policy Analysis for Public Decisions* (North Scituate, Mass.: Duxbury, 1979), ch. 2.

4. Nonteleogical valuative criteria, independent of consequences, are also used in evaluating policies, but they do not require the same concern with methods or with models of causation.

5. *The Social Function of Social Science,* ch. 4.

6. e.g., John Harsanyi, "Bayesian Decision Theory, Rule Utilitarianism, and Arrow's Impossibility Theorem" (Berkeley: Center for Research in Management Science, University of California, 1978).

7. Edith Stokey and Richard Zeckhauser, *A Primer for Policy Analysis* (New York: Norton, 1978), chs. 9 and 10.

8. Michael W. McKinney and Duncan MacRae, Jr., "Survey Assessment of Monetary Demand for Publicly Provided Goods: Recreation," Discussion Paper (Chapel Hill: Institute for Research in Social Science, University of North Carolina, 1978).

9. Angus Campbell, Philip E. Converse, and Willard L. Rodgers, *The Quality of American Life* (New York: Russell Sage, 1976).

10. Milton C. Weinstein and William B. Stason, *Hypertension: A Policy Perspective* (Cambridge, Mass.: Harvard Univ. Press, 1976).

11. Howard Raiffa, *Decision Analysis* (Reading, Mass.: Addison-Wesley, 1968).

12. See Stokey and Zeckhauser, ch. 11; and Shiv K. Gupta and John M. Cozzolino, *Fundamentals of Operations Research for Management* (San Francisco: Holden-Day, 1974), chs. 6-8.

13. Ralph L. Keeney and Howard Raiffa, *Decisions with Multiple Objectives: Preferences and Value Tradeoffs* (New York: John Wiley, 1976).

14. E.S. Quade, *Analysis for Public Decisions* (New York: American Elsevier, 1975), p. 94.

15. Genevieve W. Carter, "Measurement of Need," in Norman A. Polansky, ed., *Social Work Research* (Chicago: Univ. of Chicago Press, 1966).

16. Philip M. Morse, ed., *Operations Research for Public Systems* (Cambridge, Mass.: MIT Press), pp. 5-6.

17. Kenneth Webb and Harry P. Hatry, *Obtaining Citizen Feedback* (Washington, D.C.: Urban Institute, 1973).

18. Bruce L. Gates, "Needs-Based Budgeting: Considerations of Effectiveness, Efficiency, and Justice in the Delivery of Human Services" (presented to the APSA annual meeting, San Francisco, 1975).

19. Eugene P. Odum et al., "Totality Indices for Evaluating Environmental Impact: A Test Case—Relative Impact of Highway Alternatives," in Marlan Blissett, ed., *Environmental Impact Assessment* (New York: Engineering Foundation, 1976).

20. James W. Vaupel, "Muddling Through Analytically," in Willis D. Hawley and David Rogers, eds., *Improving the Quality of Urban Management* (Beverly Hills: Sage, 1976), pp. 190-197.

21. See Quade; and Stokey and Zeckhauser, part 2.

22. Richard Levins, "Fundamental and Applied Research in Agriculture," *Science,* 181 (1973), 523-524.

23. Gabriel A. Almond and Stephen J. Genco, "Clouds, Clocks, and the Study of Politics," *World Politics* 29 (1977), 489-522.

24. Nelson N. Foote, "Putting Sociologists to Work," in M.J. Demerath III, Otto Larsen, and Karl F. Schuessler, eds., *Social Policy and Sociology* (New York: Academic Press, 1975), p. 229.

25. Raiffa.

26. Francis M. Bator, "The Anatomy of Market Failure," *Q.J. of Economics,* 72 (1958), pp. 351-379.

27. Lewis F. Richardson, *Generalized Foreign Politics* (British Journal of Psychology Monograph Supplements, Vol. 23, 1939).

28. David Braybrooke and Charles E. Lindblom, *A Strategy of Decision* (New York: Free Press, 1963).

29. Vaupel, pp. 202-204.

30. Raiffa, pp. 27, 42.

31. John Neter, "How Accountants Save Money by Sampling," in Judith M. Tanur el al., *Statistics: A Guide to the Unknown* (San Francisco: Holden-Day, 1972).

32. Peter H. Rossi and Katherine C. Lyall, *Reforming Public Welfare* (New York: Russell Sage, 1976), p. 20.

33. John P. Gilbert, Richard J. Light, and Frederick Mosteller, "Assessing Social Innovations: An Empirical Basis for Policy," in A.A. Lumsdaine and C.A. Bennett, eds., *Evaluation and Experiment* (New York: Academic Press, 1975).

34. Henry W. Riecken and Robert F. Boruch, eds., *Social Experimentation* (New York: Academic Press, 1974).

35. Donald T. Campbell and Julian L. Stanley, *Experimental and Quasi-Experimental Designs for Research* (Chicago: Rand McNally, 1966).

36. Arthur S.Goldberger and Otis Dudley Duncan, eds., *Structural Equation Models in the Social Sciences* (New York: Seminar Press, 1973).

37. Douglas A. Hibbs, Jr., "On Analyzing the Effects of Policy Interventions: Box-Jenkins and Box-Tiao vs. Structural Equation Models," in David R. Heise, ed., *Sociological Methodology 1977* (San Francisco: John Wiley, 1977).

38. Joseph A. Pechman and Michael Timpane, eds., *Work Incentives and Income Guarantees* (Washington, D.C.: Brookings Institution, 1975).

39. Richard A. Musgrave and Peggy B. Musgrave, *Public Finance in Theory and Practice* (New York: McGraw Hill, 1973).

40. John B. Rackham and Theodore Reynolds Smith, *Automated Mass Appraisal of Real Property* (Chicago: International Association of Assessing Officers, 1974).

41. William A. Niskanen,*Bureaucracy and Representative Government* (Chicago: Aldine, 1971).

42. McKinney and MacRae.

43. Edward J. Beltrami, *Models for Public Systems Analysis* (New York: Academic Press, 1977).

44. Eliot Freidson, *Profession of Medicine* (New York: Dodd Mead, 1970).

45. Gordon P. Whitaker, "Citizen Participation in the Delivery of Human Services" (presented at the conference on Participation and Politics, Tutzing, Federal Republic of Germany, 1978).

46. Peter B. Bloch, *Equality of Distribution of Police Services* (Washington, D.C.: Urban Institute, 1974).

47. James C. Miller III and Bruce Yandle, eds., *Benefit-Cost Analysis of Social Regula-

tion, (Washington, D.C.: American Enterprise Institute for Public Policy Research, 1979).

48. Kenneth C. Land "Social Indicator Models: An Overview," in Kenneth C. Land and Seymour Spilerman, eds, *Social Indicator Models* (New York: Russell Sage, 1975).

49. Herbert Kaufman, *Administrative Feedback: Monitoring Subordinates' Behavior* (Washington, D.C.: Brookings Institution, 1973).

50. Gary S. Becker, "Crime and Punishment: An Economic Approach," *J of Pol. Economy,* 76 (1968), 169-217.

51. Duncan MacRae, Jr., ch. 8.

52. Thomas R. Dye, *Politics, Economics, and the Public* (Englewood Cliffs, N.J.: Prentice-Hall, 1966).

53. James M. Buchanan and Gordon Tullock, *The Calculus of Consent* (Ann Arbor, Mich.: Univ. of Michigan Press, 1962).

54. Theodore J. Lowi, "Four Systems of Policy, Politics, and Choice," *Public Administration Rev.,* 32 (1972), 298-310.

55. p. 299.

56. p. 300.

57. See Arnold J. Meltsner, "Political Feasibility and Policy Analysis," *Public Administration Rev.,* 32 (1972) 859-867; and Eugene Bardach, *The Implementation Game* (Cambridge, Mass.: MIT Press, 1977).

8

RESCUING EVALUATION RESEARCH THROUGH ADMINISTRATIVE EXPERIMENTATION

Thomas J. Cook
Ronald W. Johnson
Mary M. Wagner

One of the most damaging charges that can be leveled against policy evaluation research, whose raison d'être is purported to be the provision of evaluative information useful in shaping social policy, is that evaluation research as it is most frequently practiced is irrelevant to policymaking. This charge of unresponsiveness to policymakers' information needs is precisely the criticism stated at the recent congressional hearings on policy evaluation held by the Senate Committee on Human Services.[1] The consensus in that body was that evaluation research is not proving to be useful to the management of social programs.

What accounts for this perception of the unresponsiveness of evaluation research? What changes can be made in the conduct of evaluation research to alleviate the criticisms cited and increase the usefulness of evaluation research to policy development? More important, what can those of us who are committed to evaluation research as an effective tool for policymaking do to alter this condition?

AUTHOR'S NOTE: *Development of the system for experimentation discussed here was supported in part through a contract between the Research Triangle Institute and the Experimental Technology Incentives Program (project number 6-35756). Appreciation is also extended to Dr. Quentin W. Lindsey for his contribution to earlier drafts of portions of this article.*

To address these questions, it is first necessary to clarify what is meant by *responsiveness*. Here we suggest that to be responsive, evaluation research must first focus on the right questions, and then supply valid answers. By "right questions" we mean those questions or issues that are central to the decision-making concerns of program administrators. By "valid answers" we mean conclusions regarding cause-and-effect relationships within the program being evaluated which are supported by empirical evidence. The interrelatedness of these two tasks is apparent, and their challenge on the surface does not seem insurmountable. Why, then, are so few of the products of evaluation research found to be responsive to the needs of those for whom ostensibly they are designed? It is our contention that part of the responsibility for the unsatisfactory nature of many evaluations lies with the procurers of evaluations, generally program administrators, in the preconditions they set on the conduct of research. The precondition we are most concerned with here is the *timing* of the decision to evaluate a particular program.

Too often the need for evaluation is recognized well after a program has reached the implementation stage. At that point, the program administrator's most pressing need may be for information to support an increased budget request or to justify the program's continued existence. The administrator might then call in a person from the department's evaluation staff or from one of the numerous outside research organizations to perform an evaluation of the program. The limitations placed on the researcher by the ex post facto nature of the evaluation request severely constrain the quality and scope of the information the evaluation can provide. These limitations are evident both in the questions that can be addressed and in the nature of the possible answers that can be provided.

In particular ex post evaluations suffer three key defects. First, they cannot consider effects of program treatments or methods that were not implemented. That is, programs not designed with evaluation criteria in mind typically implement the one treatment alternative thought to be most likely to succeed. Therefore, information on treatment alternatives or methods of improvement cannot be forthcoming. Second, ex post evaluations cannot accurately capture the state of program recipients or the host environment prior to the onset of the program treatment. Proxy measures or reconstructed data regarding pretreatment conditions are often subject to severe biases of different kinds, and their use therefore weakens the information the evaluation potentially can provide. Using ex post control groups in place of data on the precondition of the treatment group requires matching techniques that, to be valid, must accommodate matching on all characteristics that may affect the outcome of the treatment. Such perfect knowledge rarely, if ever, exists.[2]

Finally, ex post evaluations also have difficulty capturing post-treatment effects. Administrative limitations on the quality and nature of data collected during program treatment dictate which of the intended and unintended effects of the program can be adequately measured. If record keeping procedures, for example, regarding the identification and whereabouts of program clients are inadequate, it may be impossible to locate an adequate sample after the treatment has been administered in order to evaluate long-term effects. The time constraints placed on researchers as to when an evaluation must be "finished" can also preclude the identification of long-term program effects, which, by definition, take time to be demonstrated and do not necessarily follow the fiscal year cycle.

While these three do not exhaust the list of problems attending an ex post evaluation, they are sufficient to demonstrate that the chances for evaluation to produce information responsive to decision makers' needs can be severely hampered from the outset, regardless of the good intentions and expertise of the researcher. It also should be noted that the good intentions of a program administrator who is often not completely free to determine the timing or context of evaluation are not sufficient either. The alternative to ex post evaluations would be to recognize the need and value of evaluation research at the *outset* of program development rather than as an afterthought.

Incorporating an a priori recognition of the value of evaluation into the design and implementation of a program makes that program not only a mechanism for providing a public good but also a vehicle for producing high-quality, valid information on what "works" in addressing a social problem. Public programs then become instruments for *experimenting* with theories regarding effects of various treatments (i.e., program types) on specified social problems. To serve that function, it is imperative that the design, implementation, and evaluation of a social program be conceptualized as a fully integrated set of activities pointing toward the rationalization of the overall policy development process.

Turning public programs into social experiments involves alterations in the process of designing and implementing programs. A system for social experimentation is outlined in Figure 8.1 The purpose and functions of this system are discussed below.

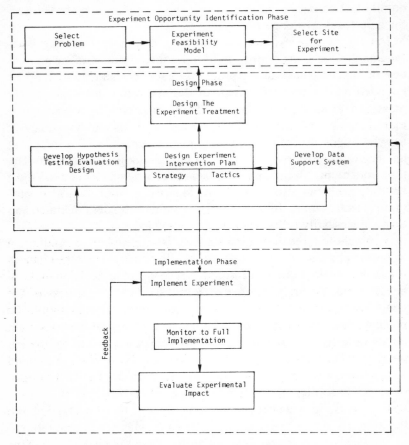

Figure 8.1   System for Experimentation

A system for experimentation has the purpose of providing information which enables policymakers to formulate decisions relating to social programs. To best serve these policymaking needs, the system must supply valid information regarding policy actions at various levels and along several dimensions, including: (1) the state of the environment prior to the experiment, (2) the nature and extent of the treatment embodied in the experiment, (3) the process by which the experiment is implemented, (4) the state of the environment after the experiment, and (5) the causal linkages between the treatment embodied in the experiment and before and after treatment conditions. For any policymaker, the system is only as good as the causal inferences that can be drawn from it.

A design for a system that enables policymakers to formulate decisions based on experiments thus must start with the question of how to establish causal relationships with appropriate degrees of validity. Field experience can suggest the basic variables to be examined. By relating field experience to pertinent literature, an experimental setting can be envisioned that combines the necessary sampling considerations (site selection), experimental conditions (treatment design matched to site), and testing procedures (evaluation design, data collection and analysis) essential to effective intervention and to system development. In place, the system supplies as by-products various types of policy-relevant information not necessarily based on full-blown hypothesis tests and not necessarily identifying causal relationships. But the system design must be holistic for the central purpose of supplying causal information based on various forms of hypothesis testing.

The major phases of the experiment system are (1) *experimental opportunity identification,* which addresses questions of the feasibility and appropriate organizational location of experiments, (2) *experiment design,* which involves designing both experimental treatments and their evaluation and (3) *implementation,* which produces the evaluative information on the effects of the treatments. Each of these phases is discussed in greater detail below.

(1) EXPERIMENTAL OPPORTUNITY IDENTIFICATION

Two tasks are involved in identifying an experimental opportunity. First, a social problem is defined and the behavior which demonstrates the problem is observed and described. Then, potential organizational locations for an experimental program dealing with the problem are reviewed, an appropriate site for an experiment selected, and a commitment to experimentation established. In carrying out both of these tasks, a model of an environment within which experimental programs are appropriate is used in determining the feasibility of experimentation with various social problems and the potential locations identified. Factors which are considered in ascertaining the feasibility of experimental programs include:

(a) *Social:* adverse public or agency attitudes toward social experimentation, unfavorable press coverage; high visibility of the experimental program or the problem it addresses.

(b) *Economic:* relative cost of mounting an experimental program, resources in general.

(c) *Political:* government support for experimentation, time-related factors in experimentation; sensitivity of policy issues.

(d) *Institutional:* specificity of existing programs and service delivery system: institutional history of and attitudes toward existing programs and experimentation within organizational setting.

(e) *Legal:* legal restrictions on random assignment; legal restrictions on the use of no-treatment control groups; legal framework of program operations.

(f) *Methodological:* control of conduct of impact measurement; range and quality of available data; location of random assignment within program operation.

(2) DESIGN ACTIVITIES

When the problem to be addressed through experimentation and the potential organizational location of the experiment are selected, four major design tasks can begin.

(a) Design of treatment variations. When a social problem is observed and described, competing theories regarding conditions that can be manipulated through policy decisions to influence or improve the problematic behavior can be reviewed, and those which seem most capable of producing an intended effect can be selected. Program variations are designed explicitly to test in a specified context the competing theories regarding what policies produce desired effects under specifiable conditions. This design specifies the program variations; procedures for distributing recipients among the variations; level, intensity, or length of treatment; and data collection procedures extending from the pretreatment condition until a point at which effects of the treatment are hypothesized to be evident. The design activity is intended to produce a treatment which has clear implications regarding both the development of an intervention plan and the testable hypotheses associated with the treatment. The treatment is designed so that the hypothesized causal relations subsumed in it (i.e., that the treatment as designed and implemented will

produce the response specified in its underlying theory) are clearly articulated as a basis for developing the evaluation design. The result of this activity is the design of a treatment appropriate to its environment, the specification of the procedures required to implement the experimental program, and a specification of the hypotheses implied by the treatment (i.e., the causal theory underlying the treatment) in terms of producing desired impacts.

(b) Design of the intervention plan. Careful design of an experimental treatment will not guarantee adequate or appropriate implementation in the field. In most cases, an administrative experiment will be conducted in the field setting by the regular employees/officials of the participating organizations. Critical control of treatments, treatment conditions, and major data collection activities will therefore be at least partially out of the hands of those who design the experiment. Thus, the implementation plan is at least as much a political design for securing the cooperation of key personnel in the experimenting organization as it is a description of procedures. The full plan for implementation of the treatment includes a specification of procedures, responsibilities of participants, schedule of activities, and an estimation of resource requirements for full implementation of the experiment.

(c) Evaluation design. The evaluation design will test the hypothesis that the treatment selected as the object of experimentation can have specified effects in the specified implementation environment. Tasks include: (a) clearly articulate the hypotheses to be tested (e.g., what are intended consequences and what might be some unintended consequences at each point of experiment impact); (b) define the comparative evaluation framework (e.g., pretest-posttest evaluation or cross-site comparison); (c) develop controls to maximize internal validity; (d) develop indicators of impacts (e.g., what measure of the consequences can be used); (e) develop instruments for collecting data dictated by the indicators; and (f) develop an analysis plan for analyzing and presenting evaluation findings. Conducting these activities requires that the experiment implementation and evaluation components be closely linked so that the design and measures accurately reflect the nature and intended effects of the treatment and can feed into the intervention plan.

(d) Design data collection instruments and procedures. A critical component in the evaluation system is the data collection subsystem.

In general, the subsystem must be responsive to data needs associated with the implementation of the experimental treatment and the implementation of the evaluation design. Several specific activities underlie the development of the data collection instruments and procedures: inventory existing data; develop data collection plans and instruments for extant data; develop data generating capability to collect new data to supplement extant data; develop procedures for ensuring the reliability and validity of collected data (i.e., data quality control).

(3) IMPLEMENTATION ACTIVITIES

When careful design of the experimental treatment and its accompanying implementation plan, evaluation and data collection systems have been accomplished, the experiment is ready to be implemented in the field. The system provides for two activities to accompany the implementation of the experiment.

(a) Monitor implementation of the experiment. Careful monitoring of the conduct of the experiment in the field is required so that (1) any deviation from the original design can be noted and its effects on performance determined, and (2) the process of implementation itself can be documented, with any obstacles or facilitating influences identified so that implementation of future experiments can be enlightened by experience, and (3) any threats to the internal validity of the evaluation can be documented and appropriate controls instituted. This monitoring function provides up-to-date information regarding the progress of on-going experiments.

The monitoring process is accomplished best by a combination of design personnel and personnel in the organization actually conducting the experiment. To the implementation personnel, the experiment is most likely to be seen as an additional burden in an already overcrowded work schedule. Including the personnel who will implement the design in the design and planning processes may accomplish two objectives then. First, the personnel most familiar with the program's operation have an opportunity to place realistic constraints on the experiment and often to suggest innovative solutions to design and implementation problems. Second, participation in the design gives those personnel a stake in the careful execution of the design. In essence, the administrative experiment depends on "real time" "real life" conditions for its success or failure and its ultimate value in policy planning.

(b) Feedback of evaluation results into the implementation of the experiment. Evaluative results which are not used in the improvement of the program at hand do not justify their costs. A plan to assure the utility of evaluation products and their incorporation into the implementation process at the appropriate points should be incorporated into an experiment. This activity will entail: (1) the development of procedures for evaluation feedback to facilitate corrective adjustments in the treatment, intervention plan, evaluation design, and data system so that both the experimental treatment and the evaluation reach maximum effectiveness and utility; and (b) the monitoring of the "adjusted" implementation to measure changes/improvements in impact.

Although this experimental system appears straightforward and its potential for improving the quality and utility of information produced by program evaluations appears high, it would be naive to think that bringing about this improved condition is a simple task. Boruch,[3] Campbell,[4] Fairweather[5] and others have been consistent advocates of the virtures of social experimentation, while articulating clearly the difficulties involved. Numerous social experiments have actually been mounted in such areas as health policy, public welfare, criminal justice, and population fertility. Researchers at the Research Triangle Institute are also in the process of developing and implementing a system for administrative experimentation under contract to the Experimental Technology Incentives Program of the National Bureau of Standards. These actual applications of the administrative experimentation approach have demonstrated both its benefits and its pitfalls. Above all, it has been made clear that it is not enough simply to argue for a process of experimentation. What is required is a significant change in attitudes of those involved in social program administration toward their respective roles, and an alteration in the organization of functions and authority of program administrators and program evaluators.

Social experiments exist in a *political* environment as well as a social environment. The Kansas City Preventive Patrol experiment evidenced this fact when community reaction to the different levels of patrol forced a halt in the research in order better to fit the research into the context of the community serving as the experimental site. The New Jersey Income Maintenance experiment is a classic example of an experiment that was in large part compromised by factors external to the actual conduct of the experiment that affected the potential validity of the experimental findings (e.g., the enactment of state welfare laws that were, in some instances, more favorable in terms of benefits than the treatment conditions).

These examples demonstrate that even when the intent to social experimentation is strong, differences in perspective, priorities, and relevant pressures among various interested groups can cause the outcome of the experiment to fall short of expectations. Part of the problem comes down to the fact that in many cases those who have responsibility for design of the experiment and the understanding of the implications and requirements of the design for the program are not those who have responsibility for implementing the experimental programs.

A redefinition of the roles and powers of the administrator and evaluator is required to bridge the gaps between them. Rather than viewing themselves as having separate functions and priorities, the experimental process asks that each move toward defining himself or herself as a policy experimenter. What this requires of both a program administrator and a program evaluator is a shared commitment to the solution of a societal problem. To support actively social experiments, one must first admit that the answer or answers to a social problem are unknown or at least unclear. The intent of a program is, then, to find out what works in addressing a problem, not to demonstrate that a solution exists and that a problem can be solved if only sufficient funds are invested in a particular program. A program administrator is asked to shift his or her loyalty from a particular program and the treatment it advocates, and instead pledge his or her support to problem solving itself. The administrator is asked to share his other authority in designing programs with the evaluator so that the treatments that are implemented accurately test the social theories and provide the most useful information for shaping policy.

The evaluator is asked to forego the comfort of being an outsider. He or she is expected to take responsibility for the program itself, not merely for the reporting of its results. The evaluator must help design programs, not just evaluations, monitor their implementation to assure their fidelity to design, and then report their outcome in a manner than can be used in the ongoing redesign and reevaluation process. The evaluator must, in this process, enlist for the long term.

Those responsible for program funding (i.e., legislators and central budget offices) also must accept the notion that problem solving—rather than guaranteed solutions—is being funded. This is a higher risk commitment in the political sense because it denies the rhetoric of "selling" solutions to tax-weary constituents. However, the payoff is in a more honest, and the only real, chance to learn what works and what does not work. Both administrators and funding officials have to cooperate in avoiding the temptation to deal with social problems by announcing the funding of major new "solutions."

One implication of this need for shared authority and responsibility in an experimental system between program administrators and program evaluators is that the difficulties attending the common practice of hiring "outside" evaluators will become even more problematic. A more hopeful approach may involve a concerted effort to develop an experimental capability internal to programs and agencies. This capability may be achieved through several channels. Evaluation researchers who are committed to experimentation may enlist for a tour of duty with a program agency in order to develop its experimental arm. Agencies may release personnel or funds for use in planned program variations and their evaluation. If the responsibility for the unresponsiveness of much of current evaluation research rests with both its buyers and suppliers, surely the responsibility for improving the quality of evaluation through experimentation must also be shared.

What we have tried to do in this chapter is outline a general problem of policy development and suggest an approach, social experimentation, which appears to offer a promising alternative to current practices. By integrating the design, implementation, and evaluation of social programs into an explicit experimental framework, the problems discussed in the paper are, if not eliminated, approached from a perspective which makes them tractable. Future research should be more nearly definitive in explicating the application of the principles of experimentation that will eventually support the social experimentation approach. It is our hope that this brief chapter will serve to advance the effort.

NOTES

1. October 6, 1977.

2. F.M. Lord, "A Paradox in the Interpretation of Group Comparisons," *Psych. Bull.*, 68 (1967), 304-305.

3. See, for example, Robert Boruch, "On Common Contentions About Randomized Field Experiments," in Gene V Glass, ed., *Evaluation Studies Review Annual* (Beverly Hills: Sage, 1976); and Henry W. Riecken and Robert Boruch, *Social Experimentation: A Method of Planning and Evaluating Social Intervention* (New York: Academic Press, 1974).

4. See, for example, Donald Campbell, "Reforms as Experiments," *Amer. Psychologist*, 24, (1969).

5. See, for example, George W. Fairweather, *Methods for Experimental Social Innovation* (John Wiley, 1967).

6. Ronald W. Johnson, "Social Policy Planning in a Federal Structure: A Social Hearing Strategy," in *Evaluation and Program Planning* (forthcoming).

9

PROBLEMS AND PROSPECTS FOR EVALUATION

Frank P. Scioli, Jr.

The 1970s have been marked by severe crises in the fiscal conditions of state and local governments. Inflationary costs of goods and services have plagued governmental officials responsible for program administration and have led them to devote increased time and attention to ways in which they can deliver services without overburdening taxpayers. The financial resources needed to deliver the diversity of basic services expected of state and local governments have grown from a 1954 level of $27 billion to a level in 1977 exceeding $200 billion. This drastic increase has forced state and local officials to grapple with ways to assess program efficiency and effectiveness so that hard decisions might be reached regarding resource allocation and resource distribution.

State and local governments are not alone in facing these challenges, for the federal government is replete with the same problems. What is unique, however, is the diffferent roles that the levels of government play in the formulation, implementation, and evaluation of policies aimed at responding to social problems. The federal government less often administers ongoing operating programs and instead formulates broad social program strategies and then distributes moneys to the states and localities. It is the state and local governments which have a direct role in the administration of a social

AUTHOR'S NOTE: *Any opinions, findings, conclusions, or recommendations expressed in this publication are those of the author and do not necessarily reflect the views of the National Science Foundation.*

program and the provision of services to intended clients.

At all levels of government arguments are being made for improvements in the efficiency and effectiveness of service delivery. These arguments invariably translate into a plea for increased attention to policy evaluation. This chapter will be restricted to a discussion of several of the problems inhibiting policy analysis at the state level as well as the prospects for overcoming them and recommendations for facilitating the tasks.

By now, the components of systematic evaluation analysis are clear and understandable.[1] We know that in assessing program impact there has to be a specification of objectives that the program is to accomplish. Further, these objectives, whether associated with the administrative features of program implementation (procedural objectives), or with the intended changes in the behavior of the clients of the program (outcome objectives), must be stated in a way that allows empirical measurement. We also know that there has to be a set of program activities established or identified to deliver the program and that this involves identification of clients to be served as well as program personnel, site selection, and procedures by which services are to be delivered. We know, too, that a cost analysis should be undertaken so that cost estimates associated with specific program activities are known. Here the objective is to uncover not only recurring costs such as salaries, employee benefits, maintenance costs, and the like, but also fixed costs such as land, physical plants and facilities, personnel training to start the program, and research and project planning expenses. Finally, we know that to establish whether the program is having any impact, the analyst must develop data points which have variously been termed "performance indicators," "effectiveness measures," or "productivity measures." The need here is to select multiple indicators of program performance which are related to the objectives of the program and are valid measures of program impact. This done, the analyst has reached the point where he can identify changes in the sociophysical environment that occurred because of the program under study.

In conjunction with the research procedures noted above, various methodologies have been proffered to insure that the most systematic path is taken to unravel the cause-effect enigma implicit in attempting to link a program activity with a behavioral change. The objective in choosing a research design is to select one which best serves to discount the plausibility of other variables, or factors, as the principal causal agents for results obtained. The procedures available—and it is not the purpose here to extol the virtues of one over another—range from simple work-load data gathering, through quasi-experimental techniques such as time-series analysis, all the way to the sophistication of experimental design methodology.[2]

State policy analysts are familiar with the above considerations; they know what evaluation is. They know that without evaluation judging the relative worth of programs is a subjective rather than a scientific enterprise. They know that they have to be about the business of evaluation. Yet every evaluation project is an event indeed. And a rigorous evaluation endeavor is as rare a bird as one can find. Now as state policy analysts as a group are not evil, or unintelligent, or incompetent, we have to ask, why is this so?

Among the major problems inhibiting program evaluation at the state level, the following must be discussed: data collection, data measurement, resource limitations, bureaucratic survival, and finally research focus.

PROBLEMS IN POLICY EVALUATION

DATA COLLECTION

In considering a particular program, whatever it might be, the state policy analyst ultimately comes to the question "How well are we doing?" Thus, a number of terms have become familiar to the analyst: Management by Objectives (MBO); Planning, Programming, and Budgeting (PPB); Effectiveness-Efficiency Analysis; and, most recently, Zero-Base Budgeting and Sunset Legislation.[3] It is not the intention of this chapter to review these techniques, for readily available to the curious is a profusion of articles both blasting and praising these various approaches. Suffice it to say that they are all well-meaning attempts to evaluate the extent to which a policy or program achieves its intended objectives, and thus dictate that the analyst bring evidence to bear to inform decision makers. In social science jargon "evidence" translates into "data." And so we come to an even more basic question: "What data are needed, and how can they be obtained?"

The collection of data is not a well-loved job. Yet it consumes great effort and time, and is, of course, essential to any evaluation. It might be compared to precinct work in a political campaign. Few people like to go out in the rain and ring doorbells or stand on street-corners passing out pamphlets, but no one involved in a campaign would say it could be won without these distasteful activities.

What makes the problem of data collection even more troublesome is that its relationship to the evaluation is not always clear. In a proper evaluation one feels that the decision about what data should be sought comes from the design of the evaluation project. But very often the availability of certain kinds of data and the problems in collecting other kinds of data dictate the evaluation itself. This happens most often when evaluation has not been built into the project. Often the data needed for a thorough evaluation are not obtainable once a program has been set into motion. Planning beforehand helps to assure the collectability of the data needed. Otherwise, one must be content with what one has at hand, placing severe limitations on the scope and reliability of the evaluation.

Whatever the data, three characteristics are essential: accuracy, completeness, and comparability. These three characteristics make the collection and recording of the data time consuming and picayune work. Since evaluations are generally not built into the program structure at its inception, record keeping procedures and minimal follow-up strategies to track clients are generally haphazard or absent. The notion of developing reliable data bases that allow comparison of program impact cross-sectionally or longitudinally requires considerable foresight and investment of financial resources so that persons are trained to keep good records, develop baseline measures, and establish instruments that permit longitudinal assessment of program impact. State program field offices are facing continual dilemmas of denying services to demanding clients or reducing their own administrative costs. That administrative costs are the first to be realized deemphasizes research and development activities for program evaluation. These administrators are so harried in delivering services within their own region or district that they cannot even begin to think of comparing service delivery strategies with other districts within the state. Thus, the proverbial "catch 22" prevails: scarce resources demand that critical decisions are necessary regarding service delivery and cost effectiveness, yet the very data gathering and analysis activities that can inform these decisions is a luxury activity rather than a regular program feature.

DATA MEASUREMENT

Data in themselves are meaningless. They must be part of a design that translates them into useful components. And indeed, a significant limitation in program evaluation is the problem that surrounds the use of the data.

How does one develop performance indicators that adequately link policy action with a measurable outcome? This demands that quantifiable measures be developed with necessary data to operationalize an effectiveness and/or efficiency model. The major difficulty inheres in trying to capture the full richness associated with the term *effectiveness*. More often than not, effectiveness measurement has been limited to assessment of production levels that programs elicit and has resulted in the development of a set of workload measures surrounding questions such as: How many persons receive the particular service? How frequently is the service provided? How many staff are assigned to serving the client? What percentage of the staff is purely administrative? This is not to suggest that these questions should not be raised or that they result in irrelevant information gathering. Rather, it is argued that such questions must be supplemented with measurement devices that allow the detection of more subtle phenomena associated not just with the quantity of the service but with the quality of the service as well. It is these qualitative phenomena that pose the most serious measurement challenge for the evaluator.

If we consider human services programs at the state level we gain rapid appreciation of the task facing evaluations of such programs. The question of the best organizational apparatus for delivering state social service programs has occupied a significant amount of time of state officials. This debate generally centers upon whether state human service programs work more effectively when all services are integrated under one umbrella agency or when they are in various autonomous agencies. Rarely does the discussion focus on measureable improvements in the quality of service provided to clients. Instead, improvements in administrative procedures and financial accounting practices are cited as factors leading to increases in numbers of clients served and/or cases processed. These workload measures thereby become the effectiveness indicators used to judge agency success.

Most recently, efforts have been directed at assessing client satisfaction with services provided.[4] Surveys are conducted to examine attitudes of clients about services they receive. The attempt to include clients' attitudes in evaluation does broaden the scope of a given project. It tries to get at the "quality" component of the services that we were before discussing. But it in itself presents more questions, because surely the relationship between the attitudes elicited and the behaviors exhibited must be made clear. Mr. X might receive his food stamps on time but be annoyed by Miss Y's manner in handing them over to him. Mrs. A has been waiting with some hardship for her food stamp clearance for several months but, impressed by Mr. B's courtesy on the phone, feels everything possible is being done to facilitate her case. If Mr. X's attitude is negative and Mrs. A's attitude is positive, what does that tell us about the goods delivered? Has quality been measured, and if so, the quality of what? Should it matter if Mr. X is unhappy, if the agency delivered what it was set up to deliver; or if Mrs. A is happy, and it has not?

Questions such as these return us to the fact that the data elicited and the intention of the project must be linked. Evaluation forces an agency to articulate what it wants. The objectives must be clear, or no evaluation can make much sense. And for that matter, neither can the agency. Rarely, however, are program objectives cast in a way that they lend themselves easily to operationalization. Policymakers frame objectives in general rhetorical terminology that has appeal to the broad public clientele that they serve. The policymaker seldom states objectives such as "reduction by 20 percent in the placement changes of children with foster parents" or "increase in reading comprehension level of high school students by 30 percent." Instead, broader terms such as "meaningful environments" for foster care children or "high quality" education are used. In many instances state education policy, to cite one example, will require "competency assessment" for the high school diploma and will not give a clue about what this means. Thus, the very nature of the policy formulation process itself pits the policymaker against the policy analyst, for the analyst must develop gauges to establish meaning for the concepts established in a particular policy.

RESOURCE LIMITATIONS

Evaluation, like anything else, costs money. There is expense involved in staffing departments for evaluation, in coordinating a unit whose responsibility is first and only the evaluation of programs, in setting up the methodological procedures; in short, all phases of evaluation entail a certain outlay of funds. People begrudge that amount of money needed for evaluation, thinking it more vital that it be spent on the program itself. It is difficult to convince people concerned with their programs that the money spent on evaluation is money well spent. Seldom are people aware that the evaluation component of their project will save money in the long run. Thus, rarely are the funds for a first-class evaluation set aside. Instead, smaller resources are allocated, resulting in part-time staffing and no central purpose.

Perhaps the most limited resource in evaluation is the trained evaluator himself. When one thinks about the number of programs a state delivers, evaluation of them all would require a veritable army of evaluators. Even if this army could be maintained, where would it come from? It used to be that if an evaluator could recognize a computer and use a statistic he was in business. Today, an evaluator needs a broad interdisciplinary background and a thorough understanding of social science methodology. He needs to know not only the more familiar social science tools such as survey research methods and interviewing procedures but also time-series analysis, cost-benefit economics, and experimental design principles. Implicit in each of these skills is an appreciation of complex measurement problems and familiarity with multi-variate statistical methodology. Clearly, the trained evaluator is at a premium.

No one has it in mind to replace current state personnel with trained evaluators. But everyone working in a program, from the director to the people in the field, ought to be conscious of accountability. The consciousness that does prevail is that of being fiscally accountable. (One should not misspend funds. Agency programs designed to spend "X" amount of money should not spend "X + $100." The money assigned to "X" should not be spent on "Y.") But the money is a concern in and of itself. Systematic evaluation, on the other hand, links objectives to outcomes. Phases of operation cannot be done in isolation but require a new kind of thinking about the *whole*. Systematic evaluation is relatively new, and many personnel are not used to

operating in terms of objectives and measurable outcomes. Therefore, state personnel need to be educated into thinking along these
lines. Dissemination of journals, workshops, in-service programs—
all the educational tools needed to develop this new consciousness—
draw further upon the states' already limited resources.

BUREAUCRATIC SURVIVAL

In less civilized times a messenger bringing bad news to royalty
automatically got his tongue cut out. We have progressed far beyond
that barbarity, so much so that now there is no such thing as bad news.
Or rather, bad news is no news, which does present a problem to the
evaluator. If his job depends on the existence of the program, and his
boss' job depends on the existence of the program, how is he to
evaluate it without bias? As Charles Peters has said in a recent article,
"Locked deep in the nucleus of each department and civil servant,
determining behavior as reliably as DNA, is the double-helix of
Survival."[5]

The success or failure of the staff becomes intrinsically bound to
the success or failure of the program. If that program is known to be a
disaster, what is the fate of the staff? If the evaluator is built into the
program, how can he divorce himself from it in order to carry on an
objective evaluation? If he is an "outsider," hired specifically for
evaluation purposes, how willing will the program manager and other
personnel be to give him the freedom he needs to undertake a reliable
evaluation? It seems that the very nature of bureaucratic structure is
anathema to program evaluation. Once the state has set an agency in
motion, its ultimate goal seems to be survival, with service-delivery
only secondary to its own importance. Until service-delivery agencies can be so structured and personnel so convinced that their main
goal is the delivery of services to the public and that programs are
simply vehicles toward that end, evaluation will be difficult to conduct. The marriage of the staff to the program in the sacred church of
the bureaucracy is a strong impediment to program evaluation.

RESEARCH FOCUS

Another problem of evaluation is an old problem and a general
problem. It concerns the age-old competition between theory and
action. We find this division everywhere. Every academic discipline
has its so-called "thinkers" and "doers," and nowhere is this distinc-

tion more visible than in the area of evaluation and public policy.

In science it is common to talk about basic versus applied research. Who has ever heard "basic" and "applied" mentioned without the "versus" in-between? It is thought that the scholar ought to concern himself with the development of reliable and testable general theories. These theories while they may have to do with public policy in the broad sense may or may not have bearing upon particular cases at any given time. The public policymaker, however, is concerned with particulars. He needs to know how general knowledge is translated into particular action useful in specific situations. No matter how intellectually satisfying a theory may be, if it cannot be operationalized when he needs it to be, what good is it to him?

The scholar sees knowledge as cumulative, needing time to develop his theory and conduct his research. Time is not limiting but necessary to the unfolding of his plan. But to the policymaker, time is a series of points by which certain decisions have to be made. He does not use time; he works within it.

Then, too, the policymaker does not want to know too much. As a private citizen, he may be as curious as any other, but his job as a public policymaker is to know that which can be acted upon. There is no sense doing research if the results produced can't be useful afterwards. If money is to be spent on an evaluation, he wants to know that the results will be amenable to policy decisions, that they will help him know what direction to take in the future.

Hence, the evaluator has to mediate between two worlds. His training has probably given him the world view of the scholar, but his particular expertise hinges on his own ability to make himself useful to the policymaker. He must somehow make himself comfortable in that association without abandoning the rigors of scientific research. He must "think" so that others may "do." The last thing any policymaker wants is an evaluation project which ends with a "to be or not to be," no matter how rich the components of the question.

PROSPECTS FOR POLICY EVALUATION

Despite the serious problems that beset the initiation of program evaluation, certain forces are advancing the prospects of their solution. Some of these forces are external to state government, and some are internal.

Perhaps the most general force and the most necessary one is an increased interest in evaluation from the top levels of government. It has been recognized that to make evaluation work, the demand for it "must emanate from top policy and decision levels."[6] In the recent presidential election campaign, President Carter made accountability a major campaign issue, advocating zero-base budgeting as a method of program evaluation. The president's persistence on this issue derived from his experience in the state of Georgia while governor.[7] Such interest from the top goes a long way toward creating a "performance consciousness" in agencies of all branches of government.

The seemingly general notion of performance consciousness translates itself into quite specific actions. It can mean the difference between a policy that is just allowed to happen and one that is directed and controlled. Performance consciousness can mean the difference between a vaguely worded policy and one whose direction is stated specifically. An agency imbued with performance consciousness will be aware that its program's main events ought to be intended consequences, and measurable, and that its unintended consequences ought to be identified and anticipated.

The consciousness of performance is dependent, of course, on the technical ability to carry on an evaluation. Another external force and one directed toward this end is the increased interest on the part of universities in the science of evaluation.

Universities are graduating increasing numbers of students trained in this area. In a recent survey of chairpersons of political science departments awarding advanced degrees (M.A., Ph.D.) and directors of interdisciplinary policy studies programs, 74 percent of those responding answered "yes" to an item inquiring whether their department, program, or university awarded any special degrees related to policy studies other than the M.A. and Ph.D. in political science.[8] This is particularly relevant since "policy studies" was clarified for respondents to mean "the application of political and social science to the study of the causes and especially the effects of alternative public policies."[9] Moreoever, 64 percent of the respondents indicated their institutions had an organized interdisciplinary policy studies program. Although a systematic analysis of the curricula in these programs is not available and the extent to which they offer formal training in the various aspects of policy evaluation (e.g., measurement, research design, analysis) is not known, the survey did indicate that respondents felt the need for more attention to evaluation and impact studies. Given the growing demand in state government for personnel with formal training in policy analysis and familiarity with policy evaluation methodology, graduates of these programs will enter government equipped with skills to undertake evaluations. In this way a force external to state government can yield a base of persons inside government who possess the "performance consciousness" referred to earlier, coupled with the necessary technical skills.

In order to facilitate "retooling" of extant personnel in state government, several training programs have emerged that afford the individual a concentrated learning experience in policy evaluation research and methodology. Noteworthy in this regard are the summer training programs which have been offered over the last several years at Northwestern University and at the University of Massachusetts, Amherst. These programs entail six to ten weeks of intensive training in evaluation for state government personnel who are able to obtain leave from their positions and who are accepted into the programs.

Also important to the consciousness of evaluation and the accompanying skills is the appearance of numerous journals and books focusing on policy analysis and policy evaluation. *Evaluation, Policy Studies Journal, Policy Analysis, Evaluation Quarterly, Handbook of Evaluation Research* and *Evaluation Annual* are a few of many sources developed specifically for the person interested in policy analysis and evaluation. This body of literature provides a forum where researchers can publish their findings and policy people can express their concerns and ideas. It is thereby a meeting place of research and policy, facilitating the exchange of information so vital to a growing discipline.

Several federal agencies have also played unique roles in advancing productivity research and evaluation analysis. One of these was the National Center for Productivity and Quality of Working Life, established by Congress in 1975 as an independent federal agency. Although this agency's concerns were primarily for productivity stimulation at the federal level, its impact was meant to be felt at the state and local level as well.

Although the center is now disbanded, its studies have shown that improved productivity in the long run is dependent upon a commitment to improve services coupled with clearly delineated lines of accountability.

The Research Applied to National Needs Program (RANN) of the National Science Foundation was another federal vehicle which advanced policy evaluation programs. RANN's Fiscal Year 1978 Budget to the Congress[10] included a $23,000,000 proposal for a Productivity Subactivity, which included a $7,400,000 Public Sector Productivity Program Element, and a $10,000,000 Public Policy Program Element.

The Productivity Subactivity had as its objective the provision of "an improved scientific and technical basis for increasing total factor productivity in the public and private sectors."[11] Among other things, it called for "research designed to improve the measures of total factor productivity."[12] Moneys for the Public Sector Productivity Program Element were intended to provide "valid, reliable, and usable analyses and measures of the effectiveness, efficiency, and equity of public service delivery systems."

In 1973, RANN distributed a solicitation for policy research on the effectiveness, equity, efficiency, and responsiveness of organizational arrangements for the delivery of services in metropolitan areas. As a consequence, four investigations were funded in the substantive areas of police, fire, solid waste collection and disposal, and public health. The police, fire, and solid waste investigations are still underway and are all developing and testing measures to evaluate the extent to which services are being provided effectively and efficiently. A major part of these investigations is the development of evaluation indicators to measure the concept's effectiveness and efficiency. In addition, a project in the state of Washington is directed toward the development and implementation of a productivity measurement system for assessing effectiveness of service delivery organizations within the Washington state government. In the first part of the research, productivity measures were developed and implemented to assess service delivery in two agencies in the State Department of Social and Health Services. The current research activities involve analysis of data gathered during the project and assessment of the problems and prospects for introducing productivity measurement into a state government system.

Since the design model emphasizes measurement for the purpose of program evaluation, including both efficiency and effectiveness, the Washington state research team, through the Office of the Governor, has been very active in establishing an information exchange with other state governments interested in undertaking rigorous program evaluation. A key feature of all of these efforts is that in addition to providing a technically competent research product, the researchers also provide a handbook for state and local officials responsible for the particular substantive area (police, fire, and so on). The aim here is to insure high potential for utilization by government officials so that they can continually evaluate the effectiveness of their programs. Thus, it is clear that, like the Center's perspective, RANN's research strategy recognized the close association between productivity and accountability, and that any concern with productivity must include an accompanying commitment to advancing policy evaluation efforts at the state and local level.

The RANN program was disbanded in February 1978 and replaced with the Applied Science and Research Applications (ASRA) Directorate. The Division of Advanced Productivity has given way to the Division of Applied Research. This new division supports a wide range of activities in the public policy fields. While having a wider focus than the Division of Advanced Productivity, it will continue to encourage research into productivity and related concerns.

Evaluation efforts in the Department of Housing and Urban Development (HUD) and the Department of Health, Education and Welfare (HEW),[13] to mention just two, are also underway. HUD, for example, is currently supporting a research project to develop a *Productivity Handbook* on the tools and techniques for local and state government productivity.[14] This handbook is being developed so that it can provide the policy analyst with the information needed to understand the techniques, tools, procedures, and problems of implementation involved in evaluating city, county, and state government functions.

The functions to be addressed run the gamut from public safety and human resources to environment, transportation, and recreation.[15]

All of the above activities directed toward improving evaluation efforts can be conceived as being external to state and local government. The states themselves are also organizing activities to advance evaluation through the efforts of newly created evaluation units within the states. Particularly noteworthy in this regard is the Legislative Program Evaluation Section (LPES) of the National Conference of State Legislatures (NCSL). LPES was established in 1973 and became formally affiliated with the NCSL in 1975. The initial purpose was to provide a focus for professional development and communication between state legislative staffs engaged in program evaluation. The LPES *Bylaws* list the following three purposes:

(1) to enhance the art and science of legislative program evaluation;
(2) to enhance professionalism and training in legislative program evaluation; and,
(3) to promote the exchange of ideas and information about legislative program evaluation.[16]

At the annual NCSL meeting in Kansas City in August 1976, three substantive panels were prepared by the LPES as part of the formal program. Two of these panels dealt specifically with the application of quantitative techniques to state program evaluation. The section also publishes a newsletter, has established a training program with the Council of State Governments, and now through the Eagleton Institute of Politics at Rutgers University is operating a "Clearinghouse" which keeps on file legislative program evaluations of member states. Each evaluation report is abstracted to document information on the scope and emphasis of the evaluation, the measures of program performance used, the analytical techniques employed, the major findings, and the major recommendations.

At present, LPES membership includes 185 professionals representing 41 agencies in 30 states. Of course, within the member states there are great differences not only in evaluation techniques employed and in the scope of the studies but also in the organization of evaluation units in the states, ranging from the independent commission or committee type to the core staff to the legislative auditor type.[17] The LPES clearinghouse, therefore, is a good vehicle for presenting these different evaluation procedures, allowing comparisons, and fostering sharing among the states.

SUGGESTIONS FOR ACTION

We have discussed the problems of policy evaluation as well as some of the more encouraging programs now underway to contribute to evaluation efforts at the state level. It now remains to map out some recommendations to ensure continued development of policy evaluation.

(1) The federal government should get its house in order with regard to evaluation. Fundamental to the development of evaluation procedures at the state and local levels is its development at the federal level. It is encouraging to note that the current chief executive is the first governor to hold that office since FDR, and is consequently versed in management and state needs. The president should press for evaluation procedures at the federal level (e.g., Zero-Base Budgeting and Sunset Legislation) which will set the stage for further activity at subfederal levels.

(2) The federal government should encourage state evaluation in the form of a categorical program of aid to the states but not at the expense of general revenue sharing funds. We have mentioned that a lack of commitment to evaluation and scarcity of funds have combined to thwart evaluation research. Federal commitment to evaluation (Suggestion #1) along with forced funds into evaluation research will provide the incentive and opportunity for the states to increase their technical capacity.

(3) Mobility assignments should be encouraged. Intergovernmental and intraagency exchanges of skilled personnel is one way of making maximum use of scarce personnel resources. Such personnel not only lend their expertise to the problem at hand but also leave their methods behind for continued use by permanent personnel.

(4) State executives should require measurement of output and regular reporting of program impacts. We have discussed problems of data gathering in this paper. Good reporting builds the data bases for future systematic evaluation. The possibility for developing incentives toward this end should be given serious consideration as a key to rapid development in this area.

(5) There should be increased research on the topic of public management at the state and local levels. University efforts to engage in such research should be encouraged vis-a-vis grants from the federal level and entry into agencies at the state and local level. Insight into the area of management is inextricably bound to the problems of productivity and evaluation. (7) Greater understanding of the field of management at the state and local level will yield progress in evaluation as well.

(6) Productivity levels should be decentralized. Evaluation should not be merely the addition of a budget function in the large picture. It should be dealt with on the department level. Individual departments must commit themselves to it, for here is where the data generates from and here is where the policies are applied.

Greater efforts should be made to disseminate and coordinate information on evaluation. To date, no single agency at any level—federal, state or local—exists that has the resources or mandate to be such a clearinghouse of information.

(8) Push for evaluation projects where they can best be applied so that credibility for the enterprise will develop. We should not all of a sudden be evaluating every program in sight. We should evaluate only those that allow evaluation and lend themselves to it given the resources and technical ability we have to start with. Our data gathering should be incremental, not "pie-in-the-sky," so that we have a careful building of data bases with a longitudinal component. As evaluation consciousness grows and evaluation techniques develop, evaluation projects can expand and multiply accordingly.

CONCLUSION

We began this chapter rather pessimistically with a catalog of the problems besetting proper and systematic evaluation of government agencies. We somewhat overcompensated perhaps with a listing of some promising activities in the area of evaluation research. We conclude with a sort of compromise, suggesting a few specific ideas that would encourage policy evaluation and ending with what may seem to some less than an all-out commitment. The commitment, however, is complete, though set within the parameters dictated by an already existent structure that must with patience be made to yield to the inevitability of policy evaluation.

NOTES

1. The proliferation of items on the topic in recent years is so pervasive that we will note only a few sources for the interested reader: Edward A. Suchman, *Evaluative Research* (New York: Russell Sage, 1967); Thomas J. Cook and Frank P. Scioli, Jr., "A Research Strategy for Analyzing the Impacts of Public Policy," *Admin. Sci. Q.,* 17 (1972) 328-339; *Standards for Audit of Governmental Organizations, Programs, Activities and Functions* (Washington, D.C., U.S. General Accounting Office, 1972); Henry W. Riecken and Robert F. Boruch, eds., *Social Experimentation: A Method for Planning and Evaluating Social Intervention* (New York Academic Press, 1974; Kenneth M. Dolbeare, ed., *Public Policy Evaluation,* (Beverly Hills: Sage, 1975).

2. See, for example: Harry Hatry et al. *Practical Program Evaluation for State and Local Government Officials* (Washington, D.C.: Urban Institute, 1973); Charles N. Brownstein, "The Experimental Evaluation of Public Policy," in Charles O. Jones and Robert D. Thomas,

eds., *Public Policy Making in a Federal System* (Beverly Hills, Sage, 1976), pp. 19-38; Frank P. Scioli, Jr., and Thomas J. Cook, eds., *Methodologies for Analyzing Public Policies* (Lexington, Mass.: Lexington Books, 1975).

3. For a recent review, see the "Symposium on Management by Objectives in the Public Sector," *Public Administration Rev.*, 36 (January-February, 1976); and *Zero-Based Legislation* (Hearings Before the Task Force on Budget Process of the House Committee on the Budget), (Washington, D.C.: Government Printing Office, 1976).

4. Two excellent examples are Kenneth Webb and Harry P. Hatry *Obtaining Citizen Feedback: The Application of Citizen Surveys to Local Governments* (Washington, D.C.: Urban Institute, 1973); and Daniel Katz et al., *Bureaucratic Encounters: A Pilot Study in the Evaluation of Government Services* (Ann Arbor: Institute for Social Research, University of Michigan, 1975)

5. "How Carter Can Find Out What the Government is Doing," *Washington Monthly,* 8 (January, 1977), p. 12.

6. *The Status of Productivity Measurement in State Government: An Initial Examination* (Washington, D.C.: Urban Institute 1975), p. 190.

7. For an interesting reply to a position paper on human services, see the article by the then governor, Jimmy Carter, *Evaluation* (Spring, 1974), pp. 6-7.

8. *Policy Studies Directory* (Urbana, Ill.: Policy Studies Organization, 1976), pp. 7-27.

9. p. 8

10. *RANN Fiscal Year 1978 Budget to the Congress* (Washington, D.C.: National Science Foundation, 1977).

11. *RANN Fiscal Year 1978 Budget to the Congress,* G-111-1.

12. *RANN Fiscal Year 1978 Budget to the Congress,* G-111-1.

13. A recently funded study on social service agency evaluation capabilities in ten sites will soon be available. The Principal Investigator is Edward Baumeier, Social Welfare Research Institute, University of Denver, and the study "Assessment of State and Local Government Practices" was supported by the Department of Health, Education and Welfare, Office of the Assistant Secretary for Planning and Evaluation.

14. The HUD grant for this project is to the National Academy of Public Administration, Washington, D.C. The Project Director is Eckhard Bennewitz.

15. There are also a number of private groups such as the International City Management Association (Washington, D.C.), Public Technology, Inc. (Washington, D.C.) and the Committee for Economic Development (New York, New York) which, among their other objectives, strive to increase productivity efforts at the state and local level by conducting research, having conferences, and issuing reports. See *Improving Productivity in State and Local Government* (New York: Committee for Economic Development, 1976), and *Measuring the Effectiveness of Basic Municipal Services.* (Washington, D.C.: Urban Institute and International City Management Association, 1974).

16. *"Bylaws of the Legislative Program Evaluation Section of the National Conference of State Legislatures," LPES Report,* January 1977, pp. 14-15.

17. For an excellent review and discussion of the differences in evaluation units, see Mark L. Chadwin, "The Nature of Legislative Program Evaluation," *Evaluation,* 2 (1975), pp. 45-49.

10

REALITIES OF PUBLIC POLICY ANALYSIS

Peter House
Joseph Coleman

Public policies are often elusive beasts. They can range from decisions to go to war to the way civil servants should interact with the public. What is policy for today may not be valid tomorrow. Although it is often confusing, this seemingly endless flux is the way we tend to operate, at least at the margin. In fact, the purpose of public policy is to make "steering corrections in the ship of state" and to change them as the "weather" requires. Although hundreds of policies, big and small, are formulated and modified every day, the perception of "how things are done" typically appears stable. The reason for this is that these numerically large numbers of policy shifts are relatively small compared with the numbers of existing institutions and operations they attempt to adjust.

Most individual public policies seemingly have little direct effect on how most of us live, which is fortuitous or sad, depending on one's viewpoint. On the other hand, the direct and secondary impact of many individual policies and the combined impact of the multitudinous decisions made by all the public sector decision makers have profound impacts on the way we live our daily lives. They should

AUTHOR'S NOTE: *We gratefully acknowledge the helpful reviews of this chapter by many of our colleagues.*

realize how great an effect their actions usually have on individuals and strive for informed and thoughtful decisions.

Formulation of a public policy that deals with a complex and far-reaching issue is normally supported by analysis of the source of the issue, criteria for setting the policy, alternative decisions that might be made, the impact of these decisions and the institutions and groups affected. The way such an analysis is carried out can often significantly affect the final policy decision. In this chapter, we explore some practical aspects of public policy analysis, recommend a general approach to analysis, and suggest ways that policy analysts could be more appropriately trained. We feel that implementation of these suggestions will improve the analysis of proposed public policies and contribute to more effective policy decisions.

A public policy will be defined here as a governing principle, plan, or course of action made by an authority in a government entity. Normally the public policymaker is appointed or elected to a position of authority. This contrasts with civil servants who usually perform the analysis, although the latter sometimes exert a good deal of policymaking authority or influence. Public policy analysis will be defined here as an analysis of a proposed public policy that generates and presents information so as to improve the basis for public decision makers to exercise their judgment.

ANALYTICAL PROCESS

It is unfortunate that what is taught nowadays as "policy analysis" often has little to do with how such analysis is actually practiced. The neatly reasoned and structured process portrayed in text books does not exist, whereas forces often not articulated are at least as important to the establishment of policy as any rigorous, formal, highly quantitative or empirical analysis. The mismatch between theory and practice is not unique to policy analysis, however.

Like almost everyone else who has been seriously interested in how to do policy analysis, we also have examined the literature for applicable techniques and guidelines. Methods abound, nearly all borrowed from a variety of more traditional disciplines—economics, systems analyses, operations research. One of the clear perceptions obtained in such a search is that almost all guidance derived from these fields recommends highly analytical and technical methods for supporting policy decisions. On the other hand, the literature of public administration provides largely descriptive solutions, usually relegated to personnel or administrative matters. Guidance from the policy science field is often so highly structured that public policies appear rational—the products of models and computers that presumably have so effectively removed the biases and politics of human judgment and interplay.

The search for guidance becomes increasingly disappointing as one gains experience in actually producing public policy analyses in the real world and relies on this experience to pinpoint methods that might be useful or workable. On the other hand, to be fair, analysis of major public policies is an incredibly complex process. In some cases, it resembles more an art than a science; in many decisions that must be made daily, it is.

This feature of policy analysis suggests that almost every situation is unique and attempts to structure the process and add a dimension not useful to the actual practitioners. This is an overstatement, but it does suggest that some attention should be paid to those practicalities that often make application of conventional paradigms messy. We shall address a few of these practicalities and discuss how one could structure the academic training of policy analysts and organize a public policy analysis shop in light of such realities.

The process of analysis begins when a decision maker calls for an analysis on which to base a policy decision. What follows depends on consideration of a variety of factors that can influence the way the analysis is performed and used. We wish to examine these factors to highlight the reality that policy decisions normally are based on more than application of analytical skills and methods.

A final policy decision may have little to do with the options suggested by rigorous analytical techniques. A mystique has arisen in the public (and, often, private) bureaucracies that seems to attribute supernatural capabilities to the various quantitative techniques which had their roots in systems analysis and operations research. In spite of the fact that few policies have been formulated solely by following these techniques, texts and college curriculae perpetuate myths surrounding the importance of their use. One technique, mathematical programming, is representative. This method requires specification of (1) the present situation, (2) the final situation desired, and (3) a listing of the so-called boundary conditions preventing immediate solutions. Computer programs are devised to demonstrate to the policymaker "the" solution which would yield the greatest payoff, or the least loss. How handy it would be to have a computation show, unequivocally, what should be done.

As a matter of fact, if the situation surround the decision to be made is accurately and adequately described, and the goal correctly articulated, the future forecast correctly, and the boundary conditions completely specified, then the computer model's results might indeed suggest the decision or decisions that ought to be forthcoming. Unfortunately, such a capability hardly ever suffices for public policy analysis. Consequently, policy analysis must depend upon the skills of humans who use less than perfect tools to articulate the possibilities for resolution of an issue that requires a decision. The ways that this can be done are myriad and yet depend on a traditional set of factors that must be considered for a credible job to be done. Many of these are obvious and are stressed by those who promote policy analysis as a highly structured science, i.e., data, models, information. These might be defined as pertaining to the "supply side" of policy analyses. There are, however, a set of other "real word" factors that nearly always are taken into consideration. Let us examine them.

We begin with some definitions of terms. There will be no attempt exhaustively to define these terms, but an effort will be made to give the reader some indication of a class of variables that, although not expressly considered in specific analyses, are nonetheless often critical to the actual impact of the resulting policy and, therefore, should be considered when the policy is being analyzed. Most experienced decision makers intuitively incorporate these factors into the total decision process. Thus, we might say that such factors pertain more to the "demand side" of policy analysis than to the "supply side." We categorize them as circumstantial, conditional and methodological:

- *Circumstantial*—the milieu extant at that time a policy is being reviewed, internal or external to the policy unit. Such factors as an agency's present policy position, the current public attitude toward such items as the environment, the unemployment rate all could be considered to be policy related but beyond the scope of an individual policymaker's ability to influence fully or directly. These types of factors are not expected to change greatly during the course of an analysis.

- *Conditional*—the provisional situation under which the analysis is performed. Examples are the amount and kind of resources available for the analyses, the time before the analysis is needed, and the personality or approach of the person receiving the information. These factors are often set at the beginning of an analysis and could be changed during its course.

- *Methodological*—the method or methods adopted to perform an analysis. There is rarely any clear-cut methodology that is ideal for performing policy analysis of public issues, although entire professional careers are often spent trying to develop particular approaches. Methodologies range from so-called optimal solutions, produced through one or more computerized algorithms, to those produced through a form of "disjointed incrementalism," a sort of muddling through approach.

POLICY ANALYSIS IN PRACTICE

It is our contention that many policy analyses do not address relevant questions or do not do so in a fashion that would lead to viable solutions. Let us look into some of the practical factors that are often not considered when policy analysis is taught or practiced.

- *Matching Issues and Resources*. The question of appropriate criteria for welfare eligibility can hardly be expected to be analyzed with the same resources and fervor as the question of a revised budget for a minor government unit. Although this comparison is extreme, it does remind us that most public decisions could be considered as policy or as providing a basis for policy formulation. More sophisticated and complex methodologies and analyses are required for the more difficult policy decisions. Determining the amount of resources to be devoted to an analysis of a given issue is an area that needs more attention and development. The matching of issues and resource is often a difficult task, even for those experienced in analysis. It has been suggested that preliminary screening and consideration of analytical alternatives be examined before significant resources are devoted to an analysis.

- *Approach of the Decision Maker*. Although almost never mentioned explicitly, the form and content of a policy analysis is often influenced greatly by the known or anticipated desires and demands of the decision maker for whom it is being prepared. This may take on many manifestations. When the recipient perceives himself to be an expert in a particular area, analysts preparing policy papers for him sometimes find their responsibilities change from merely performing an analysis to participating in a professional contest to use the "appropriate" assumptions and recognize the "proper" alternatives. Although such a situation might result in better policy analyses being performed, it might just as easily result in more elegance in the form of the analysis, which is not commensurate with the importance of the ultimate decision. Elegance is a luxury ill-afforded in the time-pressured policy area.

At the other extreme, there is the policymaker who is often not familiar with the technical aspects of the arena in which the decisions are required to be made. In these circumstances, policy papers have to be made more detailed and sometimes more tutorial.

Then, there is the decision maker who cares little for analysis and tends to use policy analysts as general staff, including the job of post hoc justification of preconceived policy decisions. Lastly, we should mention the decision maker who has a tendency to "satisfice," to require sufficient analysis only to render a decision that is "good enough."

- *Time for Resolution.* The policy analyst normally operates under a restrictive tyranny of time. The analyst refers to the situation in which "the policy window is open," meaning that the analyst may be intellectually in favor of carrying out long-range research, thereby improving the quality of data bases and methods, the realities of life often do not allow such a course of action. On issues worthy of attack, a decision will be made whether or not an analyst completes an analysis. An obvious and immutable rule for an effective policy group is that an analysis must be ready before the final policy decision must be made.

  Consequently, issues that are complex with little time for examination may get analyses whose reliability is open to question. Even so, these analyses should be the best that can be performed under the circumstances. If the analysis is periodically revised, as, for example, was the assessment of the environmental impacts of the U.S. National Energy Plan, analytical tools can be expected to lead to more reliable results, allow shorter turnaround time, and yield more comprehensive and sophisticated analyses.

- *Resource Limitations.* Just as little time may be available for an analysis, so, too, the resources to carry it out may be limited. It might be hypothesized that the government should allocate resource levels that are appropriate to the value of the policy decision at hand. This could mean that millions of taxpayer dollars should be spent for some public policy analyses. However, the vagaries of the political process often make it difficult to allocate adequate resources to the variety of proposed policies. Also, in reality, adequate funds are rarely available. For most proposed policies, a small portion of a pre-determined policy analysis budget is initially allocated to carry out the studies.

But money is not the only resource required. Probably the rarest commodity in analysis is talent—the talent to perform sophisticated, balanced, insightful analyses under extreme pressures and usually in a short time. Talented analysts can get to the heart of an issue quickly. Because of familiarity with general issues, they can relate a current issue to others in the policy stream at that moment. In addition to their technical skills and political sense, analysts need to have more than their share of luck, given the uncertainties of the political process. Whatever comprises the elusive components of (analytical) talent, policy analysts are difficult to find, to train, and to keep sufficiently challenged for long periods of time.

- *Presentations.* Few who teach or write about policy analysis seem to understand that communication is fundamental in the policy-making process. It is most apt to be neglected in the staff presentation of the analysis to the policymaker, who then must communicate the results and their bases to peers, superiors, and the public. Because policymakers have different levels of training and skills, and differ widely in personality and motivation, they differ in how they would like information presented to them. If briefed, should it be formal or informal, a one-on-one, or a team briefing, highly technical or result oriented? If written, should it be one page or twenty, options or recommendations, memorandum, technical or tutorial paper?

Policymaker and staff should settle on the mode for presentation of analytical results in the design phase of an analyses. The quality, depth, and type of each analysis will depend on the specific mode of basic communication. Even then, the situation may remain fluid, and the policy climate may shift while the analysis is underway.

The policy staff leadership or person responsible for presenting an analysis to a decision maker should have a clear understanding of what the analysis is about, the approach and methods used, the quality of the data bases, and the realities of the policy climate in which the decision must reside. During the presentation, questions and feedback from the decision maker should be answered directly in the context of the analysis performed. Without this approach, credibility and efficiency suffer, especially as the time for a decision draws near.

If the topic of communication is broached at all during the teaching process, new analysts are taught how analysis *should* be presented. Such lessons are likely to suffer from excess formalism, and bias toward "educating" the policymaker on background and method. In a world where the policymaker must wade through large amounts of information daily, effectively presented policy analyses should emphasize a clear understanding of the issues and choices in a short time. The information should be packaged specifically for the use of the policymaker regardless of the preferences of the analyst. And to the greatest extent possible, the policymaker and the analyst should be on the same "wave length."

- *The Analysts.* The federal bureaucracy often suffers from an imbalance of jobs to be done and people to do them. Nowhere is this more apparent than in the average policy shop, where the tasks are numerous and usually of high priority with short time fuses. In addition to the number of tasks that are assigned, a complicating factor is the variety of approaches that are required to dispense with the broad set of tasks. A query may be handled by the analyst spending an hour writing a letter, or by a team of three or four analysts working full-time for two weeks. Usually there is no way to predict how many tasks or what level of effort will be required from a policy shop. It is difficult to forecast staff resources required for analysis, both type and quantity, until an issue is presented and the policy climate in which it resides is examined.

Policy shops may require the assistance of outside consultants, to smooth out the surges of demand for analysis and permit better allocation of limited manpower and resources. Consultants should be used to supply such things as expert advice and data-gathering services in specific areas on an as-needed basis. The policy staff should provide the basic analytical capability for addressing policy issues. General policy analysis expertise should remain in-house. Use of contractors simply as an extension of policy staff should be avoided. In practice, the distinction between these assignments sometimes blurs. However, the credibility of a policy shop breaks down when it seems that the policy staff has contracted out much of its analysis; little appears to be required by the in-house staff but to manage contracts and route paper. Nevertheless, the policy staff ought to bear sole responsibility for the analyses they present to the decision maker.

Also, there is the question of who should develop the options for a policy maker—internal staff or outside consultants. Particularly important for government decisions is, who is responsible for representing the public interest, government worker or contractor? The answer to this question should be evident.

- *Objectivity.* Maintaining objectivity in the course of doing an analysis is a constant problem for policy staff. Normally, civil servants are expected to approach their work with a high degree of objectivity, since they are to be impartial with respect to the public they serve. Therefore, government analyses attempt to be objective in their work, fully expecting that the decision maker, usually politically appointed, will factor in the decision the necessary political realities. But objectivity for an organization person is often a subjective concept, as, Rufus Miles and others has so aptly stated. Miles' Law states, "Where you stand depends on where you sit." It is his contention that no person can totally rise above his institutional perspectives and responsibilities when asked to perform in a statesman like fashion. Both analyst and decision maker should remain aware of this reality in going about their work.

- *Brushfires.* No discussion of the realities of public policy analysis dares omit the "brushfire" issues. The actual day-to-day job of the professional policy analyst consists of responding to crises—real or imagined—that are important to a policymaker. The response to most such crises are "pick and shovel" jobs, and require little more than a telephone call or two to verify the situation, gather data, and' prepare the informative issue paper or response. The highly sophisticated, technically demanding, event-shaping analyses so often discussed in the literature usually arise only a few times each year. But, they appear often enough to challenge the more creative analysts who inhabit effective public policy shops.

MATCHING REALITY AND THEORY

Obviously, not all of the facets of policy analysis as it is practiced have been covered. However, one purpose of this chapter is to begin a dialogue with those who teach the policy sciences and public administration to suggest that the realitites surrounding public policy

analysis in practice are often very different from those portrayed in
the literature. In the spirit of assisting change, we suggest two types
of modifications—one in teaching policy science and another in organizing to practice it. These suggestions may already be known to
many readers, but are repeated here to advocate that more emphasis
be placed on their adoption.

- *Training*. The teaching of policy science and analysis is a recent
  phenomenon. In fact, there are relatively few schools across the
  country where students can major in the subjects, and most of these
  are at the graduate level. More characteristically, policy sciences
  are covered in a department or school of public affairs. Practical
  considerations do not require that policy instruction be a part of a
  formal policy curriculum, but at least a few courses which address
  policy should be taught in the social sciences, engineering, economics, and public administration departments. Although the specific topics taught in any one of these places would depend upon the
  department and the school, it seems clear that a certain minimum
  set of concepts, methods, data handling, and practicalities should
  be covered.

- *Teaching, not Preaching*. Policy analysis came into vogue in the
  1950s and 60s and developed through extensive use of the concepts
  of systems analysis and operations research. These were the days of
  "whiz-kids" at the Pentagon, a resurgence of faith in the solutions
  offered by science and technology, the New Frontier, and the slo-
  gan "If we can get you to the moon, we can . . . [the reader is to
  supply the appropriate words]."

  It is the opinion of many, then and now, that the officials who
  make public policy are inept, relying on guesses—or worse, on
  falsified information—to make decisions. An often repeated theme
  has been that the practitioners of policy analysis should move aside
  and let the new policy science specialist, armed with methods and
  models, show public officials how analysis and decision making
  should be done.

  Our plea is that instead of building more abstract and rhetorical
  arguments for how analysis ought to be done, more time should be
  spent in preparing future analysts to perform in the situations in
  which actual decisions are made. This is not to say that no time
  should be spent in improving the state of the art in practical policy
  analysis, but that less niggling and armchair philosophizing should
  be done in this field.

- *Case Studies.* The teaching of business administration, pioneered in such places as Harvard, makes extensive use of case studies of actual business situations tailored for the classroom. Similar courses in the field of public administration exist, but there appear to be few in the field of policy analysis.

  One possible reason for this paucity of case histories on the evolution of public policy is that this sort of history is often subject to "laundering" for public consumption. The behind-the-scenes dealing, the repetitive analyses often focused on irrelevant minutiae, the glaring errors of analysis, the influence of personalities, the politics of the issue, the happy coincidences, the sheer bad luck are left out. And yet, as we have noted above, these events so often are principal elements that influence specific policy decisions.

  Two improvements seem to be warranted. First, a series of candid case studies should be prepared so that the parties involved are not embarassed, but are provided full disclosure of the details of how a policy was analyzed and decided on. Business schools have augmented their case studies with the formal technique of mock governing. Possibly, some form of role playing in the public sector could be equally useful to the students. Second, a meaningful work-study program where students become involved in a more realistic policy process should be developed.

  Since many policy issues are delicate and full disclosure is not readily available even after a considerable length of time, and since they require a certain degree of trust on the part of those involved, along with commitment to goals or ideals of the group, case studies and on-the-job training will not be easy to implement. And yet, if we do not begin to move toward this approach, we shall continue to be guilty of teaching analysts to seek change in the system of policy analysis without ever understanding many of the realities that have significant influence on the system.

  In the end, the people who pay for the inadequacies of the educational system are those who are taught by it. If the educators alone are to revolutionize the system, they are almost surely doomed to frustration and failure. Chief among administrative realities is that all large bureaucratic systems eventually become designed to resist change, particularly the type of change which is driven by frontal assaults.

- *Techniques.* In spite of our complaints that students are taught to an excess that policy analysis can actually be done in a purely analytical fashion, we do believe they should be well grounded in the analytical techniques that are fundamental to practicing their art. However, a few curriculum improvements, of the type mentioned in this paper, might be considered with additional warning. Many schools, in an attempt to soften what appeared to be an overly rigorous engineering perspective to policy studies, have introduced a course or two aimed at giving students a broader purview, giving them a glimpse of the so-called "big picture." Care has to be taken that this worthwhile trend does not go too far and that students not turn out to be better grounded in how to make use of an analytical result than in how to do the analysis.

More to the point, research should be undertaking to devise better methods of teaching and performing policy analysis, so that the less quantifiable, more dynamic and realistic factors can be melded into the analysis. Parallel to, or perhaps subsequent to instruction in rigorous techniques, less rigorous methods need to be taught. Guidelines, as contrasted to methodology, might be experimented with. In spite of the analytical assaults sometimes mounted on complex issues, the key elements on which the issue is decided are often of a political nature. Superb analysis may go wanting when decision alternatives are not clear-cut.

More attention should be paid to presentation of results and to understanding the needs of particular policymakers. Term papers, theses, or articles—time-tested teaching devices—could be replaced by issue papers and decision memoranda based on samples from the policymaking world.

- *Formalism.* Attempting to discover order and structure in one's endeavor is a feature of the scientific approach, the constant seeking of a natural law or set of underlying principles to explain the occurrence of a set of phenomena, thus allowing generalization and prediction.

  Unfortunately, in policy analysis, the attempt to catalogue problems, techniques, or analytical methods can lead to excessive formalism. Structuring a problem into well-defined categories may make for analytical neatness and may be required to permit the analyst to utilize a particular set of analytical tools, but such structuring may not result in a useful approach to provide analytical support for decisions on real-world problems.

  Our goal should be to teach the new analyst not to structure an issue analysis merely to fit a "pet" technique in his kit bag but to reduce it to those few significant variables upon which a decision should be based and then to decide which one of the analytical tools most aptly fits the issue at hand. Horvath has expressed this point a bit differently. He feels that we need to give more emphasis to the problems of reducing real-life complexities to manageable abstractions: why, how, error limits, and so on.

SETTING UP A POLICY SHOP

Having made some suggestions on what should be done to improve the teaching of policy analysis, let us turn to a description of where such analyses will be carried out in the public sector. A better understanding of how a policy analysis group should look and operate might make it easier for those who teach or for those who are learning to relate the technical details of analytical methods to ultimate performance. Unfortunately, even here the real world refuses to yield to the neatness one might like when describing how such analyses are performed.

In truth, we might be judged guilty of what we have accused others of, namely, describing what ought to be rather than what is. Our only defense is that many policy operations are a mix of all of the functions we will describe; our discussion is to facilitate understanding. In the end, to escape the judgment of being "armchair philosophers," we discuss a situation where such a structure is actually in operation.

We sketch here what we believe is necessary, in an institutional sense, to operate an effective policy analysis group or shop. At the outset, to be highly effective, policy analysis has to be performed by a captive in-house group, augmented as required by outside specialists in particular areas. There also should be those within the organization who at least keep up with, if not produce, new methods and new data sources, or a policy shop becomes intellectually bankrupt and outdated relatively quickly. In general, there are at least three levels of effort required in an effective policy shop; policy analysis, impact assessments, and methods and data research.

- *Policy Analysis.* The analytical group should be almost totally involved with identifying and analyzing issues and producing the responses, briefings, and reports which communicate their work to decision makers. The group should be fully engaged in issue analysis and yet have a large enough staff to enable a sufficient division of labor, with experts in the various disciplines that must be covered to adequately serve the policymaker.

Much of their time will be spent keeping abreast of the continually changing public policy climate, attending meetings, participating in task forces, and reporting on issues of concern to the policymaker. They are constantly communicating—orally, in formal briefings, or in writing. Their expertise allows them to respond to simple queries on policy issues efficiently, although this is clearly not the most exciting part of their job. They prepare issue papers that consist of a statement of the issue, a paragraph on background, several alternative actions that could be taken, an analysis of the impacts of these alternatives and a timetable for action.

Finally, the policy analyst is expected to prepare comprehensive reports on major current issues, examining the issue in depth. Although most of the work to prepare these studies could be handled by an analyst, given sufficient time, in practice often such is not the case. Even if analysts are experts in an area, they often have to seek help, which can range from requesting information from a colleague to contracting for the preparation of background papers and the assembly of pertinent data. Further, issues have an unpredictable flare-up factor; controversy or interest in an issue may become so intense that the analyst is unable to keep up with the output demanded. However, the analyst is held responsible for preparation of the analyses and the presentation of findings, regardless of the sources of the information used in the analysis.

The individuals who make up policy groups are usually motivated less by the drive to make professional contributions than by being in on the decision making process. They build up a network of analysts and other contacts in a variety of other organizations, realizing that this network is an essential elements in their efficiently responding to a broad range of issues.

- *Assessment*. Longer-term, incisive impact assessments should be obtained in another section of a policy shop. Staff in the assessment group have the responsibility for carrying out the more complex, in-depth analyses which are the essential grist for the policy analyst. At times, assessments force issues into the open. A well-reasoned, documented assessment can bring to light an issue not currently under consideration and focus it for the policy analyst to consider.

Topics chosen for assessment require experience, sensitivity, and a degree of clairvoyance. Ideally, no assessment would be undertaken unless it was in support of a policy analysis. However, because the analyst suffers from shortening of vision (policy myopia being an occupational hazard) brought on by the brushfire realities of the job and because there is a purposely defined mismatch between the time lines of policy analysis and impact assessment, the interaction of policy needs with assessment outputs is frequently charged with serendipity. Although continual communication between the policy and the assessment groups is needed, this is less likely to focus on specific assessments than on sensitizing the assessment people to the form and content of an assessment if it is to contribute to a relevant policy issue.

Assessments can be large interdisciplinary projects taking several years to complete and requiring a considerable expenditure of resources, or they can be short enough to feed directly into the policy stream. The output of assessment work generally has a wider audience than the policy analysts.

Whether the people who work in the assessment shops actually prepare assessments is a question of style and workload. It is our preference to have those who manage specific assessments also publish in the same area. Managers of government policy shops are readily aware that manpower shortages can often reduce the staff to contract managers. If the professional contract managers also do research, however, the continual development of their talents has several obvious advantages. These reseachers command greater respect from the people who are performing contract work for them. There is also less chance of shoddy, poorly reasoned work sliding by, both because the research manager is more apt to be on his professional toes and because the contractor is apt to sense this, too. If the assessments manager is a recognized expert in a relevant field, he is also an asset not to be overlooked by the policy analyst, who is often looking for experts with whom to consult.

One important function of the assessment group is to act as a repository of methods, data, and information that have been used in previous studies, or are being developed or researched. The availability of previous works, new and improved methods, and data resources means not only that the capability to respond rapidly to policy issues is enhanced but that the quality of such response is improved with each new assessment adding to the knowledge base.

- *Research.* Few areas have more theoretical attention and lead to less skilled application than policy research. Because resources are always scarce and the rewards from research distant and uncertain in a policy shop, the natural tendency, shortsighted as it may be, is to undercut research and focus on more pressing immediate matters. If policy-oriented research is tied to the policy shops and if the projects undertaken satisfy policy needs or assessment requirements anticipated in the future, then the research has a high potential for immediate and longer-range payoff. Most of the research in an active policy shop ought to be directed toward methods development, data manipulation, or aimed at insights into comparative analysis, presently a difficult field to quantify for complex issues.

The symbiosis suggested by melding the three areas of policy analyses, assessment, and research into one shop has obvious and significant benefits. Its greatest danger is that all groups will be drawn into fighting brushfires. The opposite problem of having the activities focused on research projects is not as great in an active shop, but cannot be ignored.

One method of handling these problems is to place these requirements in separate units of the organization, based on the strategy that the functions require different skills and so their separation is logical. On the other hand, by some mixing of staff from the different units on specific projects, the dangers of over specialization is minimized and individual analysts are able to do some intellectual dabbling in order to keep their skills sharp. No single approach will fully overcome the inherent organizational barriers to cooperation among separate units in a policy shop.

SUMMARY

We have attempted to examine some of the current shortcomings in the practice and teaching of public policy analysis and focus on ways to achieve more productive and effective analyses. Since highly trained people are involved in public policy analysis activities, both inside and outside of government, there exists an excellent opportunity for preparing young analysts for the type of public policy work they are most apt to engage in. The result could be that the intial work they produce is more useful and the disappointment and disillusion they now tend to experience is much reduced. We have indicated some steps toward more honest teaching and organization, which could minimize the wasted talent and productivity. In the end, the big gainer is the public, who will get the quality of analysis that it feels is currently being paid for.

SUGGESTED READINGS

Coates, Joseph F. "What Is a Public Policy Issue?" *Judgement and Decision in Public Policy Formulation*. AAAS Selected Symposium 1 (1978), pp. 34–69.

Coates, Joseph F. and Vary T. Coates. Letter to the Editor (on graduate training and research on public policy). *Policy Sciences*, 9 (1978), 229–235.

Kerr, Donna H. "The Logic of 'Policy' and Successful Policies." *Policy Sciences*, 7 (1976), 351–363.

Lindblom, C.E. "The Science of Muddling Through." *Public Administration Rev.*, 19 (1959), 79–88.

Majone, Giandomenico, "On the Notion of Political Feasibility." *European J. of Pol. Research*, 3 (1975), 259–274.

Majone, Giandomenico, "Technology Assessment and Policy Analysis." *Policy Sciences*, 8 (1977), 173–175.

Mettsner, Arnold J. *Policy Analysis in the Bureaucracy*. Berkeley: Univ. of California Press, 1976.

Miles, Rufus E., Jr. "The Origin and Meaning of Miles' Law." *Public Administration Rev.*, 38 (1978), 309–403.

Quade, E.S. *Analysis for Public Decisions*. New York: American Elsevier, 1975.

Salisbury, Robert H. "The Analysis of Public Policy." *Politics, Policy, and Natural Resources*. Ed. Dennis L. Thompson. New York: Free Press, 1972, pp. 65–84.

Vaupel, James W. "Muddling Through Analytically." *Policy Sciences Review Annual*, Vol. 1. Beverly Hills: Sage, 1977, pp 44–66.

11

POLICY RESEARCH:
INDUSTRY OR SOCIAL MOVEMENT?

Edward W. Lehman

Not so long ago, my colleague, Dennis Wrong, quite rightly punctured the hubris of those he called "the *post* boys," those who are "defining our age as post-industrial, or post-bourgeois, or post-capitalist, or post-modern, or post-economic, or post-Christian, or post-Marxist, or post-traditional, or even post-civilized." He concluded: "Enough posts abound in contemporary social thought to build a picket fence!"[1] Nevertheless, it is impossible to deny that significant shifts have marked the landscape of all advanced societies. "Posts-" have become handy intellectual markings that many of us employ to designate these changes, although as signs they are better at telling us where we have come from than where we are going.

Yet virtually all "post-" analyses proclaim an alteration in the pivotal activities of advanced societies as a key ingredient of modernity. We have witnessed a more rapid growth in the production of services than of goods and a faster increase of service occupations than of manufacturing ones. Most important, however, the new age is decisively set off from earlier ones by a knowledge explosion and the

AUTHOR'S NOTE: *This chapter was written with support of NIMH Grant No. 5 R12 MH 27900 to the Center for Policy Research, Amitai Etzioni, principal investigator.*

growing dependence on specially created knowledge by both private and public power holders and decision makers. Daniel Bell, the chief prophet of "postindustrial society," says:

> After the Second World War, the scientific capacity of a country has become a determinant of its potential and power, and research and development (R & D) has replaced steel as a comparative measure of strength of the [world] powers. For this reason the nature and kinds of state support for science, the politicization of science, the sociological problem of the organization of work by science teams all become central policy issues in a post-industrial society.[2]

Too much time and energy have been spent on debating whether these changes are of the same magnitude as the transition of feudalism to capitalism. Not enough attention has been given to what we all can agree has happened: Today, large-scale bureaucratic enterprises—most especially the state—rely on endless streams of new data in order to back their power and to pursue ever broader yet subtler goals. In the past, comparable agencies depended more on conventional wisdom, received knowledge, traditional technologies, and long-standing bookkeeping and accounting procedures.

These changes rekindle interest in the *sociology of knowledge,* an ordinarily arcane subspecialty devoted to delving into the interplay between how a society's members organize themselves and what they believe, value, and feel. This branch of sociology generally has been the province of those of a more speculative or theoretical bent. However, the current interest is with one of its most practical questions: How is knowledge for decision making best created, transmitted, and utilized? The most crucial locus for inquiry here has been the modern state, for this superbureaucracy serves as the main arena where the "big decisions" for society are hammered out. Thus, the perennial concerns of the sociology of knowledge are being expressed practically, that is, in an escalating call for more effective government policies and for a greater capacity to monitor and evaluate present programs. This amounts to asking: What are the institutions through which modern polities "think"; how are they organized; and how do they affect societal guidance?

"Sprouting up to offer answers," according to *Society,* "are numerous organizations and groups that claim expertise in cost-benefit analysis, program and policy research and evaluation, and various other analytical and crystal-ball skills."[3] Not surprisingly, the United States, the last most potent citadel of "free enterprise" and entrepreneurship, is at the hub of the policy-research revolution. Moreover, in the U.S., this revolution has features of both a social movement and an industry.

SOCIAL MOVEMENT VERSUS INDUSTRY

On the face of it, interpreting the proliferation of policy research centers in social movement or in industrial terms seems contradictory. A social movement perspective rivets attention on "a set of opinions and beliefs in a population which represents preferences for changing some elements of the social structure and/or reward distribution of a society."[4] The degree to which movements assume organizational expression—as well as the precise forms they take—varies widely. Clearly, the policy research revolution has social movement traits insofar as it is spearheaded by intensively trained enthusiasts who declare that society can (indeed, *must*) be seen and reshaped, using the tools of the behavioral sciences, operations and systems research, or a myriad of other new social and administrative technologies. In Marxian terms, this outlook would be said to consist of both an ideology and a praxis.

Yet policy research has also become a major American industry. Currently, the federal government spends over $100 billion a year on grants and contracts to "experts," usually lodged in policy research institutes or corporations. Indeed, Guttman and Wilner tell us that a "perusal of the Washington, D.C. Yellow Pages suggests that they are the largest industry in the nation's capital. A recent edition lists about 120 'economic and social researchers,' 90 'economists,' 150 'educational researchers,' 400 'management consultants,' and 15 'urban affairs consultants.'"[5] But not all the "producers" in the industry have bloomed recently; a few have been around for more than a generation. Although I use the term "industry" because all the "firms" generate an analogous package of products, not all "the firms" are part of the business, for-profit sector. The remainder call themselves "nonprofit," although many bear an uncanny resemblance to their for-profit cousins. Others look remarkably like traditional university-based social science research institutes.

A common thread unites the interpretations of policy research as a social movement and as an industry.[6] It permits us to understand more clearly the origins, morphology, products, and consequences of this striking phenomenon. This thread is deliberately macrosociological and interorganizational insofar as it casts the critical unit of analysis as a population of organizations rather than research organizations taken singly. Such a perspective demands that we see society and polity as providing the infrastructure which policy research organizations (and the overall movement and industry) use and depend upon. Especially critical is how the flow of projects, money, facilities, and personnel articulates with policy research activities and the organizational forms they take.

Reliance on the dual metaphor of movement and industry prevents us from being boxed in by macroeconomic assumptions which tend to treat noneconomic variables as disconcerting "noise" in the system. Macroeconomics would hold us too tightly to the view of policy research as merely what is produced by the aggregate "firms" in the "policy research industry." But the addition of a social movement perspective leavens understanding in two ways. First, it prevents us from neglecting the unique historical forces that propelled policy research activities. Second, it provides us with a mechanism for dealing with the extraordinary diffuseness and breadth of product-lines in the policy research sector.

HISTORICAL FACTORS

The first point signals that conventional macroeconomic analyses of industrial growth and diversification and of firm expansion and specialization cannot do justice to the historical vortex which molded the policy research revolution. To see the revolution in social movement terms more easily centers attention on the unique events around which history often pivots. In other words, analogies to the growth of other major industries (e.g., automobiles) yields more confusion than clarification. Conventional economic models of industrial development cannot account adequately for the upsurge of government interest in the creation and use of practical knowledge over the past four decades. A grasp of the events surrounding World War II and its aftermath renders a far sharper portrait of what has happened.

Without question the critical episode which towers over all other events of the period is the founding of Rand (an acronym for research and development) in 1947. Rand began as a task force inside the Douglas Aircraft Corporation during World War II. Its original charge, upon becoming a separate corporate entity, was to develop techniques for the Air Force's air wave tactics and strategy. Very rapidly, this "nonprofit" corporation became the Air Force's principal advisory arm although it also conducted research for other government agencies, perhaps most notably the Atomic Energy Commission. More recently, Rand, in line with a national trend, has expanded its horizons to domestic policy spheres, although defense research remains its single most important concern (if volume of contracts is any indicator in such matters).

Rand's unique reputation was solidified by a single, now legendary, project. In 1951, one of its top political scientists, Albert Wohlstetter, undertook a study for the Air Force to find the most efficient way to acquire and build overseas air bases. That same year, Congress had appropriated about $3.5 billion for air-base construction, nearly half of it for facilities overseas. Gradually, Wohlstetter's team came to recognize the faulty premises upon which planning for overseas bases was built. No consideration had been given to their vulnerability to conventional or nuclear attack. After much politicking and resistance, the Air Force revised its strategy to fit in with Wohlstetter's recommendations. Most observers agree that Rand's willingness to challenge its ultimate patron's most cherished assumptions not only revised strategic military planning but also saved the Air Force at least a billion dollars. Needless to say, this study and Rand as an overall model had strong reverberations for federal policy research initiatives on both the military and domestic scenes. RAND's reputed success was generally attributed to two factors: detachment of researchers and pundits from direct federal bureaucratic control coupled with a "special" relationship between Rand and the USAF, a relationship in which high levels of continuous funding and contact were believed to breed trust and mutual understanding. This bond became a paradigm for other defense "think tanks." In the euphoria of the War on Poverty, numerous aspirants for the status of "domestic Rands" sprang up. The Urban Institute, founded in 1968, was explicitly described as an "Urban Rand."

Thus, the model of industrial development in which many small "cottage" enterprises are later superseded by a few, large bureaucratic and more specialized firms does not hold for policy research. The industry began with a large, well-financed enterprise precisely because it was also a social movement launched under federal auspices. Clearly, the governmental sector which served as the springboard for the new industry-movement was not chosen at random. America in the mid-twentieth century was only willing to focus federal wealth and political initiative behind military and foreign policy explorations. A War on Poverty only became possible after policy research had apparently proven its mettle in the cold war on communism. (Of course, the quagmire of Vietnam later came to cast doubt on the utility of cold war planning.)

DIVERSE PRODUCTS

The second reason for mixing industrial with social movement analyses is, you will recall, to cope with the complexity of organizational products. Industries are usually defined in terms of a closely linked array of goods or services which they produce. But policy research organizations generate a spectrum of outputs which makes it difficult to pin the label "industry" unambiguously. Use of the term "think tank" illustrates the diversity of products. Some policy institutes (e.g., Rand, Brookings, the Center for the Study of Democratic Institutions) wear the tag "think tank" unequivocally because they provide a setting where policy pundits cogitate, exchange ideas, and issue position papers. Other policy institutes cannot be considered "think tanks" at all since the major activities include proposal writing, data generation and analysis, and the preparation of final reports under the pressure of writing more proposals.

However, the outlines of a possible universe of centers becomes clearer if we see policy researchers as marching under the banner of a social movement. Social movements, after all, are marked more by a commitment to a Great Cause than by a grinding out of narrowly defined organizational products. Yet even supplementing an industrial perspective with a social-movement one does not totally resolve the problem. No consensus exists about the nature of the universe. Virtually everyone agrees that places like Rand and the Brookings

Institution belong to the universe. But what about organizations which began as, and continue to play, management consulting roles (e.g., Arthur D. Little) or those who still do a considerable amount of traditional social science research (e.g., Institute for Social Research)? Should one include only established institutes, or should fledgling agencies also be in the universe? How about centers engaged in training graduate students or conferring degrees (e.g., the Wright Institute)? What should one do about organizations whose official mandates are policy research but who freely acknowledge that some of their investigations are basic research (e.g., the Center for Policy Research)? Is policy research only prospective (i.e., geared toward new programs) or is it also retrospective? That is, is evaluation research an integral part of policy research or not? How loosely (or tightly) ought one to define research? Should we use strict academic standards for scientific research and hence risk excluding advocates such as the Hastings Center or the Center for the Study of Responsive Law? Finally, if we include "advocacy" centers, how broad should the political spectrum be? For instance, if social movements aim at changing the social structure, what does one do with conservative "think tanks" such as the American Enterprise Institute or the Hoover Institution at Stanford University?

Analogies to social movements are also helpful here. A social movement usually has one or more organizations at its hub, but it is set off from workaday bureaucracies because it has access to other persons and groups on its periphery who are not part of the core organizations. Similarly, the policy research field consists of a "hard core" of obvious institutes and a larger number on the periphery that shade over into other types (management or social science research, public advocacy work, evaluation research, policy research training). I believe that policy research as a social movement compels us to include these relatively peripheral enterprises in any analysis and not to focus exclusively on hard core institutes.

COMPARING INSTITUTES

Of course, the organizations in such a universe differ from one another in ways other than "product-line." They vary widely in such commonsense traits as age and size. In a recent study, Anita M.

Waters and I found that the 33 policy centers we sampled ranged in age from 90 years to 1 year, in staff size from 3,000 to 6, and in annual (1976) revenues from $104.6 million to $70 thousand.[7] However, despite the magnitude of these variations, age and size alone do not yield useful directions for getting a better understanding of the dynamics of the policy research revolution.

Another strategy for trying to get a handle on the phenomenon is in terms of two conflicting models of successful policy research. One model extols the university-based social science research bureau as the ideal type for reliable policy analysis. The argument here is that an academic setting, with its flexible structure and highly professionalized staff, generally turns out research of superior quality. Not surprisingly, those advancing this prototype are themselves usually social scientists with university affiliations.[8]

Others, however, argue that the academic ethos is a poor guide for workable policy analysis, indeed that academic criteria tend to confuse the difference between basic and policy research. The latter should be as concrete as possible, whereas basic research seeks the most generalizable findings. Moreover, the erratic and unpredictable shift from grant to grant by academic researchers, it is held, fails to provide the continuity and the follow-through that policy research demands in order to have practical import. Thus, the second model of successful policy research points to structures of a more stable, permanent, and formal character.

The differences between the polar models for policy research are often couched in terms of profit versus nonprofit or entrepreneurial versus academic research. Such an approach is still commonsensical in that it invokes a typology based on the assessment and language of "everyday" actors. Yet, some nonprofit organizations share key traits with for-profit institutes. Moreover, entrepreneurship is hardly absent from academic research settings. Indeed, entrepreneurship is often a vital "profit-making" mechanism in ostensibly not-for-profit corporations.[9]

Sociologists are generally more comfortable in analyzing and comparing organizations in terms of structural properties, i.e., in terms of how the parts of the system relate to one another. In my own research, I have found it convenient to contrast policy research centers in terms of the internal locus of control of major goal-decisions, i.e., those key decisions about what kinds of research projects to pursue and how available funds are to be allocated. Thus, Anita Waters and I distinguished among four types of control structures which set off policy research institutes from one another: bureaucratic, semibureaucratic, semicollegial, and collegial.

Bureaucratic centers have their pivotal goal-decisions (i.e., research priorities) shaped mainly by a central administration. Yet, as professional organizations, even the most bureaucratic policy centers are generally not so hierarchic and formalized as the typical business concern. In our own research, all of the officially for-profit centers and the majority of institutes with a heavy defense focus fall into a bureaucratic mold. Examples are Arthur D. Little, Mathematica, Rand, and Institute for Defense Analyses. We also found that bureaucratic centers are the oldest, largest, and best-funded units and that the age, size, and economic viability generally decrease as we move toward the collegial end of the continuum.

In semibureaucratic centers, an elite group of senior professionals emerges as a source of strategic decisions. Here decisions are ordinarily made in concert with the highest-ranking administrators. Although the bureaucratic category contains a contingent of formally nonprofit centers, our research indicated that all semibureaucratic cases (as well, indeed, as all semicollegial and collegial ones) are exclusively nonprofit. The Brookings Institution is perhaps the quintessential semibureaucratic center.

Semicollegial structures fall between the semibureaucratic and purely collegial categories. We found university-based centers to be concentrated in either the semicollegial or collegial categories, although both contain a variety of other nonprofit types. Key priorities in semicollegial settings are set by the senior staff acting as a kind of committee-of-the-whole. Wisconsin's Institute for Research on Poverty is an example of a university-linked semicollegial center, and the Center for the Study of Democratic Institutions and the American Enterprise Institute are two nonacademic instances.

In the purely collegial case, responsibility for designing and running research projects devolves mainly on principal investigators. Decisions here are atomistic in the sense that one investigator's choices are not coordinated with and do not impinge directly on those of others. Most organizational groupings exist only for the lifetime of an individual project. Much the same goes for personnel: There are no organizational careers; staff is recruited anew for each project, not from a pool of career-oriented employees. This pattern prevails because of the centrality of principal investigators who must solicit their own research funds and hire their own staffs. Our research suggests that collegial institutes are far more *transient* than the other three types mainly because of their newness, small size, and precarious funding. Buffalo's (SUNY) Center for Policy Studies is an example of a university-based collegial center, and the Center for Policy Research illustrates an independent nonprofit type.

Of course, bureaucratic and collegial elements are found in all four control types. The issue is one of relative proportions. Even senior researchers in bureaucratic settings have some responsiblity for "drumming up new business." Yet this factor becomes more and more the central trait as we move toward the collegial end of the continuum where it emerges as the decisive feature. Conversely, collegial centers have the rudiments of a central administration, but this element becomes the dominant factor only when we reach the bureaucratic category.

THE LARGER SYSTEM

However, the analysis of policy research as a blend of social movement and industry traits requires that *external structure* also be looked at. Once society and polity are treated as the infrastructure within which policy research occurs, a study of how policy research institutes organize themselves internally will not suffice, for the needs and demands of the state have a decisive effect on the interior life of these centers. How institutes obtain revenues and the types of relationships they forge with the government impinge on control structure, probably a host of other administrative and professional arrangements, and most certainly, the kind of impact they are likely to have on policy.

Stable, ongoing funding is a blessing to which all policy research centers aspire. All else equal, their viability grows with the size of their financial cushion against the vagaries of the grantsmanship economy and the mercurial good will of potential benefactors. Stable, long-term funding takes several guises. Internally generated revenues are the most stable of stable funds. Large endowments (preferrably invested in high-yield stocks and bonds) loom most significant here, although fees from publications and conferences sometimes also play an important role. The Brookings Institution is often seen as an exemplar of this happy state of affairs. By deliberately remaining of moderate size and setting aside unrestricted foundation grants and individual bequests, it has tripled the proportion of its income from endowments as well as publications, rentals, and conference fees since 1965 and now draws over half its annual revenues from such sources.

The consequences for Brookings' structure are significant. Endowment and related income are centrally controlled and allotted to areas of research officially designated by the board of trustees. Yet the independence such income affords allows the senior staff members considerable latitude in molding their own research interests. But Brookings is an exception rather than the rule. No other major center approaches Brookings' ability to rely on endowment.

In some instances, the federal government provides the cushion of stable funding. Whatever the legalities, this is the real grounding of support for the major defense "think tanks" such as Rand and the Center for Naval Analyses. These institutes are marked by bureaucratic control structures, permanent departments, and a regular staff. These arrangements allow the same top personnel to interact regularly with key defense officials (often former colleagues).

As I noted previously, the 1960s saw a push to replicate defense-style "think tanks" on the domestic front. Thus, the Urban Institute was begun in 1968 with special funding from HUD and HEW with the pious hope that it would emerge as the Urban Rand. Other institutes, such as the University of Wisconsin's Institute for Research on Poverty, have also sprung up with similar ties to domestic agencies. Most of these places have also been able to establish relatively stable, permanent structures because of such long-term financing; however, they tend not to be as hierarchical as the defense "think tanks." In the study of 33 policy research institutes, those with stable federal funding for domestic purposes were generally semibureaucratic in form.

Stable support from private foundations produces much the same pattern. For example, the Washington-based Resources for the Future has a relationship with the Ford Foundation reminiscent of special governmental links—ongoing support and interaction between researchers and funding agency personnel—except that the foundation's grants to RFF are largely unrestricted. Ford currently provides about 90 percent of its revenues. These circumstances allow an institute to initiate almost all its own programs and to abstain from contract research. At the same time, continuous support over many years (a quarter of a century in the case of Resources for the Future) has permitted considerable centralization of control, at least in administrative matters.

These forms of stable funding have another effect which is as important as the fiscal cushion they provide. Reliable, long-range support, in the forms I have just described, tends to be *nonprescriptive*. That is, the grantor does not spell out every job-and-title of the recipient's obligations but rather yields the latter considerable leeway in interpreting the mandate. The granting agency does not always intend to be nonprescriptive, but long-term relationships ultimately require a large dose of mutual tolerance and trust. Wohlstetter's triumph over Air Force intransigence was no fluke nor merely the product of the inherent virtue of facts. It was the most plausible outcome of the mutual dependence which had built up between the Air Force and Rand. At the opposite extreme, one finds federal contract research (or RFPs—Requests for Proposals), for which fledgling for-profit enterprises are forced to struggle. Contract research is usually short-term and is highly prescriptive, i.e., detailed in research objectives, confining in design, and extremely constraining in budgets and timetables.

All of this clearly suggests that stable, long-term funding is also a critical indicator of a "special relationship" with federal agencies. Indeed, some critics charge that a "revolving door" of staff exists between federal decision makers and policy research centers akin to the links between regulatory agencies and the industries they allegedly supervise. Waters and I studied this factor by asking administrators at each of the 33 centers how many former staff members are now in federal service and how many present staff members were formerly in the federal government. We then added the two to gain a revolving-door index. Centers with scores of 20 or more are assumed to have a rapidly turning revolving door with the federal government and those with scores of under 20 a slowly turning one. Not surprisingly, bureaucratic institutes are most likely to use the revolving door, collegial institutes are least likely, and semibureaucratic and semicollegial organizations are somewhere in between.

Proximity to the nation's capital has also been mentioned as a possible sign of a "special relationship." Here again, bureaucratic centers hold a place of prominence. Eight of ten bureaucratic agencies in our sample have offices in or around Washington, D.C. Five of the eight are branches. Four of these five happen to be the largest centers in the study. Thus, bureaucratic centers—the largest, oldest, most formal, and best funded institutes—have the greatest access to the federal government, both through the rotation of staff and physical proximity. If such ties affect policy, then bureaucratic centers have a decided edge over other types.

IMPACT

But who and what in the policy research field are most likely to affect government activity? Of course, phrasing the question in this way presumes that an impact exists. In fact, there is a curious split in thinking on this matter. Critics of the American system—both on the left and the right—ascribe near omnipotence to "think tanks," whom they see as agents of villianous elites. From the right, the cry goes up for a counterbalancing "conservative Brookings," with the American Enterprise Institute and the Hoover Institution scurrying for the mantle. The fears of the left have received their most recent expression in a Nader-sponsored study by Daniel Guttman and Barry Wilner. Their book's title is *The Shadow Government*. The subtitle leaves no doubt about the authors' views of policy research: *The Government's Multi-Billion-Dollar Giveaway of Its Decision-Making Powers to Private Management Consultants, "Experts," and Think Tanks*.

The view from inside the system could not be more different. Senator William Proxmire regularly makes headlines with his "Golden Fleece Awards," which are attacks on allegedly trivial or impractical research into which the government has been pouring money. The rallying cry from within the federal bureaucracy is "research utilization." Those unfurling this banner point to the mountains of unread, undigested, or unfathomable reports gathering dust in the files and archives, and lament the prospects that most sponsored research will never have any impact. Periodic conferences about research utilization appear. More and more agencies require "utilization and dissemination plans" as an integral part of research grant proposals.

The truth, as usual, probably lies somewhere in between. No intricate research design is needed to zero in on the centers with the most clout. Brookings, Rand, and a few of the other think tanks with strong ties to DOD are obvious candidates for centers with the ability for exceptional impact. On the other hand, in this sprawling industry-movement, most federal grants and contracts unquestionably bring forth reports destined for the governmental equivalent of the dead-letter office. The operation of the grantsmanship economy has a dynamic of its own which the informational needs of federal decision makers touches upon only occasionally. My own research corroborates this hunch. Waters and I created an Impact Ranking Scale, based on responses to our questionnaire by 33 center administrators. Respondents were asked to nominate their institutes' most influential public policy products. In the few cases where no nominations were made, we let secondary published sources do the nominating for us. Items were checked for accuracy and ranked on the following scale:

0 = No impact;

1 = Conferences or workshops, minor demonstrations;

2 = Information, testimony or reports to government agencies, courts, or legislative committees;

3 = Changed administrative routines or procedures, minor legislation;

4 = Helped shape key decisions, strategies, or tactics of agency or legislature;

5 = Helped create major programs or new agencies.[10]

Most of the 33 institutes have had some policy impact: all but four have Impact Ranking scores of at least 2. However, the overwhelming majority do not exhibit *exceptional impact* (by which we mean scores of 4 or 5). Eleven of the centers have had *modest impact* (score of 0 to 2); 14 have had *significant impact* (scores of 3); and eight have had exceptional impact. Only two institutes, Brookings and RAND, received a maximum score of 5.

Perhaps our most significant result was to link greater bureaucratization to successful policy impact. We found a step-by-step reduction in the proportion of centers with major impact as one moves from bureaucratic to semibureaucratic to semicollegial and, finally, to collegial. A similar pattern appeared when we computed median Impact Ranking scores for each control type. (See Table 11.1.) Such a finding should not surprise us in light of the data which indicate that bureaucratic centers are the largest, oldest, best funded and most formally structured institutes and that they have the most "special relationships" to the federal government. Indeed, these "special relationships," although linked to bureaucratization, also have independent effects. Purely collegial centers, on the other hand, offer a set of ad hoc arrangements which are too transient for exceptional impact.

Table 11.1   Control Structure of Policy Research
Institutes and Impact Ranking (n = 32)*

Control Structure	Number of Institutes with:			Median Impact Ranking
	Modest Impact (0-2)	Significant Impact (3)	Exceptional Impact (4-5)	
Bureaucratic (N=10)	0	5	5	3.5
Semibureaucratic (N=5)	0	3	2	3.3
Semicollegial (N=11)	6	3	1	2.0
Collegial (N=6)	5	1	0	1.5

SOURCE: Lehman and Waters, in *Policy Analysis, 15 (1979), 217.*
*One case did not fit the classification scheme

These results may seem self-evident, but, at first blush, they also appear to fly in the face of two other recent studies. Bernstein and Freeman report that "academic" centers as opposed to "entrepreneurial" ones are more likely to produce evaluation research of superior quality.[11] Insofar as academic probably correlates with collegial and entrepreneurial with bureaucratic, do the two sets of findings necessarily contradict each another? I think not, because Bernstein and Freeman were trying to explain differences in the rigor of research styles whereas Lehman and Waters were in the business of accounting for variations in clout in Washington, D.C. Indeed, a complementarity may exist between the two bodies of data. This potential has led Stuart Nagel to suggest, in the 1978 edition of *Policy Research Centers Directory,* "What might be ideal are more research centers that combine the qualities mentioned by Freeman and Bernstein with the impacts mentioned by Lehman and Waters." However, it is also plausible that adhering to the orthodoxies of contemporary social science methodologies may actually dilute the prospect of being heard by decision makers. At the very least, it may make packaging acceptable recommendations more difficult.

Carol Weiss has found that government decision makers report being influenced strongly, but indirectly, by academic research.[12] Do her data contradict the association between bureaucratization and impact? I think not; rather they point to additional implications of policy research which have not yet been tapped fully. Policy research has many potential consequences. The direct shaping of policies is one of these, and influencing the mind-set of officials is another. The latter consequence may have an effect on policy albeit an indirect one. The indirect effects of policy research centers are a vital issue for future research. Weiss' study touches on one key sector in this regard, but it is not the only possible one. Policy research has other potential consumers than government officials. More research needs to be done on how it is filtered to the general public and whether and how it molds public opinion. The advocacy centers set up by Nader and his raiders have unquestionably reverberated on public opinion. But how about other centers? Moreover, "critical communities" such as interest groups, the mass media, academics, and "unattached intellectuals" all are consumers of policy research. How such communities acquire and use information—and the impact of such activity on public policy—warrants detailed study.

CONCLUSIONS

We can jettison all the "post-whatever" labels, but we cannot deny that advanced societies have entered a new stage in recent times. Centers which churn out the rather diffuse array of products which we have come to call "policy research" are an integral aspect of that new era.

But are these institutes permanent fixtures or a passing fad? The recognition that policy research is simultaneously a social movement and an industry helps answer this question. Such a perspective makes the role of the state and the larger political system central. Once we see that we have only experienced the beginnings of the activist state, we will have to agree that policy research is still in its infancy, too. Particular centers may disappear, but the industry-movement will expand.

In short, the state will continue to grow, and hence so will policy research. The activist state is an insatiable consumer of information, but an activist orientation may also widen the gap between needed and available information even while society's pool of new knowledge increases. Moreover, dependence on information can be addictive: larger and larger doses are needed to keep the user content. The trappings of rational planning have become more central to political life. Modern political leaders are unwilling to rely on muscle and bluff alone to get their way. They want to know as much as possible about alternative courses of actions. They expect policy research to produce this type of information. Thus, the informational capacity of today's world is expanding, but it has difficulty keeping pace with the state's yearning for the veneer of rational sophistication.

The addiction to information fosters strong pressures for a tighter bond between the state and the creators of policy research. The "special relationships" between federal agencies and large, more bureaucratic, and better established centers (which our research and the work of others point out) attest to the potency of these pressures. The fact that bureaucratic centers and those with special relationships have the most immediate policy impact provides added testimony for the pressure for tight bonds. The linkage between DOD and the major defense "think tanks" are the most visible prototypes of such a relationship but certainly not the only intances.

Those with a narrow "managerial" outlook may applaud such ties and advocate more of them. Yet sociologists have known for some time that too snug a fit between information-creators and decision makers can also weaken the prospect for more effective social policy.[13] For one thing, fusing information and decision centers can lead to information blockages so that the right data fail to get to the appropriate decision makers. In addition, it may mean that political leaders will hear only what they want to hear. The quality of information will be impaired unless reports are allowed to contain "heretical" proposals, and this cannot occur within the bosom of the state.

Thus, too tight a bond between policy research and the state means that some alternatives will not be explored. It goes without saying that the bias here is decisively in favor of the most powerful and privileged elites. Yet, I am not calling for "disestablishment" of policy research as a remedy. Perhaps we need Rands—both military and domestic. But we also need centers that are outside the "special relationships" I have been speaking about. Each Rand needs to be balanced by an Institute for Policy Studies, which raises unpalatable questions and offers unfashionable solutions. Less dramatically, fledgling collegial institutes with a greater academic orientation also must be encouraged, even though their direct impact on policy is more modest. As I have indicated earlier, such centers may influence officials indirectly and stimulate the "critical communities" which are indispensable elements of a viable democracy.

Of course, providing support for "heretical" and fledgling institutes means that there will always be a utilization crisis. More position papers and reports will be generated than policy makers will ever be able to incorporate in the decision process. However, if only the "establishment" institutes receive backing, then we may be fostering a new power elite which is infinitely more threatening to a democratic system than the military-industrial complex ever was. In the new era the modern world has entered, a society that cannot ask the right questions or falters in getting the best information will ultimately fail.

NOTES

1. Dennis H. Wrong, "On Thinking About the Future," *Amer. Sociologist*, 9 (1974), 27.

2. Daniel Bell, *The Coming of Post-Industrial Society: A Venture in Social Forecasting* (New York: Basic Books, 1973), pp. 117-118.

3. "Social Science and the Citizen," *Society*, 14 (1977), 8.

4. John D. McCarthy and Mayer N. Zald, "Resource Mobilization and Social Movements: A Partial Theory," *Amer. J. of Sociology*, 82 (1977), 1216.

5. Daniel Guttman and Barry Wilner, *The Shadow Government: The Government's Multi-Billion-Dollar Giveaway of Its Decision-Making Powers to Private Management Consultants, "Experts," and Think Tanks* (New York: Pantheon, 1976), p. 4.

6. McCarthy and Zald's article, which treats social movements *as* industries, is instructive in this context.

7. Edward W. Lehman and Anita Waters, "Control in Policy Research Institutes: Some Correlates." *Policy Analysis*, 5 (1979), 201–221.

8. See, for example, Ilene N. Bernstein and Howard E. Freeman, *Academic and Entrepreneurial Research* (New York: Russell Sage, 1975).

9. See Amitai Etzioni and Pamela Doty, "Profit in Not-for-Profit Corporations: The Example of Health Care," *Pol. Sci. Q.*, 91 (1976), 437-441.

10. Both researchers independently ranked every institute's nominations. The agreement rate was almost 90 percent (29 of 33). In no case were discrepancies greater than one point on the scale. Discrepancies were resolved by way of a conference in which responses on the questionnaire were reviewed in light of published materials about the institute.

11. *Academic and Entrepreneurial Research.*

12. "Research for Policy's Sake: The Enlightment Function of Social Research," *Policy Analysis*, 3 (1977), 531-546.

13. See, for example, Amitai Etzioni, *The Active Society: A Theory of Societal and Political Processes* (New York: Free Press, 1968); and Harold L. Wilensky, *Organizational Intelligence: Knowledge in Government and Industry* (New York: Basic Books, 1967).

12

THE GAP BETWEEN KNOWLEDGE AND POLICY

Karin Dagmar Knorr

THE GAP BETWEEN KNOWLEDGE AND POLITICAL ACTION

The "gap" between knowledge and political action[1] has long been a topic of discussion for social scientists. Depending upon the theoretical perspective adopted, it has been associated with a conflict of norms and values between scientific and political institutions,[2] with different organizational forms underlying bureaucratic and professional patterns of activity,[3] or with the difference between "power" as characteristic of political systems and "knowledge" as characteristic of science.[4] The work of these as well as other authors[5] implies that the difficulties of establishing smooth relationships between the political and the scientific field derive from the different organizing principles of the subsystems involved. The most recent attempts to specify some of these principles are by Luhmann and Bourdieu.[6] Accordingly, Luhmann conceives of the scientific system as governed by the control mechanism *(Steuerungsmedium)* of "truth" as opposed to the mechanisms of "power" and "money" ascribed to the

AUTHOR'S NOTE: *I am heavily indebted to Paul Lazarsfeld and H.G. Zilian for their help in designing the study and for their comments on an earlier draft of this chapter. I also want to thank Donald Pelz for his suggestions and criticism, and to the Institute for the Study of Social Change,University of California, Berkeley, which facilitated the writing of this chapter.*

political and economic systems respectively. The scientific system is characterized by predominantly cognitive principles which operate toward eliminating deficiencies of knowledge and information. Truth, in contrast to power, is not a zero-sum resource. In other words, there is no constant sum of truth in the sense that the knowledge claims of one scientist must necessarily conflict with those of others in the area. This implies that there are no structural constraints which prevent cooperation in science, as opposed to the political system. Luhmann's approach suggests a contrast between *cognitive* (scientific) and *strategical* (political) action from which we can derive some of the problems alluded to when we talk about the gap.[7] However, I have argued elsewhere that scientific research is *not* primarily a cognitive undertaking.[8] On the contrary, it involves all the dimensions of an *agonistic practice*[9] we commonly attribute to more apparently social and competetive systems. Bourdieu's theory of scientific agents sheds light on some of the characteristics of this practice. According to Bourdieu, the scientific field is the locus of a competitive struggle for the monopoly of scientific credit—a credit that is at the same time scientific competence *and* social authority. The individual scientist's position in the field defines the moves he is apt to make, and, consequently, also his attitude towards political decision-making bodies. With this approach the gap between knowledge and practical action must be associated with the quasi-economical investments made by scientists and decision makers in fields which determine those investments. Investments once made will orient future action toward symbolic returns, such as gaining an impact on the "scriptures" of a field[10] or advancing in a political career. Given investments and the predominant impact of a field or "system" as stressed by both Luhmann and Bourdieu, what would we expect the interaction between social scientists involved in contract research and government agencies which finance this research to look like? Will potential conflicts be resolved through mutual adaptation proportional to the pressure that is exerted by the parties involved (such as economic pressure on the part of government agents and "reputational" pressure on the part of well-recognized scientists)?[11]

Traditionally, the above question was couched in terms of dysfunctional problems of adaptation which arise in accordance with a consumer-client model of the interaction between policymakers and social scientists.[12] In the present context, the focus is shifted to a model that emphasizes the actual *practice of production* in the respective scientific and political field. If this practice determines external arrangements, we would expect a certain amount of *subversiveness* to rule the scene of mutual interaction. In other words, we would expect the investments made in the respective field to assume priority over interests promoted by an "external" party (such as the government sponsor for the social scientist), a priority which is covered up by protective strategies. In order to establish the thesis, we have to show that scientists *and* decision makers succeed in utilizing the project according to their *own interests* to an extent unanticipated by the respective partners. The gap between knowledge and political action exists; the data which follow suggest that it might not exist to the disadvantage of both parties.

METHOD AND DATA

This chapter seeks to illustrate the degree of subversiveness as enhanced by the exigencies of the political and scientific field by drawing from seventy face-to-face interviews done in 1974 with medium level decision makers in Austrian federal and municipal government agencies (all located in Vienna) who were directly involved with contract research. The persons identified constitute a more or less complete set of government contractors in the city of Vienna, where more than 50% of Austrian social science government contract research is financed.[13] The study included only government officials who had financed at least one finished project in a social science discipline in the years preceding 1974. The distribution of projects over disciplines is as follows: sociology (51%), economics (24%), educational sciences (13.5%), urban and regional planning (4.5%), political sciences (4.5%) and others (2.5%). The frequency of projects classified as sociological reflects the predominance of social research and opinion surveys in government contract research. This should be kept in mind when reading the following analysis.

Responses from government officials are contrasted with data obtained from a survey of 628 Austrian social scientists done in 1973-1974, which included a set of questions equivalent to those that had been asked of the decision makers. The questions analyzed here refer to the "most recent finished research project" in which the scientist was involved. Needless to say, the same definition of social science which centers around the disciplines mentioned above (including psychology, contemporary history, and business administration) was used for both groups of respondents.[14] The population of social scientists analyzed for the present purpose excludes those researchers who had not done a contract research project during the respective years.

The present chapter relies on both responses to open-ended questions recorded on tape and answers given to standardized formulations. In accord with the goal of the present chapter, researchers and decision makers were asked to indicate the intended audience of their research and financing efforts, the scientific and other interest they realized in the project, the criticism they associated with various aspects of the research, and the degree of actual and perceived utilization of research results. The data illustrate the alleged subversiveness by showing how both parties profit from the exchange, mainly in terms of their own interests, and how this remains hidden to both of them. To highlight the discrepancies, answers from decision makers and social scientists are juxtaposed in the respective tables.

SYMPTONS OF THE GAP: INTENDED AUDIENCE OF RESEARCH PROJECTS

Table 12.1 shows the resulting distribution of answers by social scientists and financing government officials to a question as to the audience for which the results of the project were primarily intended on the part of the researcher. The question was introduced as a measure of the actual compliance of researchers with government officials' demands, given that the latter—in a government financed contract project—would certainly want themselves or the financing authority to be the main addressee of the project outcomes.[15] By confronting government officials with an equivalent question, it is learned to which degree government officials actually perceived this to be the case in the most recent social science project financed by them. As the table indicates, less than half of the scientists but more than three-quarters of the political officials hold the financing organization to be the main addressee of the study. Conversely, 18.5% of the scientists indicate that they intended the results primarily for the scientists of the respective specialty, but only 5% of the government officials had the same impression when confronted with the project report (see Table 12.1).

Table 12.1 Intended Audience of Contract Research Results According to Social Scientists and Sponsoring Government Officials

Main intended audience of project results	Reported by social scientists % Respondents (N = 259)	Reported by gov't. officials % Respondents (N = 67)
The scientific community of the respective speciality	18.5	5.0
The political decision makers or financing government agency	44.0	76.9
The general public	20.1	0.0
The groups concerned by the study	17.4	18.1

NOTE: The wording of the question to the scientists was as follows: "What target group did you mainly intend to address with your results?" The respondents had the choice to indicate one of the categories mentioned in the table. With government officials, answers were measured on a 100 point scale which was dichotomized at a cutting point of 50 for the present purpose.

It is interesting to note that not one of the government officials, yet about one-fifth of the scientists refer to the general public as of primary interest. As expected, social scientists working within universities are less inclined to accept political decision makers as their major reference group, even if financed by them in order to solve a practical problem. And although they seem more oriented toward the general public than nonacademic researchers, they are less interested in those actually concerned by a study.[16]

INTERESTS REALIZED
IN CONTRACT RESEARCH

The above results can be refined by examining the answers of social scientists and government officials as to the perceived degree to which (1) scientific interests of the social scientists, (2) their eventual social policy interests, and (3) concrete interests of the financing authority have been realized in a project. Again, we presuppose that political authorities financing a contract project will *intend* their cognitive and utilization interests to primarily guide the research—

which is not the same as saying that the researcher has to accept the financing authority's definition of the problem. It is interesting to note from Table 12.2 that a majority of government officials apparently *do* feel that their interests were primarily taken into account in the project (approximately 70% say their interests have been realized to more than 50%); and it is no less interesting to find that on the average only 34% of the social scientists (i.e., *less than half* of the percentage of government officials) say they actually *did* give the financing authority's interests such priorities (see Table 12.2).

Table 12.2   Realization of Different Interests on the Part of Social Scientists in a Contract Research Project as Claimed by Social Scientists and Perceived by Sponsoring Government Officials

Interests on the part of social scientists % Realized	Reported by social scientists % Respondents (N=240)	Perceived by gov't. officials % Respondents (N=87)
Scientific interests of the social scientists		
0	14.2	22.4
1–49	40.6	58.3
50–99	31.0	16.3
100	14.2	3.0
Social policy interests of the social scientists		
0	48.5	48.5
1–49	39.7	43.9
50–99	10.5	7.6
100	1.3	0.0
Concrete interests of the financing government agency		
0	31.8	9.1
1–49	33.9	21.0
50–99	29.3	54.7
100	5.0	15.2

NOTE: The wording of the question to the social scientists was as follows: "To which extent could scientific or other interests be realized in this project?" The respondent was asked to distribute 100% on the alternatives included in the table and on the alternative "Interests of the respective financing government agency as reinterpreted by you." The last alternative was excluded in the questionnaire addressing government officials; consequently, the data are not reported. The percentages are summarized here such as to keep extreme answers (0% and 100%) separate.

More striking perhaps is the fact that about one-third of the social scientists (31.8%) admittedly did *not* realize *any* interests of the financing organization in that project, yet on the average only 9% of the contracting agency's officials say the project did not meet any of their intentions. In accordance with this, more than 80% of the government officials believe that purely scientific interests granted to social scientists did not dominate in the project (i.e., have been realized to less than 50%)—a percentage which contrasts with the slightly more than 50% of social scientists who did not give scientific interests their priority. In general, both groups seemingly "overestimate" the realization of their own respective interests. Or, if we concede that both groups have a sound knowledge of what they actually gained from the project, one would have to say that the degree of *subversiveness* on the part of scientists in actually using the money for a realization of their own interests goes largely unnoticed on the part of the government officials, as does the degree to which the latter succeed in using the project to meet *their* intentions. The groups are *most* in agreement when evaluating the realization of interests which are of *no* direct concern to either one of them, i.e., when estimating social policy interests. Here, almost half the social scientists as well as half the government officials do not see any social policy interests realized in the project—which reveals something about the nature of the problems dealt with in government contract research and about the fact that there will be no subversiveness once the interests of none of the parties are at stake in a given area.

Table 12.3 confirms university researchers to be much less inclined to give priority to the concrete interests of government agencies and to have a higher probability to transform project designs according to their own scientific interests. However, it should be noted that even in the case of nonacademic research more than 50% of the researchers do not give government authorities' interests a priority (realization of interests less than 50%).

Table 12.3   Realization of Different Interests in a Contract Research Project by Social Scientists in Academic and Nonacademic Settings

Interests on the part of social scientists % Realized	Reported by social scientists in academic settings % Respondents (N=142)	Reported by social scientists in nonacademic settings % Respondents (N=98)
Scientific interests of the social scientists below 50%	46.1	67.4
50–100%	53.9	32.6
Concrete interests of the financing government agency below 50%	71.6	57.2
50–100%	28.4	42.8

ANTICIPATED AND ACTUAL CRITICISM
OF SOCIAL SCIENCE RESULTS

Our results so far have allowed us to illustrate the gap between the perceptions of members of the political and scientific system with respect to their actual points of contact and interconnection. Furthermore, we have seen an obvious success on the part of scientists and decision makers in adapting a piece of research for their own intended audience and interests, a fact that goes largely unnoticed. The following tables address the question as to what social scientists actually know about policymakers' *evaluation* and *utilization* of their results. We asked the social scientists what irritated them most with respect to the government agency's reading of their report, and we asked government officials what they and their superiors (if any) criticized most heavily in the report.[17] As Table 12.4 indicates, the amount of criticism on the part of government officials is in general *underestimated* rather heavily by social scientists. Furthermore, aspects criticized most often by government officials *do not match* those aspects for which most criticism is anticipated by the scientists (see table 12.4).

Table 12.4   Government Officials' Criticism of Final
Project Reports and Criticism Anticipated by Social
Scientists

Kind of criticism	Anticipated by social scientists % Respondents (N=240)	Made by gov't. officials % Respondents (N=67)
Results offer nothing new	8.9	43.1
Results are not concrete enough	26.0	51.1
Results contradict the expectation and opinion of government officials	15.6	36.7
Results are not in accordance with previous expert reports	6.3	38.5
Results might involve political difficulties	10.9	63.0
Results are too difficult to understand because of jargon	20.3	36.2

NOTE: The wording of the question to the social scientists was as follows: "Please think of the final project report. What kind of criticism on the part of government officials have you been mainly concerned with when writing the report?" Respondents were asked to indicate all categories which applied. The question to the government officials ran: "Please think once more of the final project report. What did you or those mentioned below (referring to supervisors or others not analyzed here) criticize it for?"

Table 12.4 testifies to a substantial lack of feedback about the kind and extent of criticism project reports attract from government officials. For example, less than 10% of the social scientists fear that their results might offer nothing new to their government sponsors, yet more than 40% of the sponsors actually criticize the project report, claiming that it did not offer anything new to them. Or, only approximately 10% of the social scientists anticipate that the results might involve political difficulties for the sponsors, but more than 60% of the government officials actually criticize the political inadequacy of results. Some aspects of the project are of primary concern to social scientists for their aptness of attracting criticism—like the fear that the results might not be "concrete" enough. Even there, the government officials criticizing this aspect outnumber to a large extent the percentage of scientists concerned with this criticism. The last aspect is, however, one of the rare cases which occupy about the same rank (as measured by the highest number of respondents citing it) in both populations.

In general, the different weight given to single items in the respective population and the social scientists' underestimation of the amount of criticism not only suggests a lack of information on the part of the latter but also indicates different standards of evaluation. As an example, many social scientists might consciously neglect political difficulties implied by their results while adhering to criteria imposed by their field and interests. The social scientists' general underestimation of criticism suggests that government officials do not communicate their critical reactions to the scientists. We will find this underestimation confirmed when we compare the perceived (on the part of social scientists) and actually reported (on the part of government officials) utilization of social science knowledge.

UTILIZATION OF
SOCIAL SCIENCE RESULTS

If responses of government officials can be trusted—and in order to make sure that they can be, standardized questions were supplemented by open-ended questions designed to allow us to learn "what actually happened"[18]—there is only a minor degree of absolute non-utilization of social science results. On the other hand, in any type of utilization explored, the percentage of social scientists who perceive their results as being "wasted," since never used, always remained above 60%. As implied previously, social scientists do not know much about the extent to which their results are being utilized. In a mutually sustained consumer-client definition of the situation, the relationship ends when the report is delivered to the financing agency. In addition, utilization on the part of the client will involve further processing of social science results in the political field. In other words, social science results will provide part of the basic material which is selected and transformed in the process of producing political decisions. This kind of utilization will be hardly visible to the social scientists, however. What emerges from a political mode of production in a political field is no longer a purely (and recognizably) scientific fact. Nor will government officials necessarily tend to emphasize the scientific origin of the hybrid, given that they need to highlight and legitimate their *own* competence and efficiency.[19]

Table 12.5 shows that utilization is most underestimated in the case of "basic information and support for measures and programs intended," a category that suggests further processing at a "decision-preparatory"[20] stage of the political production process. It is important to note that the first 3 kinds of utilization listed in table V as well as the last 2 items do correlate much higher with each other than items

Table 12.5   Extent of Nonutilization of Social
Science Research Results as Reported by
Government Sponsors and Social Scientists

No utilization in terms of:	Reported by government sponsors % Respondents (N=58)	Perceived by social scientists % Respondents (N=202)
Translation into significant practical action (1)	37.9	60.3
Basic information and support for measures and programs intended (2)	14.3	60.2
Sponsoring of further research (4)	38.2	70.8
Invitation of the scientists for advising or consulting purposes (5)	46.4	79.8

NOTE: The wording of the question to the government sponsors was as follows: "How were the results of the project utilized in the following respects?" The respondent was provided with the categories included in the table. Social scientists were asked: "As far as you know, how did the government sponsor utilize the results? Please indicate all categories that apply." Since positive answers were further elaborated in the questionnaire in a way irrelevant for the present context, the table gives the figures for definite nonutilization in both cases.

from the first set with those of the second set. Correlations between the first three items of table 12.5 range from .65 to .71, those between the first set and the second set are between .21 and .38, and the correlation between the last two items is high again: .54. This seems to imply two alternative action strategies of potential users: social science results are *either* directly translated into practical measures *and* used as information support *and* made known in the organization in question, *or* they lead mainly to the sponsoring of further research and to further "consulting" of the scientist.

Table 12.5 is confirmed by Table 12.6 which contrasts the degree of perceived and actual change of opinion experienced by government officials in connection with project results. Agreement is highest in the case of a "very strong"—and presumably more visible—change of opinion on the part of the decision maker. Interesting to note, the percentage of government officials who claim to have undergone at least a moderate change of opinion about a problem based on project results is fairly high (approximately two-thirds of the respondents), despite the critical attitude as documented in Table 12.4

Table 12.6 Extent to Which Government-Sponsored Opinions Changed Through Social Science Research Results as Reported by Government Sponsors and Perceived by Social Scientists

Degree to which opinion about the research problem changed with results	Reported by government sponsors % Respondents (N=58)	Perceived by social scientists % Respondents (N=169)
Strong or very strong change of opinion	8.6	10.7
Change of opinion in single respects	56.9	38.7
No change of opinion	34.5	50.6

NOTE: Government officials were asked to what degree they had changed their opinion about the problem area on account of the project results. They were provided with a 5-point Likert scale. Social scientists were asked "Did the government sponsor change his/her opinion about the problem on account of the project?" and provided with the above categories.

In order to obtain comparable categories, scores 4 and 5 of the Likert scale (strong and very strong change of opinion) were combined in the case of government sponsors, as were categories 2 and 3.

The last two tables—beyond yielding some insight into the actual degree of utilization of social science results in policy—provide us with a logical equivalent to the data presented in Table 12.1 and 12.2. There I was interested in showing the degree to which social scientists succeed in unnoticedly "using" a government-financed project for their own scientific and other interests by transforming it substantially. Here I intend to show the degree of actual utilization of project results in government client agencies, which apparently also goes largely unnoticed, this time by social scientists.[21] In the former case, it will be the contingencies of the scientific field which account for a certain amount of resistance and subversiveness of the scientists with a view to the interests of their government sponsors.[22] In the latter case, the reason for the scientists' underestimation of utilization may be found in the fact that the relationship between financing authority and social scientist often deliberately ends with the delivery of the report, and in the fact that government officials have a substantial interest in "reproducing" the information (under their own authorship) according to the exigencies of the political field and their concern with legitimating their activity.

DISCUSSION AND CONCLUSION: THE PRODUCER-CLIENT MODEL RECONSIDERED

The data presented here indicate substantial mutual misconceptions on the part of both government officials and social scientists in matters related to their interaction in virtue of contract research. Consequently, the data imply that the establishment of often long-lasting producer-client relationships and the mutual interaction and communication associated with it may *accentuate* rather than eliminate basic incompatibilities. Apparently, pressure such as a decision maker can exert by providing project money does *not* transform the exigencies of a scientific field into a structure congenial to the government officials' interests. Instead, such pressure will lead the scientists to attempt to fulfill those exigencies while at the same time maintaining the decision makers' confidence. The latter, while displaying this confidence, indulge at the same time in heavy criticism not communicated to the researcher, and utilize the results in a manner which allows them to integrate social science knowledge into political action without changing the loyalties and decision criteria of the respective political field. It appears that both parties succeed fairly well in profiting from each other, yet the reason for this does not seem to be mutual *adaptation*. Thus, the scientists do not "adapt" in the sense of becoming primarily concerned with the solution of the social and practical problems at issue in the study, nor do they allow their sponsors' interest to dominate their research. And the government officials do not adopt the results they are presented with in the sense of accepting them as serious grounds for their decisions. Rather, they incorporate the results wherever they "fit" in the cycle of political production, and there is enough criticism at hand whenever such a procedure might be challenged. The misgivings entertained by government officials may well operate as a protective belt[23] which so far has successfully prevented social scientists form assessing the kind and extent of utilization of their results. What we have to accept is that there is no use in deploring the existence of the gap and in pondering over strategies for better mutual adaptation. We need to see that both parties succeed continuously in bridging the gap by using the other party's services while guided by their own interests and while assuring the continuous functioning of the respective action systems, i.e., the scientific and political fields. The problem, as posed in the literature, turns out to be misconceived. The producer-client model does not specify subversiveness as a central aspect of the exchange between social science and policy making, nor does it suggest reprocessing of social science results in the sphere of political production as a dominant form of utilization. The logic of utilization lies in what is *done* with social science results; the present paper is an attempt to direct the attention towards such a logic.

NOTES

1. Many of Lazarsfeld's writings address the issue of the gap. See, among others, Paul F. Lazarsfeld and Jeffrey G. Reitz, *An Introduction to Applied Sociology* (New York: Elsevier, 1975), especially ch. 5; and Paul F. Lazarsfeld, "Uber die Brauchbarkeit der Soziologie," in Leopold Rosenmayr and Sigurd Höllinger, eds, *Soziologie, Forschung in Osterreich* (Wien: Verlag Hermann Böhlaus Nachf., 1969), especially p. 27.

2. See Robert K. Merton, *Social Theory and Social Structure* (New York: Free Press, 1968), chs. 17-20. See also André Cournand and Michael Meyer, "The Scientist's Code," *Minerva*, 16 (1976), 79-96. The ethical question of the scientists' concern about the application of their work is described by Edward Shils in *The Intellectuals and the Powers and Other Essays* (Chicago: Univ. of Chicago Press, 1972), especially II.7-II.10.

3. See Richard W. Scott, "Professionals in Bureaucracy: Areas of Conflict," in Howard M. Vollmer and Donald L. Mills, eds., *Professionalization* (Englewood Cliffs, N.J.: Prentice-Hall, 1966), pp. 265-275; and William Kornhauser, *Scientists in Industry: Conflict and Accommodation* (Berkeley: Univ. of California Press, 1962).

4. See Derek K. de Solla Price, *The Scientific Estate* (Cambridge, Mass.: Belknap, 1965).

5. See Joseph Ben David, *The Scientist's Role in Society* (Englewood Cliffs, N.J.: Prentice-Hall, 1971); Helmut Krauch, *Die organisierte Forschung* (Berlin: Luchterhand, 1970), Hans Jürgen Krysmanski, *Soziales System und* Wissenschaft (Düsseldorf: Bertelsman Universitatsverlag, 1972); Alvin M. Weinberg, Reflections on Big Science (Cambridge, Mass.: MIT Press, 1968); Carol Weiss, "Improving the Linkage Between Social Research and Public Policy" (delivered at the Vienna Roundtable on the Market of Policy Research, Vienna, October 1975).

6. See Niklas Luhmann, "Selbststeuerung der Wissenschaft," in Niklas Luhmann, ed., *Soziologische Aufklärung* (Opladen: Westdeutscher Verlag, 1971), pp. 232-252; Pierre Bourdieu, "The Specificity of the Scientific Field and the Social Conditions of the Progress of Reason," *Social Sci. Information,* 14 (1975), 19-47.

7. It is characteristic of strategic-tactical argumentation, unlike cognitive argumentation, that meaning is transferred at two levels concomitantly; on the level of explicit content of what is said and on the level of the implicit meaning the message has in the tactical policy of the sender for realizing his interests. "Political" deciphering must primarily address the second level; politically appropriate answers must be given on the basis of a correct understanding of the implicit meaning of the message in the sender's strategy.

8. See Karin D. Knorr, "Producing and Reproducing Knowledge: Descriptive on Constructive? Toward a Model of Research Production," *Social Science Information,* 16 (1977), 669-696; and "The Research Process: Tinkering Toward Success or Approximation of Truth? Prelude to a Theory of Scientific Practice," *Theory and Society,* 8 (1979), 347-376.

9. It might be possible to construct the difference between the political and scientific systems as a difference between an *antagonistic* system based upon oppositional conflict and an *agonistic* system based upon generalized, abstracted, and competitive conflict. The term *agonistic* was introduced into the area by Bruno Latour and Stephen Woolgar, *Laboratory Life* (Beverly Hills: Sage, 1979).

10. The "scriptures" of the field are the authoritative writings which orient scientific research through processes of perception and categorization. These writings consist mainly of the recent literature on a topic rather than the accepted textbook knowledge. See my "Producing and Reproducing Knowledge" for a more detailed analysis of the phenomenon.

11. Examples of problems of adaptation are found, for instance, in Lazarsfeld and Reitz, ch. 6, or in Merton, especially ch. 19. Garfinkel adds a new dimension: he sketches different modes of rationality which are said to hold in scientific and everyday life and which correspond to different exigencies in both contexts. See Harold Garfinkel, *Studies in Ethnomethodology* (Englewood Cliffs, N.J.: Prentice-Hall, 1967), ch. 8.

12. Such a model is presupposed, for instance, in Lazarsfeld's analyses of utilization of social science knowledge. See Lazarsfeld and Reitz, pp. 41-43; and see the use of the notion "client" throughout the book and the Lazarsfeld's "Uber die Brauchbarkeit der Soziologie."

13. Since there are no files of the universe of government officials who finance social research, the respondents were identified by means of a snowball procedure, which cannot claim statistical representativity. However, cross-checks made with social scientists and financial authorities suggest that most of the respective population is included in the respondents.

14. The responses by government sponsors and social scientists do not refer to the same projects, but have been collected as independent average opinions of the corresponding subsystem. The comparison of the opinions is based upon the assumption that there is no systematic bias as far as the selection of projects described on the part of the sponsors and social scientists is concerned. Since both groups of respondents represent the universe (of government sponsors and social scientists), and since the response rate varied between 78% and 90% (personal interviews!), there is no reason for assuming such a bias.

15. This holds, even if the scientist is granted the right of "secondary" utlization of results in

the form of a scientific paper or a popular nonficition book. We are not talking here about sponsored basic research but about problem-oriented contract research.

16. Since the table is not included for reasons of space, let me indicate some of the figures. In academic settings, 24% of the social scientists hold the scientific community to be their major audience, as compared with 11% in nonacademic settings. The general public is cited by 23.3% in academic institutions, as compared with 15.6% in other research organizations; and 15.3% of academic scientists list those concerned by a study as primary reference group, in contrast to 20.2% of scientists in nonacademic research. See Karin D. Knorr, Max Haller, Wolfgant Zehetner, and Hans-Georg Zilian, *Struktur and Verwertung sozialwissenschaftlicher Forschung in Österreich* (Vienna, Jugend und Volk Verlag, 1980).

17. Both groups of respondents were given an identical set of alternatives from which they could choose, and in both cases there was one additional item specific to the group, which is not analyzed here.

18. An extensive analysis of open-ended questions addressing the problem of instrumental versus legitimating use of social science results is found in Karin D. Knorr, "Policy Makers' Use of Social Science Knowledge: Symbolic or Instrumental," in Carol Weiss, ed., *Social Research in Public Policy Making* (New York: D.C. Heath, 1976).

19. Lazarsfeld once pointed out that the capacity to work out and generate decisions is the most cherished competence on which government officials pride themselves. One cannot expect that decision makers will let it happen that decisions are made by social scientists, as the technocratic model of society would have it. Rather, they will use the scientist's fact and incorporate it into a product which bears their own mark or that of their agency. See Lazarsfeld, p. 25.

20. The "decision-preparatory" role of research results in decision processes is described in detail in Knorr et al., ch. 8.

21. The finding that social science results *are* utilized by political decision makers to an unexpected degree seems to become more and more established. See, for example, the results of Nathan Caplan et al., *The Use of Social Science Knowledge in Policy Decisions at the National Level* (Ann Arbor, Mich.: Institute for Social Research, University of Michigan, 1975); and Michael Useem, "State Production of Social Knowledge: Patterns in Government Financing of Academic Social Research," *Amer. Soc. Rev.*, 41 (1976), 613-629.

22. Lazarsfeld once pointed out to me that the gap in both parties' perceptions of each other as shown by our data might be an artifact insofar as the questions we asked might be interpreted differently in both systems. As already mentioned, we tried to prevent crucial misunderstandings by supplementing the standardized question approach with open-ended "talks" with the respondents. But even if there are different connotations involved in both systems (and we believe that there are, depending on the notions involved), this only proves the point of basic incompatibilities of the respective action systems.

23. The notion of a protective belt is borrowed from Lakatos, who used it to characterize protective strategies of the scientific community vis-a-vis moderately successful theories or research programs. See Imre Lakatos, "Falsification and the Methodology of Scientific Research Programs," in Imre Lakatos and Alan Musgrave, eds., *Criticism and the Growth of Knowledge* (Cambridge: Cambridge Univ. Press, 1970), pp. 134ff.

13

CREATING A POLICY ANALYSIS PROFESSION

Arnold J. Meltsner

Why all the interest in policy research and analysis at this time? Are policymakers seeking analytical help because of past failures or because good policies are hard to find? Are they simply postponing action by resorting to research? Is this interest in policy analysis just a slight extension of an American inclincation for "solving" problems? No one really knows.

Fads are just as much a part of the practice of social science as they are of other aspects of human behavior, and some observers of the social scene are wondering, in not too mean-spirited a fashion, how long-lived the current interest in policy analysis and research will be. Certainly, the many and bewildering overlapping activities of public policy indicate a field in ferment: policy initiation or formulation has something to do with suggesting policies or defining problems; policy implementation anticipates whether a policy will be realized in a less-than-benign world and as such is a variant of the study of political feasibility; policy evaluation asks what should be done with an existing policy or program; policy termination examines how to get rid of unwanted policies when an evaluation or some other means indicates the desirability of doing so; policy research generates knowledge; and policy analysis, when narrowly construed, acts as a broker between knowledge and action by developing alternative policies, or, when broadly construed, subsumes all of the above.

From what I can see, names change, but these activities and the functions they serve are fairly constant. Anticipating the future, coping with the uncertainty of decision making, and reducing the anxiety of policymakers will always be important. This will be true whether the activity goes on under the rubric of systems analysis, social engineering, or technology assessment. Thus, it is not unreasonable to assume that policy analysis, as an umbrella activity, is a more or less permanent feature of public policymaking. An appropriate question, then, concerns its institutionalization, by which I mean not only that policy analysis is practiced but that it is an activity valued by society. To understand this activity we need to identify the institutional roots of analysts and the conditions under which they and policymakers produce and consume analyses. We will have to be concerned, among other things, about issues of performance, use, and distribution.

Performance has to do with the quality and integrity of information that policy analysis supplies. Here the concern is not only with the standards and ethics of practitioners and scholars but also with the power and realism of their theories and hypotheses. Standards of performance are directly related to the quality of the base of knowledge. When that base is inadequate, as is so often the case, standards are usually relaxed under the palliative that some information is better than none. A partial corrective, showing that a little information may be dangerous, can come from peer review or from the general climate of advocacy in which policy is examined.

Despite the usual well-placed confidence in advocacy and adjustment, the system of policymakers and analysts is not always self-correcting. An inadequate analysis with faulty assumptions and logic can be converted into public policy. Right now, no sufficient organizational counterweight exists to the imperatives of policy formulation and its use of analytical expertise. Analysts, inside and outside government, are often called upon to defend preconceived policies and mythical numbers. Such work goes beyond the legitimate use of analysis in selecting or explaining policies and can involve questionable behavior on the part of both analyst and policymaker.

Error, of course, can be corrected through time and experience as a policy works itself out, but it would be preferable to have at least the known errors pointed out when policies are being formulated. Part of the problem of error stems from the diversity of intellectual perspectives that are used in analytical practice. Such diversity is a source of both strength and weakness. The perspectives of various physical and social scientists, of engineers, and of those trained in public policy contribute to a vigorous and adaptive problem-solving capacity. At the same time, the diversity of perspectives makes agreement on standards of performance difficult, and because of this lack of agreement policymakers are able to manipulate both analytical information and analysts—something the powerful have been doing to their experts for centuries. No single professional organization of policy analysts monitors performance, and no journal of record provides critical review that will satisfy various analysts and the range of their intellectual perspectives. What is important to recognize is that there is no forum for discussing or obtaining agreement on minimal or desirable standards of performance.

Use has to do with suitability: How well does the information generated by analysis meet the imperatives of policymaking? When used, policy analysis is submitted in a timely fashion and in a form congruent with the symbolic and informational requirements of policymakers. Many analysts, for instance, face the dilemma of maintaining "reasonable" standards of performance while meeting unreasonable deadlines or responding to manufactured flaps and crises. Nor are analysts always sensitive to other imperatives of policymaking, such as communicating their results in ways that will enhance understanding and improve the possibility of developing political support for their recommendations.

Related to use is concern about the distribution of analytical resources. Political actors can use information and expertise, like money, as a resource in bargaining, exchange, and achieving policy preferences. To the extent that the various actors in the political process have different access to such resources, outcomes may shift and the process itself may be questionable. Unequal distribution of analytical resources can have unfavorable consequences. When the analytical resources of the federal government are compared with those of state and local governments, for example, the distribution is skewed in favor of the federal government. Whether this puts local government at a disadvantage in achieving its policy preferences is not definitively known, but surely local governments have not had an easy time meeting the federal government's requirements for program evaluation and other informational reporting.

INSTITUTIONAL ROOTS:
ORGANIZATIONAL CONTEXTS

The value of policy analysis—whether it is used and how it is used—depends heavily on the specific organizational context. The organizational home, so to speak, not only shapes a study but acts as a gatekeeper for it. Where the work is done—at a university, a well-established nonprofit research firm, a relatively new consulting firm, or a governmental organization—makes a significant difference. As one of the central determinants of the role of the policy analyst, the organizational context significantly influences the analyst's discretion, the policy analysis agenda, the scope of the policy analysis, the range of policy alternatives that will be considered, the time constraint under which the policy analysis will be done, the allocation of resources to the policy analysis, and the relationship of the policy analysis to policymaking.

Policy analysis, when practiced as a brokering function of knowledge in governmental organizations, is, in Eliot Freidson's terms, a consulting profession. Its practitioners rely on clients or policymakers who are attracted to them to solve or do something about their problems. But as the practice moves toward social experimentation and the validation and creation of policy knowledge, its practitioners then become part of a scientific profession. Whether we call this latter practice policy research or policy science is beside the point. As in other professions, both types of knowledge creators and users exist.

In a sense, the purity of the scientific-consulting, creator-user distinction is modified by the organizational context. Consider, as an example, the standard of peer review. The policy analyst based in the university accepts this standard and submits work to peers for criticism and evaluation. The incentive system is geared to peer approval and recognition. But what happens when this scientific type goes to work for a governmental agency? The scientific type takes along his notion of peer review, which gets quickly altered by the agency's requirement for secrecy or by the policymaker's desire that the analyst remain anonymous. Thus, a merging of professional types takes place as policy analysts circulate from universities and research organizations to governmental service and back again.

Judging by the existence of analytical offices at various levels and branches of government, policy analysis has sunk its institutional roots. Consider the Office of the Assistant Secretary for Planning and Evaluation in the U.S. Department of Health, Education and Welfare (HEW). Originally started as part of the program-budgeting movement of the federal government in the 1960s, this office has survived not only program budgeting but also a number of changes in political administrations. At present it has a permanent and temporary professional staff of over 150 who work on a broad variety of social problems and programs—welfare reform, national health insurance, teenage pregnancy. Roughly half of this staff is engaged in generating analytical option papers or in responding to policy proposals that come from legislative, self-initiated, and task force work. In addition, at subordinate levels in HEW there are a variety of analytical offices; for example, seven professionals work in the Office of Assistant Director for Policy Analysis of the Health Care Financing Administration. Similarly, the Congressional Budget Office (CBO) with its staff of about 200, of which about 75 are policy analysts, has within its short four years developed clientele support from congressional committee members and staff—so much so, in fact, that following President Carter's request for a congressional assessment of the inflationary impacts of proposed legislation, the CBO was called to provide such assistance.

A great deal of policy analysis and research is also conducted by private research firms and university-based research laboratories and institutes. In order to deal with time, personnel, or financial constraints, governmental agencies resort to research and consulting firms such as the Urban Institute, the Rand Corporation, and Mathematica. Foundations such as Ford and Sloan have also encouraged policy research. The range of this policy work is as broad as government itself. For example, it involves the social research company Abt Associates of Cambridge, Massachusetts, in running housing experiments or evaluating compensatory education programs, or the Brookings Institution in developing its own version of the national budget, or an old-line consulting firm such as Arthur D. Little in its work on juvenile justice.

A survey made in 1977 showed that of the 101 graduates from the Graduate School of Public Policy, University of California, Berkeley, who went into the job market, 22 were working in research and consulting firms, 20 for the federal government, 18 for state government, 15 for local government, 14 for universities, and 12 elsewhere. Geographically they were spread out, with 50 in California, 28 in Washington, D.C., and 23 scattered around the country. In California, many graduates were working as analysts in the state departments of education, finance, and health, and in the office of the legislative analyst. A number of students had also entered local government by working for cities, counties, and regional agencies.

INSTITUTIONAL ROOTS: EDUCATION

The business of educating policy analysts, researchers, and program evaluators is growing rapidly despite the stable or declining condition of higher education. Special departments and schools have been created to teach policy analysis, and regular units, such as schools of public administration and business administration, have initiated sections or majors devoted to policy analysis and research. Moreover, specialized analytical programs ground their activities in a substantive policy area such as health, environment, and natural resources. Such programs can be found under a variety of labels; political economy, public policy, engineering and public systems, public management, and health planning are just a few of them.

From looking at the schools that educate policy analysts and researchers, it is not at all clear who is doing what. Over 200 institutions from 45 states and Canada belong to the National Association of Schools of Public Affairs and Administration, but not all of them are *centrally* involved in the education of policy analysts. Their involvements vary all the way from one introductory course in evaluation in a school of public administration to a comprehensive effort at applying systematic analysis, social science, and other disciplinary perspectives and methods as preparation for the public service and related research activities. Such examples of the latter include the School of Urban and Public Affairs, Carnegie-Mellon University; the Institute of Policy Studies and Public Affairs, Duke University (an undergraduate program); the John Fitzgerald Kennedy School of Government, Harvard University; the Institute of Public Policy Studies, University of Michigan; the Hubert H. Humphrey School of

Public Affairs, University of Minnesota; the Woodrow Wilson School of Public and International Affairs, Princeton University; the Public Management Program, Graduate School of Business, Stanford University; the Lyndon B. Johnson School of Public Affairs, University of Texas at Austin; the Rand Graduate Institute; and my own school, the Graduate School of Public Policy, University of California, Berkeley.

Such a list does not of course do justice to the many fine universities and colleges involved in analytical education. Besides the specialized schools, more traditional departments of economics, planning, engineering, mathematics, statistics, and physics have also contributed their share of analytical practitioners and scholars.

The schools that are devoting considerable resources to policy analysis do not have a common curriculum. Some confine themselves to "hard" perspectives, such as economics and operations research; others emphasize "soft" perspectives, such as ethics and politics. Some schools, however, have developed a core curriculum approach, similar to business schools, in which students from a variety of backgrounds—some in the social sciences, some not—are exposed to public sector problems and a number of social science perspectives. Students take courses in methods of policy analysis, economics, law, and political and organizational analysis. Methods usually encompass a mix of quantitative and qualitative approaches and include such subjects as statistics, decision analysis, experimental design, and modeling. The training in economics has a micro orientation and emphasizes cost-benefit analysis as well, but it can also include macroeconomics, public finance, and urban studies.

Courses in law, politics, and organizations are quite varied—sometimes emphasizing "sensitivity" in actually trying to develop skills. In my own experience, such courses develop over time, starting from a perspective close to the discipline and then gradually moving to an analytical problem-solving approach. For example, courses in political and organizational analysis may begin with fairly traditional descriptions of political institutions, policy formulation processes, and organizational theory. As instructors learn more about practical applications, they start using cases that emphasize particular problems, such as implementation, or the concept that politics involves a process of adjustment of conflicting goals and beliefs. In the mature stages of such a course, the instructor shifts away from "canned cases" that inculcate sensitivity and to encouraging students to develop their own skills of political and organizational analysis. Such encouragement takes place in the field, where students work with real clients or policymakers and have no book to consult about what happens. Indeed, students are forced to make and communicate their own predictions and judgments about political feasibility, distributive effects, and the desirability of governmental intervention in the first place. They may address questions of organizational design, reorganization, implementation strategies, and identify points of policy adjustment and compromise.

Most programs also have some type of workshop course that emphasizes policy problems—definition, searching out alternatives, and assessing consequences. The tempo of such courses is varied by imposing constraints on the time allotted for an assignment—from seventy-two hours to five or more weeks. All courses in the core curriculum sooner or later, and with different degrees of success, become problem oriented, so that working on policy questions is a pervasive feature of analytical education.

AN EMERGING PROFESSION:
THE IMPORTANCE OF IDENTITY

With all this activity both in higher education and at various levels of government, one would think that policy analysis would have come to be recognized as a profession, or at least as an occupation. But this is not the case. Sometimes the policy analyst is simply lumped together with other "staff." Sometimes the policy analyst is hidden behind such titles as budget analyst, program analyst, manpower analyst, or economist. For example, nobody in the CBO has the title of policy analyst. One can be an assistant, associate, or principal analyst, but not a policy analyst. The title policy analyst sounds arrogant or perhaps threatening. It seems that policy is what elected officials do. Even the U.S. Civil Service Commission has not established an official occupational category for policy analysts, although it is investigating what to do about those employees involved in evaluation activities.

Attaching importance to a name or title may be foolish, and no doubt people perform analytical tasks without even being aware of the name policy analyst. Nevertheless, names, besides having symbolic significance, indicate recognition by others and can be a measure of the permanence and depth of institutionalization. In order for policy analysis to be an accepted occupation, it must be sufficiently differentiated from other work activities and have its own identity.

Once we get outside governmental and research organizations, with their educational bases of support, the question of institutionalization becomes more problematical. The social and institutional context for establishing policy analysis as a valued and permanent activity does not exist. No single professional association, for example, provides an intellectual home and a locus of identity for the growing number of policy analysts regardless of where and in what way they practice their craft. True, some schools encourage the formation of alumni groups and some disciplinary professional associations have sections for those who are interested in analysis or public policy in general. A group such as the Policy Studies Organization comes to mind because it is composed mainly of political scientists and, while separate from the American Political Science Association, does arrange some of its important professional activities around the APSA's annual meeting. In addition, there are some small emerging organizations of specialists interested in communicating with each other, say, on problems of evaluation, as well as groups of social scientists concerned about the production and utilization of their work, such as the Council for Applied Social Research. Nor should we ignore the numerous substantive organizations that deal with a variety of policy areas such as health, taxation, conservation, transportation, and even earthquake engineering.

Despite this plethora of related organizations, policy analysts lack their own professional association. Indeed, the existence of these related organizations makes it difficult for such an association to emerge. These substantive and disciplinary organizations syphon off the energies and resources of potential leaders and members. By setting forth standards and paradigms, the disciplinary organizations can encourage intellectual parochialism and, as an unintended consequence of promoting the discipline, the knowledge and methodological base for the development of the craft of policy analysis is not built. Policy analysis then becomes unnecessarily circumscribed and defined in terms of a single discipline. Economists have had this effect on policy analysis in the past. Worse yet, a disciplinary orientation can lead to misdirection or at least confusion. It was not too long ago that political scientists, for example, viewed policy analysis as examining policies to understand politics and political systems. They did not focus on the selection of appropriate policies or on the application of their knowledge of politics to do so. Instead they focused on policies to improve their knowledge of politics. Today, under the rubric of policy analysis, political scientists do both.

One might argue that strong disciplinary efforts will ultimately build the requisite base of knowledge for policy. In the last twenty-five years or so, the social sciences, for example, have matured sufficiently to contribute something to policy questions. Moreover, there is much to be gained from the perspectives of the physical sciences, engineering, statistics, and operations research. We need help from the disciplines to establish a robust theoretical and empirical foundation for policy analysis. Such a future foundation built on disciplinary intentions, however, should not displace more immediate efforts at improving the state-of-the-art of policy analysis; otherwise, there may be nothing worthwhile to be institutionalized. A problem with an emerging field is that as it departs from its intellectual roots it may tend to become vacuous and lacking in substance. This is particularly true of policy analysis, which claims general problem-solving skills in resolving policy questions. That is why it is essential that disciplinary efforts complement and support the efforts of scholars and practitioners of policy analysis. Both kinds of effort are required.

Another way traditional academic disciplines undermine the institutionalization of policy analysis is through their lasting effects on professional identity. Analysts who have been educated in a particular discipline usually perceive themselves as members or students of that discipline. Having made the investment of going to school and working in a field, they are unlikely to develop a new professional identity. Regardless of the high-level positions they may occupy in government circles, they continue to think of themselves as economists or sociologists who happen to be working on policy questions. Even in the schools of public policy and public affairs where future generations of policy analysts are being taught, faculty members identify themselves by academic discipline. When someone asks, I say that I am a political scientist interested in policy and the policy process; I do not say that I am a policy analyst interested in politics.

The importance of this lack of identification with policy analysis should not be underestimated. If a field is going to prosper, it needs intellectual heroes and well-known practitioners. Besides being exemplars for the young, they set the intellectual and research agenda. Both directly and indirectly, they create through their actions the theoretical paradigm of practice and the standards of acceptable performance. Currently, however, we are dealing with a number of not necessarily compatible paradigms and standards. Many faculty members are in the peculiar position of educating students to be something they themselves neither are nor pretend to be. The situation, as one colleague suggested to me, is like a rock tumbler in which each of us grinds away at the student from our disciplinary perspective with the expectation that what comes out will be different from what went in. I hope that our polished products will identify with policy analysis and make the current lack of identification a short-term, transitory growing pain.

SHOULD WE PROFESSIONALIZE?

The steps from full-time occupation to profession are not easy, and some observers of policy analysis are not sure that these steps are either feasible or desirable. Some feel that the field is too immature, and that there is insufficient agreement on the definition of policy analysis for talking about professionalization. Some would rather wait until policy analysis pays off in better policies. Some believe that the currency of professionalization has greatly depreciated because everybody wants to be a member of a profession.

Among teachers and practitioners of policy analysis, there are those who are content to continue working under their present professional labels; others are unconvinced because they anticipate more disadvantages than advantages from professionalization. The unconvinced are quick to raise questions about other professions: Did the professionalization of social work help the workers and their clients? Would statistics and computer science have been better off if they had stayed in mathematics? Has the professionalization of business and public administration enhanced the productivity of business and government?

To students of the sociology of professions, the arguments are familiar, but they are worth considering because professionalization can all too often have adverse consequences. I have seen decision makers, because of their professional backgrounds, use extremely narrow and circumscribed criteria that result in inefficiencies and misallocation of public funds. I have known smug professionals who, secure in the mystique of their expertise, are unresponsive to their clients. And I have observed fields of knowledge become too theoretical and divorced from their origins in practical problems as they become professionalized. Thus, it is not a simple matter for me to conclude that policy analysis should move in the direction of greater professionalization.

I say greater professionalization, because policy analysis is already moving in that direction. Policy analysis already has its own technical language. It has professional schools, and these schools do have linkages to the world of work. Representatives from schools of public policy have already met, although infrequently, to discuss curricula development and other issues of common concern. Texts and cases are being published. A number of journals are devoted to the analysis of public policy questions and to the improvement of methods and teaching of analysis. In fact, there are so many that one editor is contemplating a consortium of journals to give mutual aid and comfort. This growing list of journals includes *Policy Analysis, Policy Sciences, Policy Studies Journal, Public Interest,* and *Public Policy.* In short, professionalization is a matter of degree, and the questions that concern us are: How far should we go? How formal should we become?

More professionalization means more formalization. It means a formal association or organization. It implies establishing minimal criteria for membership in the organization and perhaps for admission to the profession. It means choosing a journal of record to promote excellence and to disseminate standards. It need not go as far as requiring licenses and using the state to achieve autonomy.

What is to be gained or lost from this formalization? One way to get at this question is to ask who would benefit from such a change. The professors and the growing educational apparatus would certainly benefit. It is not particularly easy to develop courses and materials to teach the substance of policy analysis. Standard courses and texts do not work, since theory and method are best taught in the context of specific policy problems. The advantages of increased and regular exchange of teaching materials through a formal organization would surely benefit new educational programs in public policy analysis. New programs are starting to proliferate not only in this country but overseas as well, and the established schools and experienced professors have much to lose if these new programs are not successful. If the level of competency and quality of our graduates is not maintained, it could threaten the entire enterprise of policy analysis. Of course, it is possible that a small group of professors could put a stranglehold on the professional organization that might lead to premature closure and conservatism in education, but this seems a small risk to run given the prevailing openness of the field and the diversity of its participants.

Students and graduates of policy analysis programs would also gain from increasing professionalization. Medical students seldom question that there is something called *doctor,* but policy analysis students often are concerned about just what it is that they are being trained to be. This concern goes beyond the definition or scope of policy analysis and focuses on whether anybody is doing "it." Besides providing accessible role models and reducing this student anxiety, a professional association could, for example, facilitate placement for internships, field work, and eventual employment. Moreover, greater professionalization would promote clearer identity, which in turn would promote an early internalization of standards and the necessary socialization critical to effective performance. Accepting the professional identity of policy analyst, the student or practitioner might be precluded from certain jobs in and out of the public service. By saying what policy analysis is through greater professionalization, we will also be saying what it is not.

What about policymakers, the clients? Will they be better off? Will improved policies emerge from increasing professionalization? Here we get back to the issues of performance, use, and distribution. Increasing professionalization means setting standards that may or may not be capable of being enforced by the sanctions of an association. But at least the standards will be known, and as such they should have a positive effect on performance. The game playing between client and analyst should be reduced: analysts will be less like to "snow" their clients, and clients will be less likely to misuse the information of analysts. Clearer demarcation through professional means of the conflict between loyalty to peers and loyalty to clients may place some policymakers at a disadvantage, but the policy debate between partisans should improve. Whether better policies emerge from that debate is a function of many things besides the professionalization of policy analysis.

One important consideration to keep in mind is the likely effects of professionalization on the base of knowledge for policy formulation. As research is directed to policy questions and to the methods and practices of analysis, the state of the art should make rapid progress. Will that progress also bring with it the disadvantages of specialization through knowing more about less? How narrow we get or broad we remain depends heavily on the behavior of members of the profession. If scholars, for example, cut themselves off from intellectual developments in their former disciplines and other fields, then policy analysis will not prosper. A professional organization has the responsibility for establishing criteria of relevance that will ensure the linkages of analytical activities to a fairly broad base of knowledge. Whether it can do this without inundating policy analysis or making it irrelevant is uncertain.

A professional association can increase the use or suitability of the efforts of its members. It can work through its placement and other activities to ensure an equitable distribution of analytical resources. It can be a forum for policymakers to express their informational needs to practitioners and scholars. It need not be a closed meeting of professionals so intent on talking to one another that they forget what their social role is. Policy analysts need not become so insulated that they are neither on tap nor on top.

ORGANIZING THE PROFESSION

If policy analysis is to become truly institutionalized—that is, to be of lasting value to the variety of organizational contexts of present and future practice—it must become a profession in its own right. Rather than allowing its identity to be blurred by disciplinary, substantive, and organizational orientations, policy analysis must start drawing lines of definition, albeit soft ones. Focus as to scope, method, and application is necessary if policy analysis is not to succumb to shoddy practice and the insecure strength of being merely topical or a faddish.

To form a profession, the practitioners and scholars of policy analysis will have to coalesce and organize. They will have to counter the usual incentives of privatization and see the value of such association. As trained skeptics, most of us know about free riders and the difficulty of collective action, and we need no one to point out the costs of such action. But what about the benefits? Every professional organization talks about promoting and advancing its field, but what does this mean? Surely it must mean more than establishing recognized peers for ad hoc promotional committees in universities. It must also mean working for recognition outside of universities. It means developing common curricula and standards of performance. It means intellectual exchange and controversy. It means having access to a variety of ways of openly communicating with each other—conferences, journals, newsletters—to improve performance and to criticize breaches of standards and ethics.

Starting from a group of schools that share a more or less common vision, an organization could be gradually developed to promote mutual interests, such as exchanges of curricula and policy research. This group could then be extended to include policy analysis and research units both inside and outside government. Finally, the membership of the organization could be extended to all interested practitioners and scholars.

Even for mature professions with well-established organizations, tasks of quality control are never really completed or easily accomplished. Perhaps these professions become complacent about what they are and what they do. For the emerging profession of policy analysis, I see no real choice. Without standards for curricula and practice, without the ability to criticize and advance the state of the art, and without the organizational means to do so, policy analysis may continue, but it will then provide only a fraction of its potential value to society.

SUGGESTED READINGS

Freidson, Eliot. *Profession of Medicine: A Study of the Sociology of Applied Knowledge*. New York: Harper & Row, 1970, pp. 21-22 and 73-75.

Meltsner, Arnold J. *Policy Analysts in the Bureaucracy*. Berkeley and Los Angeles: Univ. of California Press, 1976.

Moore, Wilbert E. *The Professions: Roles and Rules*. New York: Russell Sage, 1970.

INDEX OF NAMES

INDEX OF SUBJECTS

ABOUT THE CONTRIBUTORS

BARBARA A. BARDES received her Ph.D. in American politics and policy from the University of Cincinnati. She is currently Assistant Professor of Political Science at Loyola University of Chicago.

JOHN E. BRANDL is Professor of Public Affairs in the Hubert H. Humphrey Institute of Public Affairs, University of Minnesota. He was Director of Minnesota's School of Public Affairs from 1969 to 1976 and has taught at Boston College, Harvard University, St. John's University (Minnesota), the University of Wisconsin, the University of the Philippines, and Sydney University. He has been a systems analyst in the Office of the Secretary of Defense, Deputy Assistant Secretary of the U.S. Department of Health, Education and Welfare, and a member of the Minnesota House of Representatives.

JACK BYRD, JR., is Professor of Industrial Engineering at West Virginia University. He is the author of the text *Operations Research Models for Public Administration* (Lexington Books, 1975) and *Decision Models for Management* (McGraw-Hill, forthcoming). Dr. Byrd is an active consultant for government and private industry. He is the author of numerous papers in the operations research literature.

JOSEPH COLEMAN received his Ph.D. in chemistry from the University of Washington. His working experience has been at the Bell Telephone Laboratories in Murray Hill, New Jersey, the National Bureau of Standards, and the Energy Research and Development Administration, now incorporated in the Department of Energy. Currently, Dr. Coleman is Deputy Director of the Office of Technology Impacts, within the Office of Environment of the Department of Energy.

THOMAS J. COOK is Senior Political Scientist at the Research

Triangle Institute, Research Triangle Park, North Carolina. He has taught at Pennsylvania State University and the University of Illinois, Chicago Circle. His research interests center on issues involved in the application of social science research methodology to the study of social policy, with particular reference to policy evaluation. He has published widely in the area and currently serves as principal investigator on an experimental evaluation of a community-based exoffender program as well as a project to develop a performance measurement system for adult criminal courts. His article in this volume draws upon the experience gained from directing a project on the design and implementation of administrative experiments in public procurement agencies.

MELVIN J. DUBNICK is currently a policy analyst with the Office of Regulatory Economics and Policy, U.S. Department of Commerce. He is on leave from Loyola University of Chicago, where he is director of the public administration curriculum and Assistant Professor in the political science department.

WERNER Z. HIRSCH is Professor of Economics at the University of California, Los Angeles. His recent books include *Law and Economics: An Introductory Analysis* (1979), *Urban Economic Analysis* (1973), *Local Government Program Budgeting* (coauthored, 1974), *Governing Urban America in the 1970's* (1973), *Fiscal Pressures on the Central City* (1971), and *The Economics of State and Local Government* (1970).

PETER HOUSE is currently Director of the Office of Technology Impacts under the Assistant Secretary for Environment, Department of Energy. He received his Ph.D. in public administration from Cornell University. Dr. House has served with the U.S. Environmental Protection Agency, the Department of Agriculture, and was a visiting scholar at the Institute of Transportation Studies, University of California at Berkeley. His research is focused on the development of gaming simulation models and studies in the area of suburban/ farmland and preferential tax assessment.

RONALD W. JOHNSON is Senior Political Scientist at the Research Triangle Institute, Research Triangle Park, North Carolina. He is the author of articles on evaluation research and policy analysis and coauthor of *Public Budgeting Systems*. He is currently engaged in a project analyzing the implementation of administrative experiments in public agencies, and is principal investigator on a study to evaluate four LEAA-funded court improvement projects.

KARIN DAGMAR KNORR is on the faculty of the Department of Sociology at the University of Pennsylvania. She formerly was at the Institute for Advanced Studies in Vienna and the University of Vienna. Her major research interests focus on the question of utilization of knowledge, especially social science knowledge, and on the analysis of scientific discourse and argumentation with a view to scientific development.

EDWARD W. LEHMAN is Professor and Chair of the Department of Sociology, New York University, and Senior Research Associate, Center for Policy Research. He is the author of *Coordinating Health Care: Explorations in Interorganizational Relations* and *Political Society: A Macrosociology of Politics*.

DUNCAN MacRAE, JR., is William Rand Kenan, Jr., professor of Political Science and Chairman of the Curriculum in Public Policy Analysis at the University of North Carolina at Chapel Hill. He is the author of *The Social Function of Social Science* (Yale, 1976) and the coauthor of *Policy Analysis for Public Decisions* (Duxbury, 1979).

ARNOLD J. MELTSNER is Professor of Public Policy at the Graduate School of Public Policy, University of California, Berkeley. He has published numerous books and articles, including *Policy Analysts in the Bureaucracy* and *The Politics of City Revenue*. He is the editor of *Policy Analysis*.

STUART S. NAGEL Is Professor of Political Science at the University of Illinois and a member of the Illinois bar. He is the secretary-treasurer and publications coordinator for the Policy Studies Organization. He is an author or editor of *Policy Analysis: In Social Science Research* (Sage, 1979), *Decision Theory and the Legal Process* (Lexington-Heath, 1979), *The Legal Process: Modeling the System* (Sage, 1977), *Legal Policy Analysis: Find-*

ing an Optimum Level or Mix (Lexington-Heath, 1977), and *Policy Studies Review Annual* (Sage, 1977). He has been an attorney to the Office of Economic Opportunity, the National Labor Relations Board, and the U.S. Senate Judiciary Committee.

MARIAN NEEF is Assistant Professor of Political Science at City University of New York Baruch College. She received her Ph.D. in political science from the University of Illinois in 1979. She is coauthor with Stuart Nagel of various books as well as articles in such periodicals as *Public Administration Review, Political Methodology, Policy Analysis, Judicature, PS, Human Behavior, Policy Studies Review Annual,* and *Evaluation Studies Review Annual.*

FRANK P. SCIOLI, JR., is Section Head for Applied Social and Behavioral Sciences in the Division of Applied Research at the National Science Foundation. He taught at the University of Illinois, Chicago, and Drew University and has published numerous articles in the major social science journals on evaluation research and methodology.

MARY M. WAGNER is Political Scientist at the Research Triangle Institute, Research Triangle Park, North Carolina. She is involved in a program of evaluation research with a particular emphasis on performance measurement for public services. She is completing her doctoral degree in political science with a dissertation involving comparative case studies of efforts to implement performance measurement systems in two local jurisdictions.